THE FURNITURE WARS

THE FURNITURE WARS

HOW AMERICA LOST

A FIFTY BILLION DOLLAR

INDUSTRY

MICHAEL K. DUGAN

Designed by and set in

Garamond Premier by

Nathan W. Moehlmann

Goosepen Studio & Press

Conover, North Carolina

www.GoosepenPress.com

Printed in the United States of America.

Visit www.Booksurge.com to order additional copies.

ISBN 978-1-4392251-0-3

＋

IN WAR, EVERYTHING IS VERY SIMPLE, *but the simplest thing is difficult. Someone who has no personal experience of war does not understand where the difficulties that are constantly discussed actually lie, nor the reasons for the brilliance and exceptional mental ability the commander must possess. Everything seems so simple: all the necessary knowledge seems so obvious, and all the deductive reasoning so insignificant that, by comparison, the simplest task of higher mathematics impresses us with a certain degree of scientific dignity.*

If one has experienced war, however, all these things become understandable, yet it remains extremely difficult to describe the invisible yet ubiquitous factor that causes this change.

Carl von Clausewitz, *On War*

＋

CONTENTS

AUTHOR'S NOTE

THE FURNITURE WARS is intended to provide an inside look at the American furniture manufacturing industry over the past fifty years. During this period, I was fortunate enough to have had a front-row seat, close to the action, and at times, I was on the stage. This gave me a closer look at the subject than a typical historian would get, but it deprived me of a certain measure of objectivity. The narrative is seen through my point of view, but the book is not about me. Therefore, I like to call it a *histoir* rather than a history or a memoir.

I arrived in 1969, a self-assured Outsider who viewed the old-fashioned, factory-oriented industry with mild disdain. I was particularly struck with the lack of marketing practices and couldn't wait to show the misinformed natives how to do it the right way. At first, my youthful attitude was reinforced by a band of MBA types, mostly from Harvard, who felt the same way. For some reason, I sensed that maybe, just maybe, the insiders were not as dumb as we thought. And by listening carefully to some veterans, I began to see that what looked like antiquated practices were, in fact, clever accommodations to the brutally competitive industry.

In furniture, every square foot of floor space, every dollar of sales, and every nickel of profit has to be fought for against countless rivals. And it has to be done with Sisyphean strength and regularity. There is no time to savor the fruits of victory, and the losses are painful. It is like war.

I kept listening and observing, and somewhere along the line I lost the Outsider's false omniscience and became an Insider. Now, all I had to do was help the Outsiders do it the right way. During this time I began as a marketing and product development manager at the H. T. Cushman Co. and moved on and up to become the vice president of sales and marketing at Pennsylvania House. In ten years I dealt with three owners and five presidents, each one unique.

By 1979, I had grown restless and I succumbed to a recruiter's call to move to the industry's mainstream and become senior vice president of sales and marketing for the S&H furniture group. The High Point group headquarters were filled with insiders, many of them highly capable, who were held in mild contempt by the outsiders in the New York corporate headquarters. Green Stamps and furniture did not mix well, and it was not a fun time in my career. I missed the maverick atmosphere at Pennsylvania House and rarely agreed with my S&H boss. Still, I was near the top of a major furniture producer and learned a lot more about the business.

Thanks to a referral from a friend, I met with a Wall Street investment banker and agreed to partner with him in the acquisition of the Union Furniture Co. in Batesville, Indiana. Around the same time, S&H was raided by Baldwin United, and a management leveraged buyout was crafted. LADD was born, and later the key managers became millionaires on paper when the company went public. Perhaps I should have stayed, but I just did not feel right there, and the people who stayed were not happy.

The Union venture led to the acquisition of Jamestown Sterling in 1982, and the fun returned. Turner moved on to bigger things, leaving me as president of my own company. His fearless pursuit of acquisitions caused a few anxious moments and eventually led to multiple bankruptcies, but Jamestown Sterling prospered through it all. It represented the furniture business at its best, a money-making niche company with a good management team. Who could ask for more?

Then one day in the summer of 1987, I took a call from a head-hunter who wanted to know if I would be interested in becoming president of a "large manufacturing company in the Southeast."

"No way," said I. "I am perfectly happy where I am."

"Are you sure?"

"Yes, I am absolutely sure."

"What if I told you the name?" he proffered.

"It wouldn't matter," I insisted. "But I am curious, of course."

"The name is confidential."

"It doesn't matter. I really am not interested."

"It's Henredon."

"Oh."

Seventeen exciting years later, I retired as president of Henredon to become a college professor and to work on this book. I hope it will help insiders and outsiders reach a better understanding of the special nature of the business. I remain convinced you must love and respect the furniture business to survive in it, and that means you cannot treat it in a cavalier manner. You either love it or you don't. There is no middle ground.

The original idea that led to this book was a decision to send a memo up the line to point out some of the mistakes I had seen repeated often during the Furniture Wars. It seemed so obvious.

I naively felt I would be able to help by pointing out some of the traps that had caught others. The memo was not received with much favor; it was not what people wanted to hear. Now, it has grown to become a 400 page book.

I have tried to be factual and objective in my narrative with malice toward none. However, it is impossible to set aside deeply felt personal impressions based on first hand observations.

Seven years in the making, this book would not have been possible without the generous help of many people. Since many interviews were conducted off the record, I cannot list them all, but several are due special thanks. Barbara Dugan for her infinite patience with me and "the book." Professor Chris Roberts of Alabama University for his tireless editing. Sheila Long O'Mara and Amy Kyle of *Home Furnishings Business* for their unflagging support. Nathan Moehlmann of Goosepen Studio *&* Press for his wonderful graphic design. Jerry Epperson of Mann, Armstrong, and Epperson for his insights and statistics. Budd Bugatch of Raymond James for his brilliant analysis. *Furniture Today* for its superb coverage of the industry. Earle Levenstein, Will Somers, Jack Curry, Jack Glasheen, and all those who urged me to stay the course and not give up.

M. K. D.

Hickory, North Carolina

THE FURNITURE WARS

INTRODUCTION

A VACANT FACTORY SITS FORLORNLY astride Spring-maid Mountain just off the Blue Ridge Parkway in western North Carolina. Outside, weeds grow defiantly through the cracks in the empty parking lots, and cobwebs surround the locked doors. Inside, it is quiet and dark. The power has been cut off. All that remains are faint memories of the products made there and the people who made them.

The facility once produced world-class Henredon furniture – prized by movie stars, professional athletes, country and western singers, and other discerning customers the world over. Henredon products even graced the homes of Presidents from Truman to Clinton. Now the factory produces nothing. Opened in 1967, this particular complex was named after the nearby Mitchell County community of Spruce Pine, 40 miles northeast of Asheville. With nearly a million square feet of floor space, it provided thousands of steady jobs for some of the state's poorest counties. It was a good place to work. Today, no one works there.

Spruce Pine is one of several hundred such facilities spread across the Carolinas, Virginia, and Tennessee – abandoned, deserted, and deprived of hope. Not long ago, these plants hummed with workers, managers, engineers, and machines making furniture and textiles, but no longer.

A few miles down the road from Henredon, Ethan Allen

opened a new plant in the 1990s that managed to stay busy. What looked like a sign of hope for American manufacturing dissipated quickly; it too closed in 2005. Alas, even this American furniture retailing powerhouse, its name artfully connected with an American Revolutionary War hero, could not avoid the move to "offshore" production.

Twenty minutes south of Spruce Pine sits Marion, home of another Henredon plant and two Drexel Heritage plants. All are shut down. Drive in any direction and you will see more empty buildings that noiselessly clutter the landscape. They once made brands such as Thomasville, Broyhill, Lane, Bernhardt, and Bassett. Not any more. Why? Because few companies still make furniture in America.

American workers who once earned decent livings producing furniture are scrambling for employment in lower-paying service jobs. The ones who view those jobs as inferior to making furniture go back to school to prepare for high-tech jobs that as yet do not exist in these counties. The community colleges are filled, thanks to government grants, but the unemployment numbers remain frighteningly high. Caldwell County, North Carolina, home of Broyhill and Bernhardt, two of the industry's biggest and best known brands, has hit unemployment levels as high as 12 percent.

Eight thousand miles from Henredon's shuttered factory in the Blue Ridge Mountains, a company in China is hiring workers and expanding its gigantic factory to make Henredon's newest collections. Henredon, which had carefully differentiated its prestigious brand by making products other companies could not copy, has now committed to a strategy of becoming an import sourcer with no domestic production. Instead of rigidly controlling its own production in-house, Henredon will outsource it to companies in Asia. These third-party vendors also make furniture for other companies.

THE BIG WAR, 1999–2006

A coalition of Asian countries – most notably China, Vietnam, Indonesia, and the Philippines – has captured the American furniture industry, and a tenuous truce has been reached. The Asians make the goods; Americans design and sell them – for now. A few holdouts have escaped the Asians, but essentially the Big War is over. American forces have surrendered. How did it happen so quickly?

It started innocently enough for Henredon in 1983, when a British antique merchant struck a deal with Henredon to import hand-carved parts from the Philippines. The impresario was Paul Maitland-Smith, who arranged to have hand-carved dining chairs made in Korea to sell in the United Kingdom and America. He found the Korean producers to be unreliable, and access to the American market was difficult. He then moved his operation to the Philippines and convinced Henredon to carry his eponymous line. He was extremely knowledgeable about antiques, had a wonderful eye for scale, proportion, finishes, and decorative trim, and could design – or, more accurately, adapt – products that consumers loved. Full of energy and charisma, he skillfully dealt with developing countries in the tradition of the British Raj. He had the hot designs but lacked access to the lucrative American market. At the time, Henredon had access to the top retailers, but its own line needed some excitement.

At first, hand-carved components were used in Chippendale-style dining chairs and Plantation-style poster beds. The items were priced well below the machine-made domestic versions and sold out quickly. The logistics, however, were troublesome. The native Philippine mahogany did not look quite right, so a better grade of lumber was harvested in South America and shipped to North Carolina to be properly dried. It then went to the Philippines to be machined, carved, assembled, finished, and shipped back to Henredon's warehouse in North Carolina. The finishes sometimes lacked the subtle touches preferred by Henredon customers; shipments were invariably late; the native wood supplies were erratic; and frankly, Maitland-Smith and Henredon did not get along very well. It was clear to furniture experts that this cumbersome process would never work. The only problems were that customers loved the products, and the values were compelling.

The experts who said imports couldn't put a dent in the U.S. furniture industry were wrong, and America managed to lose an entire industry. How it happened – and the lessons the industry failed to learn – is the focus of this book.

GLADIATORS IN COMBAT

The prospects were not always so grim for the American furniture business. It once was a prosperous, vibrant entity led by family-owned businesses run by strong-willed patriarchs. These leaders were gladiators who regularly fought like-minded gladiators in retail arenas across the United States.

The American furniture gladiators lived quite well. The wonderful United States economic system provided abundant audiences close to home, and their opponents understood the rules and used similar weapons. The government made sure the furniture markets were kept free from alien elements. It was cozy. True, the furniture gladiators had to contend with the ups and downs of economic cycles, and the game was pretty competitive at times, but it was a lot of fun because it was so freewheeling and so people-driven.

The players in the furniture game lived in a protected environment. Outsiders were repelled quickly – especially the annoying ones who knew nothing of the old ways yet insisted on changing things. When the gladiators were not fighting each other, they returned to their homes in rural North Carolina and Virginia and made furniture so nice it was considered to be truly "world class," unmatched anywhere on the planet.

Buyers from all over the globe came to North Carolina twice a year to attend an antiquated trade show called "The Market." On occasion, someone suggested that the gladiators should take their show on the road and become more global, but someone else would shoot down the idea. Besides, it was expensive to travel abroad, and, as everybody knew, the income in furniture barely covered manufacturing costs. There was little money left over for extras such as marketing and brand building. The government kept pushing for exports but offered little in the way of assistance. Even if government had pitched in, the gladiators were typically wary of government involvement with business. They viewed government as the source of endless regulations and taxes that handicapped the furniture production and made costs go up. There was truth to this perception, given that Congress tended to treat all businesses as if they were big, when in fact most are small. The government did not seem to understand the impact of its actions and kept piling on new rules, making life substantially more difficult for the furniture gladiators.

Then, the U.S. government became caught up in a policy called Free Trade and passed new legislation that made things substantially more difficult for the furniture gladiators. But, as long as the rules and regulations applied equally to all the combatants, they were grudgingly accepted.

As a result of the 1994 North American Free Trade Agreement and similar trade agreements that followed it, American gladiators had to compete with gladiators from places such as China and Vietnam. Their rules and regulations were not the same as America's. America's shields were made of biodegradable plastic; Asia's were made of steel. America's swords had to be blunt to avoid injury; Asia's were razor sharp. America was not allowed to use South American mahogany for ax handles; Asia could use all it wanted. The customary defenses no longer worked. The rules of combat changed, and the American furniture makers faced gladiators who were younger, stronger, and more determined.

Faced with an environment filled with uncertainty, the gladiators did not know where to turn. Previously, they had made world-class products. Now, they were shutting their factories while the Chinese were building new ones. Tomorrow, they would face a continuous convoy of container ships sailing from Hong Kong and Shanghai to Los Angeles and Charleston – all loaded with furniture destined for American homes. By 2005, imports accounted for 62 percent of the furniture sold in America.

WHAT WENT WRONG?

How did the Americans lose a $50 billion industry?[1] Admittedly, the Chinese were making furniture long before the Pilgrims made their first chair in North America, but the Chinese were making Asian-styled furniture for Asians, not American styles for the American market. How did they start making Western-style furniture so quickly and force such massive shutdowns so fast? Why did American gladiators teach them how? Should the blame be laid at the feet of the Free Trade movement, or were other factors in play? Without question, the rise of international trade has contributed greatly to this near collapse. American furniture makers cannot compete with Asian workers happy to earn 32 cents an hour. And American furniture makers cannot match prices with Third World companies that operate with those lower worker costs and without the federal mandates of OSHA, EPA, FICA, MACT, ERISA, OFCCP, ADA, ADEA, and COBRA. But the problems of the American furniture industry go beyond this inevitable economic force. The industry made itself particularly vulnerable to offshore competition because it had been preoccupied far too long with an internal battle for control.

CIVIL WAR, 1965–2002

Instead of establishing brand names and modernizing operations, the U.S. furniture industry has been absorbed with fighting its own Civil War. Instead of improving productivity and recruiting stronger people, it busily rejected new ideas that were "not invented here." This battle has been waged between Insiders, those who grew up in the business with sawdust in their veins, and Outsiders who often came into the business with sawdust in their brains. While the two sides were fighting to dislodge each other, the industry became myopic and lost its focus, which left it open to attack from offshore producers.

In what has become one of history's longer running corporate conflicts, an army of Outsiders has tried for 35 years to invade the furniture industry. They have little to show for their efforts. The furniture insiders put up a relentless defense, and the invaders experienced an 80 percent casualty rate. Of the 120 documented incursions by outside firms, 96 abandoned their quests – and most of the survivors would bail out if they could.[2] Fearlessly marching into the harmless-looking industry, the Outsiders expected to make money while showing the grateful natives how to run their companies more efficiently and effectively. Instead, they found the environment was more hostile than they ever imagined. The initial sense of elation they experienced when entering the venture was soon replaced by desperation as losses mounted. Eventually, this led to a sense of relief as they bailed out. Rarely did it occur to the Outsiders that they should have seen it coming. Blinded by arrogance and hampered by tightly closed minds, they often underestimated the complexity of the furniture business and disregarded the lessons of history.

Low entry barriers, combined with high exit barriers, have captured and humiliated dozens of otherwise well-run companies. The victims include some top-notch corporations: Armstrong World, Beatrice Foods, Burlington Industries, Champion International, General Mills, Georgia Pacific, Gulf & Western, Magnavox, Masco,

Mead, Singer, Scott Paper, and Sperry & Hutchinson. Conglomerates could not make it, nor could companies that make paper, bedding, fabric, appliances, pianos, steel, cement, and baby food.

Not to Reason Why

A close reading of the history on the industry from the 1960s through the current time raises a multitude of questions we hope to answer in this book. What draws Outsiders to this fragmented industry, and why do they fail to see how treacherous it can be? Why do they assume it is "ripe for consolidation," even though the reasons underlying the fragmentation remain in place?[3] What makes them think they can succeed in the face of so much evidence to the contrary, and why do they think their own lack of furniture knowledge is somehow an advantage? Why do they eventually dismiss the talented furniture people who attracted them in the first place and replace them with people who know nothing about furniture?

Because they share in the responsibility for these failures, the Insiders cannot avoid blame. Why have they not been able to show the Outsiders how to make their ideas work? Why have they rejected the good ideas as quickly as the lame suggestions? Why have furniture professionals been so slow to adopt new methods regardless of where the suggestions originated?

Is the furniture business truly unique, as Insiders insist, or is it just like other industries, as Outsiders claim when they first arrive? Is the perceived uniqueness just an excuse to avoid doing the difficult things that need doing, or is it the real reason the many imported concepts fail to take hold, just as organ transplants are frequently rejected?

No matter the questions, the answers add up to an industrial tragedy of epic proportions. The American furniture industry desperately needs new capital and new ideas. It also needs new leaders to replace those who called the doctors "fools" while rejecting the medicine that might have made them healthy. Today, the patients are sicker than ever while consumers are largely indifferent to the industry's designs, frustrated by the shopping process, and spending less of their disposable income on furniture. While the Insiders were preoccupied with keeping the Outsiders away from the town square, the Asians all but captured the whole town.

To Do or Die

This book seeks to answer these questions based on the author's more than 35 years of firsthand experience and reflection. Written from the perspective of an outsider who became an insider, it reflects the thinking of someone who has a deep passion for the furniture business. That passion was developed and nurtured within the industry, where companies fight daily battles to capture a small piece of disposable income before it is snatched away from them – a world measured in six-month cycles between semi-annual trade shows called Markets, where couches are called "sofas" and suites are called "suits." It's a world where the battle between Insiders and Outsiders is one of many being fought simultaneously, including retailers vs. manufacturers, Northerners vs. Southerners, owners vs. managers, divisions vs. headquarters, and the United States vs. the World. So, take some time and survey battlefields where the

Furniture Wars are fought. But be careful, because the battlefield is not as simple as it seems. It's the proverbial Briar Patch – a refuge for some, a painful experience for others.

This narrative is based on real-world experience in one industry but has application to many industries, especially those that must contend with Outsiders who arrive with agendas based on experience in unrelated fields. Above all, this saga has relevance to any industry that contends with foreign competition.

This story could be termed a *histoir*, part history and part memoir. It is a history as it records events of the past 40 years to reveal the many mistakes that were needlessly repeated – and to warn that the mistakes will be made again unless the lessons are heeded. It is a memoir in the sense that it deals with the personal aspects of the industry that invariably interact with the business side and vice versa. As such, it deals with a full spectrum of human emotions, including victories and defeats, fortunes made and bankruptcies declared, divestitures and divorces, and even a murder trial.

The Bottom Line

Each furniture company has many direct competitors, and each company vies with others for retail floor space and retail advertising expenditures. Consumer brand preference is weak, vendor loyalty is fleeting, and substitutions are easy. That means producers must cope with having little leverage when dealing with suppliers and customers. And it means excessive price competition exists, which means chronically low margins. The most successful companies barely reach 10 percent pre-tax return on sales. Reasonably good companies make a profit of 4 to 6 percent, and many prominent players stay close to breakeven year after year. Because the assets needed to produce these modest results are high, the returns on working capital are even worse.

Still, Insiders love the business and cannot imagine working elsewhere. Outsiders sometimes learn to love it, but they typically become frustrated and self-destruct. Rarely do Outsiders have the patience to make the needed changes, and rarely do Insiders accept the need for these changes. Recently, they both find themselves ill-equipped to defend their turf in a battle with powerful foreign forces. Rather than invade the industry, the Asians plan to shut it down.

American factories stand idle in this post-apocalyptic wasteland. A $50 billion, uniquely American industry is in disarray, and 80,000 factory jobs have been eliminated since 2000.[4] This means one in four workers has been sent home. One study said 38 percent of them could not find work, and a quarter of the ones who found jobs took pay cuts of at least 30 percent.[5] The people who held these jobs may have found work in other fields, but they are gone from the furniture industry. Does it matter? To me it does and, if you care about the traditional American way of life, it should also matter to you.

I witnessed the Furniture Wars as well as fought in them. I am partly responsible for what happened to the American furniture business, and I hope that by sharing the story of the Furniture Wars, at least part of the industry and some other industries might be saved. If not, the future of the United States seems uncertain to me, and two questions beg to be answered: Can the American economy survive without producing anything? And if Asia produces everything America needs, who will pay for it?

THE INNER WORKINGS OF AN AMERICAN INDUSTRY

The Early History of the American Furniture Industry

THE FIRST PILGRIMS CARRIED few possessions when they set sail from England for the promise of the new land. There was no room on board for furniture. After arriving in Plymouth, they grew impatient with sleeping and eating on the ground and crafted a few dining tables, benches, and beds. With no furniture imports available, the domestic "shade tree" industry of cabinet making became one of America's first industries. The earliest designs were hand-hewn, primitive, and built to last. Decorative elements were added as settlers became more affluent.

The industry expanded dramatically during the eighteenth century. Cabinet makers in Boston, Newport, New York, Philadelphia, and Virginia turned out more expensive, more decorative products for well-to-do colonists. The designs were typically pared-down adaptations of more elaborate originals from England. Although Colonial woodworkers imported mahogany, they preferred native wood species such as cherry, maple, and pine. This gave the designs a uniquely American flavor.

In the nineteenth century, advances in machinery brought about by the industrial revolution helped the industry to move beyond its cottage roots. Machine-made products gradually replaced bench-made items, and railroads made it possible to branch out of the industry's New England base. Propelled by the arrival of European immigrants with woodworking skills, furniture manufacturing centers were formed in central Pennsylvania, western New York, southwestern Michigan, and southern Indiana.

Despite this growth, the business retained its entrepreneurial spirit and competitive structure. It was relatively easy to start a furniture company, not as easy to run one, and quite difficult to sell one. The industry remained too small to attract the attention of the big-time Robber Barons, so none bothered to monopolize furniture the way they did with trains, steel, oil, and coal. The furniture industry remained fragmented, with production spread among many players and polarized with a gap between the upper end and the mass market.

The industry's westward migration turned south by the twentieth century, and Virginia and North Carolina emerged as primary furniture-producing states. By offering cheaper labor costs in a union-free environment and abundant capital, the South enticed hundreds of textile mills to move. Furniture factory owners did not physically relocate, but new investments shifted from north to south. Gradually the South became the world's most important furniture producing area – especially when an offshoot group, seeking lower-cost labor, began making promotional upholstery in Mississippi.

POST-WAR PROSPERITY

Shipments continued to grow, especially after World War I, but they were hammered during the Great Depression when demand for home furnishings disappeared. Likewise, furniture companies during World War II either closed or made wood products for the military. Bernhardt made airplane parts, for example, and the Kittinger Co. built PT boats.

The companies that survived saw unprecedented prosperity during the post-war period. For two decades sales had been depressed and capacity had been reduced. Then, in the late '40s, the Greatest Generation went to college on the G.I. Bill, married, bought houses, and filled them with furniture. Then they had children, moved to bigger houses, and filled those bigger houses with furniture, and on and on. When they finally stopped buying furniture, their children, the Baby Boomers, were ready to buy more furniture.

These Glory Days were good times for the owners of furniture businesses. If you could make it, you could find a buyer for it. Pent-up demand exceeded supply, and the industry had no offshore competitors. The economy was free of major downturns, and the industry prospered during the 1960s and parts of the 1970s. The weakest competitors made money; the strongest made a lot of money.

Sophisticated it was not, unless you consider survival in a fiercely competitive industry sophisticated. You needed little marketing.

The only technology was the adding machine in the front office. You didn't even need a brand name. All you needed were a few savvy commission sales representatives to peddle what your factory could make, or tell you what to make. A select few companies invested in a primitive form of branding, using home decorating magazines to get their names more widely recognized. Bassett, Broyhill, Drexel, Thomasville, and Lane soon became well known, and their sales growth reflected the power of brand building. Consumers equated familiarity with quality, so these mid-market brands found themselves positioned as top of the line.

The rest of the industry generally ignored the end consumer, scorned marketing, and concentrated on production. Some companies introduced mass production techniques, but it mainly meant more machines and bigger lot sizes. Most upholstery was still bench-made, as were many casegoods. In some ways, management had not moved far from its Pilgrim origins. Merchandisers continued to feature eighteenth century styles, most of which they blatantly copied from each other. Operations executives were slow to keep pace with computer-controlled machinery developments, and information technology was viewed with suspicion.

Glory Days

Yes, the industry had problems during this time, but there also was something special about the business that attracted and held onto the participants. Companies placed greater value on people than on fixed assets. The talented "two-legged" assets – people who knew how to design, make, and sell furniture – could contribute more to the company's success than any machine. There was a certain collegiality, a sharing of the experience that resulted in camaraderie. This spirit encompassed the producers and sellers as well as the related participants who supplied materials and services to the industry – fabric mills, lumber mills, chemical finishing firms, hardware and machinery producers, designers, landlords, magazines, ad agencies, accountants, and consultants.

The product also was fun to work with. It was real; it was understandable. It had no moving parts and no on/off switch. It just sat there and, at best, looked good. It made rooms and homes look better. It made people feel good.[1]

The players had the opportunity to make an impact. The industry's fragmentation meant there was no establishment, which meant your career could move quickly. Nothing would hold you back if you had talent and ambition. The companies were family owned, and the mode was entrepreneurial. In the 1950s, it was reported that 75 percent of the firms were family controlled. Mavericks were tolerated, along with a few mildly crazed people.

The industry was relationship driven, and friendships meant a lot. Making money was important, but having fun was important too, because no owner was ever accused of paying anyone too much. The industry had its curmudgeons and inflated egos, but it was enjoyable to be in the furniture business. Few willingly left it. You had to love it to be successful, and it was easy to love.

At Mid-Century

At mid-century, the American furniture industry still carried the baggage that reflected its origins. The manufacturing process resisted automation and included a heavy labor component. Quality was hard to control, because standards were hard to measure. Marketing was non-existent. Worse still, few consumers enjoyed the shopping experience, and retailers did not know what to do about it. Critics claimed that profits were sub-standard and that the industry failed to maintain its share of consumer disposable income. While it was no longer a "shade tree" industry, some said it was still stuck at the "cottage" level. As designer Norman Hekler, once quipped, "The American furniture business proudly represents two hundred years of tradition . . . unimpeded by progress."

Dartmouth professor Kenneth R. Davis in 1957 published his study of the industry's marketing practices in a remarkable book called *Furniture Marketing, Product, Price, and Promotional Practices of Manufacturers.*[2] His surprising conclusions refuted critics and demonstrated that industry profits were average or slightly above normal. Furthermore, he claimed the "inability of the industry to realize a larger share of consumers' expenditures stems from the nature of the product, not the marketing methods."[3]

Davis said the culprits are consumers, who prefer their own individualized styles instead of me-too designs stamped off an assembly line. This prevents factories from generating economies of scale from long production runs and leads to unusually large product variety. This results in excess cost and inventories. Most importantly, in view of what was to come, was his observation that classic marketing methods do not work particularly well with furniture because "the technology of marketing managers in the furniture industry . . . is dwarfed by the underlying forces of consumer taste. It is the individual firm's ability to survive as it caters to the whims of a segment of consumer taste that has made the furniture industry atomistic."[4] In other words, the fragmented structure of the industry limits the effectiveness of marketing, and the structure has been determined, not by accident, but by responding to the consumer. How unfortunate that Davis' book was not read more widely.

And what is the nature of consumers' behavior when they buy furniture? Simply put, they do not want their furniture to look like the neighbors' furniture. They want their own "look." The retailer responds by offering as many choices as possible. This usually means he cannot concentrate on any one supplier. The suppliers' sales representative responds by opening more dealers. This means no one feels loyalty to anyone else. Just as consumers want their own "look," retailers also want to "differentiate" themselves from competitors. The manufacturer responds by adding more products. This usually results in trouble servicing the broad line, which means customers must wait months for delivery. They complain to the retailer, who complains to the sales rep, who complains to the factory. Meanwhile, the sales rep also is suggesting that a second finish be added to the collection, which further exacerbates the problem. And all anybody wanted was to meet the customer's needs.

The process looks cumbersome and inefficient to outside observers, and the remedies seem obvious. The Insider knows the process is cumbersome and inefficient. But the Insider also knows that the methods used in other industries will not work in furniture as long as consumers resist standardization. The manufacturing structure mirrors the retailing structure – many players, but no one capturing enough share to control the market.

Another contributor to this odd architecture is the fact that no manufacturer has ever successfully differentiated his brand name. Furniture becomes more of a commodity than water. Water is put in a fancy bottle and given an exotic name in hopes of setting it apart from rivals. Furniture is packaged in a carton that the customer never sees, and the product's label is hidden if it has a label at all. Furniture retailers have an equally hard time separating themselves from the competition. What furniture people lack in originality they make for with ingenious skill at copying. Products, programs, and ideas are knocked off with such regularity that it is hard to sustain a unique identity, much less a competitive edge.

SURGE

In spite of its many flaws and its provincial mind-set, the furniture industry surged forward during the "go-go" 1960s. The strong economy and the demand for home furnishings lifted spirits and earnings. The business was in good shape in 1965 but continued to resist consolidation and remained highly fragmented. Upholstery producers had little in common with casegoods producers. Mass market factories and carriage trade cabinet makers had little to do with one another.

The industry also continued to show its regional divide. The old-line New England companies specialized in Colonial and Early American styles made of the solid maple, birch, and pine indigenous to the region. Pennsylvania producers took advantage of their native cherry trees to make styles they called American Traditional. In Michigan, the Grand Rapids firms loved to use mahogany and walnut to make elegant styles. Southern producers relied on wood species indigenous to the Southeast – oak, ash, and pecan – that created new looks that were weightier and more casual. Some in the industry called it the "furniture by the pound" School of Design. Construction methods combined veneers and solid woods and, miraculously, molded plastic parts were introduced. This let mass market producers introduce extravagant designs in a style called "Mediterranean." These products reinforced the belief by some that "ugly outsells pretty" and that, for many consumers, "too much is not enough." Of course, each region felt its products were superior to the others. Northerners thought veneered products were inferior to solid, and Southerners looked down on what they thought were the boring styles of Yankees.

Within the regions, each plant developed distinctive construction traits and finishing techniques that set their products apart. The problem was that these points of differentiation were so subtle that only experienced furniture people could spot them. Consumers could not.

BALKANIZATION

The industry was further divided by an alphabet soup of industry associations. The National Association of Furniture Manufacturers (NAFM) was comprised mostly of small, family owned firms up north, and the Southern Furniture Manufacturers Association (SFMA) was dominated by a few large family-owned companies down south. They were joined by the Association of Outdoor Furniture Manufacturers and by BIFMA, the Business & Institutional

Furniture Manufacturers. And of course retailers had their own association, the National Home Furnishings Association (NHFA). Rarely did these groups talk to each other, much less collaborate.

This splintering extended into the company organizations, too. Sales and Manufacturing rarely got along; headquarters and the outlying facilities often fought; sales reps and management did not trust each other; and retailers and manufacturers rarely agreed.

MAKING IT

Making the furniture was not easy. Unlike most manufacturing processes that basically assemble parts, casegoods manufacturing requires many individual processes as raw lumber boards become finished items. The lumber must be bought and graded before it is air dried and kiln dried in the lumber yard. Workers must select, buy, slice, splice, match, tape, and patch the veneers. Someone must cut the lumber to the proper sizes before it is defected, planed, and glued into panels or posts. In other parts of the factory, workers machine, carve, drill, bore, turn, tenon, mortise, and route the lumber – and all the while, that lumber is being inspected, shaped, sanded, moved, and counted. Next, workers start the sub-assembly process to build the doors, drawers, frames, and panels. Finally, the parts are joined to become the furniture it was designed to be. But it's not ready until workers complete more sanding, inspecting, and finishing.

The work takes weeks when it's done right and the lumber cooperates. Wood attracts moisture, resists bending, and cannot be forged, stamped, melted, molded, or cast. It refuses to cooperate and behave like plastic or metal. It would rather split, warp, check, splinter, and discolor.

Finally, the product is ready to be finished. This process can be quite simple for low-end goods made of printed film on cheap fiberboard. They are finished quickly and indifferently by a process sometimes called "Rip, Dip, and Ship." Fine furniture receives much more attention, with as many as 25 steps. These include combinations of sanding, bleaching, drying, sap staining, padding, ragging, sealing, sealer sanding, overall staining, wiping, uniforming, toning, distressing, speckling, cowtailing, dry brushing, spray padding, hand padding, and oven drying. Then, if everything looks right, it gets two coats of lacquer and a final rub and wax.

The upholstery operation is different. The frames can be bought or made in house with a few machines. The fabric is purchased, as are the cushions, springs, and other parts. The process requires only a few days if the raw materials are on hand. The production steps include cutting the fabric, matching and completing it to a pattern, making and applying welts as needed, sewing the fabric pieces together, filling the cushions, applying the fabrics to the outside backs and sides, and then tying it all together with the inside (front) upholstery operation. The manufacturing problem lies in upper-end goods, because there is very little repetition and everything is custom made.

SELLING IT

While workers do their jobs along the assembly lines, the sales and marketing types keep trying to sell what is in production and to figure out what new products might sell. The sales process is pretty straightforward. In April and October, manufacturers showcase their new products in large showrooms in High Point, North Carolina, at what is referred to as "the Market." Sales representatives and sales managers try to win orders for "placements" of the new goods in stores nationwide. This leads to a ritual called "Vendors vs. Emptors," in which buyers and sellers play a zero-sum game that nobody wins. The retail buyer tries to get access to as many lines as possible without ceding his valuable floor space. He wins outright if he can have access to a line but only agrees to put the catalog on display. On the other hand, the seller tries to get a huge display without agreeing to let the dealer have the line exclusively. He wins outright if he can get all the dealers in town to give him big displays. The game usually ends with compromises that satisfy neither party.

The product planning and merchandising process is even quirkier. Freelance and staff designers work with merchandisers to plan and design new collections. Sketches are drawn and mockups are built. Then samples are built just in time for the Market launch to the trade. At this point, true manufacturing costs can only be guessed at, and consumer reaction is a complete unknown. The cost of the handmade samples is very high, as is the risk of competitor copying. It means market testing with real consumers is out of the question. Ideas for new designs come from everywhere – resorts, restaurants, flea markets, antiques, movie sets, and, more often than not, a competitor's product line. Some designs sell while some do not, and no one can predict with any regularity. The surest bet is to copy something that is selling and make it for less money. This is patently unfair and unethical, of course, but so it goes in the furniture game.

Buying It

The end user was ill served by this system. The family-run producers ignored end users and relied on retailers to act as surrogates for them, but this arrangement did not work very well. Manufacturers rarely met with customers between Markets and then only with the biggest volume accounts that also may be out of touch with end users. The fragmented retail channel of distribution meant that most furniture stores were too small to have much impact. In 1965, the typical furniture store was undersized and undercapitalized. The "Mom & Pop" retail store was a fitting counterpart to the "shade tree" furniture manufacturer, because what they presented to the shopper left much to be desired. There were many notable exceptions, but a visit to most stores in those days involved dirty windows, "rack 'em and stack 'em" product displays, and predatory sales tactics. This was matched by consumer ignorance about construction, woods, finishes, and fabrics.

Is it any wonder the industry was criticized? The marketing process was like a parade without a parade route, with factory-oriented producers trying to respond to inefficient retailers trying to react to uninformed shoppers. Kenneth R. Davis concluded his book *Furniture Marketing* with a quote from economist E. A. G. Robinson on the irony of this system: "In many industries all the firms, big as well as small, could produce more efficiently were they assured a large and certain market. It is, as Adam Smith told us, the extent of the market that limits the division of labor, and it is you and I who determine the extent of the market. It was, as we all know, the rolling English drunkard who made the rolling English road."[5] It is the independent customer who has shaped the furniture industry.

Michael Porter Rules

The realities of the furniture business are inordinately difficult to grasp, yet some notable insights come from Michael Porter, Harvard's resident strategic wizard.[6] Porter says the furniture industry is highly fragmented, and companies choosing to compete within this structure must shape their strategy accordingly. Fragmentation results when no single company controls enough market share to influence industry outcomes. He advises that unless the underlying reasons for the industry's fragmentation can be overcome, true consolidation cannot occur, regardless of size. Yet the following chapters show repeated, futile attempts to consolidate it while ignoring the underlying causes. Here are some of those causes:

+ Economies of scale are rarely realized in furniture production, because bigger does not mean better. Long production runs and repeated operations do not necessarily drive down costs. Large lot sizes in furniture, called cuttings, actually disrupt product flow by tying up machinery needed for other jobs.

+ Size sometimes works against manufacturers. The typical retailer is fairly small and more comfortable dealing with a modest-sized supplier than with a large one. Because retailers seek exclusive products and steer clear of lines available to competitors, manufacturers cannot generate high volume in one style.

✝ The need to maintain a low overhead favors small, entrepreneurial furniture companies, while large firms tend to lose focus as they grow. The industry is thus comprised of a series of overlapping niches served by specialists, not generalists. One cynic called it "a confederacy of niches served by a conspiracy of dunces."

✝ Heavy creative content fuels the furniture business, and large organizations typically do not breed great creative environments. The product design function, combined with the interior design element, drives customer appeal. More often than not, these talents are provided by freelance artists who abhor big companies. This is similar to the entertainment business, which tends to attract and destroy outsiders.

✝ Fragmented consumer tastes force merchandisers to develop diverse product lines, which contribute to inefficiencies and work against standardized products.

✝ High product differentiation is desirable but hard to attain. This limits the size of the company. This is especially difficult for upscale furniture makers, who cannot sell themselves as exclusive while selling products in both "mass" and "class" markets.

It is relatively easy to start a furniture company, but not so easy to get rid of one. Economists characterize this quirk as a "low entry barrier with a high exit barrier." Marginal companies almost never go completely out of business. If they do, a new owner typically arrives in time to restart the cycle. During this period, the overriding goal is simply to meet the payroll. This leads to giveaway prices that drive down everyone's margins.

Porter argues convincingly: "It takes the presence of only one of these characteristics to block the consolidation of an industry."[7] Yet the furniture industry has multiple barriers in its way. When the odds are against overcoming fragmentation, it makes sense to accept the fact and to devise strategies accordingly.

The Bottom Line

The sum of the industry's unique issues – much competition, limited brand preference, weak vendor loyalty – means producers must cope with little leverage in dealing with suppliers and customers.

Excessive price competition exists among furniture makers because they have few retail alternatives, which means chronically low margins. Most industries have a handful of competitors who set the pace for everyone else. Economists call this model an *oligopoly*, or "control by the few." The furniture industry is closer to the model of *perfect competition*, in which no one sets the pace. By 1965 the industry was beginning to attract outside investors who would seek to be reformers in spite of its track record, or maybe because of it. Like a party on fraternity row that draws a crowd of uninvited guests, the furniture business had caught the eye of more than a few outside interests. The party started to be crashed.

Fortune magazine noted that the furniture industry had been shielded from modern management and marketing techniques by virtually automatic prosperity, thereby creating a wonderful opportunity for innovators. "An air of earnest optimism pervades the industry because for two hundred years, furniture manufacturing has preserved the characteristics of its handcrafted origin," reporter Thomas O'Hanlon wrote.[8] "Most companies are still insignificant in size, inbred in management, inefficient in production, and inherently opposed to technological change." His remarkably disdainful article blasted the industry for resisting change, being overly competitive, and pandering to the lowest common denominator in taste, producing furniture "that is uniformly uninspired and often downright ugly." For good measure, he also claimed the industry had abysmal quality, patronized its workforce, used "Rube Goldberg" assembly line methods, and followed a "scattershot approach to product development."

This confluence of incompetence and obstinacy resulted in a confusing array of products with inadequate appeal to consumers who were turned off by the whole experience. A large part of the problem, according to the article, was caused by the preponderance of small companies in the industry who could not afford to research consumers or designs. They had to rely on plain, old-fashioned intuition, without the benefits of market research. Two-thirds of the 5,350 companies employed fewer than 20 people. Only 75 or so companies had more than $10 million in sales. And the largest company, Kroehler, held less than 3 percent of the

$4 billion market. This severe fragmentation was part of the appeal to Outsiders who saw opportunity through consolidation. Grudgingly, O'Hanlon admitted that the industry managed to make money – much more, in fact, than the leaders in clothing, textiles, and appliances – but he quickly asserted that this respectable performance resulted from an elementary need for furniture, not shrewd management.

The article neglected to explain how some of these obtuse furniture people had managed to stay above breakeven, well above. For example:

✝ From 1962 to 1966, Thomasville tripled its net income while increasing sales by 70 percent. Net margins were close to 9 percent.

✝ During the same period, Drexel's sales rose 42 percent and net income rose 74 percent.

✝ Bassett's net income nearly doubled from $4.6 million to $8.9 million, while sales went from $66 million to $95 million.

✝ The best performer was a relatively small firm called Henredon Furniture Industries. It reported net income of $2.2 million on sales of $22.3 million.

A young investor named Colin Carpi thought he could foresee big changes on the horizon. As sales grew, there would be a wave of consolidation as the innovative outsiders struggled with the rigid old-line companies inside, not unlike the battle between the Athenians and the Trojans in Homer's Iliad. "I'm convinced," he told *Fortune* in 1965, "that within 10 or 15 years, 50 companies will account for 90 percent of the volume in furniture. A company with $300 million in sales will not be unusual."

THE OUTSIDER INVASION

The industry was a mess, O'Hanlon concluded. All it did was make money. Just think what it could be like if only some outsiders would give it professional management, modern marketing, and capital. Carpi and others did not hesitate to *carpe diem*. A few would study the industry to arrive at a clear understanding of its unique characteristics. Most simply assumed it was similar to other industries and would respond accordingly. Practically all of them underestimated the complexity of the business and misread its subtleties. Any lingering doubts about moving into uncharted territory were overcome by the highly favorable demographic projections for the industry. The first wave of Baby Boomers soon would be out of school and starting families. Young families typically buy furniture. Furniture companies would be in a great position to cash in on this demographic windfall. Armed with money but little understanding, Mohasco, Magnavox, Litton, Burlington, U. S. Plywood, and others marched fearlessly into the furniture industry. They all sought a quick payoff by exploiting what they perceived as slow-witted Insiders.

But the Insiders were not willing to vacate their chairs without a protest. They resented the newcomers' assertions that radical changes were warranted, and they stiffly defended their tried-and-true methods. They saw the furniture manufacturing process as more art than science, and the variable nature of wood dictated methods that were different from those used with metal. They also saw the industry as being built on relationships with customers, suppliers, workers, even with competitors, and they knew best how to nurture them. Insiders knew the industry was unique, or at least decidedly different from others. Publicly, they welcomed the new players at the table. Privately, they thought the Outsiders were crazy. Somehow, this conflict would have to be resolved, even if it meant an outbreak of The Furniture Wars.

Like a society cut off from outside influences, the industry became isolated, and the debilitating conflict between Outsiders and Insiders sapped its vitality. Instead of evolving and adopting new methods, the furniture business became stuck in time and left itself open to the more serious threat of offshore competition. Instead of reinvesting intelligently in plant and equipment, it spent its profits to pay off leveraged buy-out debts.

The net result of this infighting led to one very fragile industry, struggling to rebuild itself as its civil war fizzled to a close. Because so many companies in the furniture industry had been so preoccupied for so long with so many internal battles, they had neglected the fundamental work that needed to be done to meet the challenges of the twenty-first century. Instead of concentrating on the enhancement of their brands and the modernization of their production methods, the insiders had been engaged in repelling the wrong enemy. Meanwhile, the Outsiders had produced little more than a costly list of failed initiatives, and their ability to "get results" turned out to be nonexistent. The Insiders refused to recognize that the Outsiders had many good ideas and stubbornly held on to outmoded methods. By relying too heavily on price competition without the benefit of lower costs, margins were driven to dangerously low levels. Because of low margins, companies could not afford to make the moves necessary to break out of this "doom loop" and they were not able to attract sufficient capital to retool.

The inevitable consequence was a movement to offshore production in order to make the product cheaper by reducing labor costs. Instead of re-engineering the processes so that the required labor hours could be reduced, the manufacturers threw in the towel and transferred their old-style methods to Third World countries where the labor supply was cheap and plentiful. It was highly unlikely that the offshore model would be any more effective in attracting the consumer's attention than the original had been; it would be cheaper, but no one was claiming it would be better. Still, it was all the American furniture warriors had to go on, given the current climate of the industry.

SEVEN REALITIES,
SEVEN SINS,
SEVEN COMMANDMENTS

AMERICA'S FURNITURE MAKERS might be in better shape today had someone written a *Furniture Industry for Dummies* book with a set of clear guidelines. Perhaps a furniture rule book might have meant the Outsiders' grand visions to improve the industry would not have turned into gluttonous and overwrought disappointments. A more calculated implementation of these visions – one grounded in the undeniable principles of the furniture business – could have helped an American industry make a successful leap into the twenty-first century.

But for reasons hard to understand, the Outsiders wore blinders that kept them from comprehending the traditional principles of furniture. Why else did one after another stumble into nearly identical traps in the Briar Patch? Couldn't they at least have learned from the mistakes of the Outsiders who preceded them?

Once it became clear that the Outsiders were going to become squatters in the Briar Patch, many Insiders did their best to communicate the principles of the industry. Although the Insiders didn't like ceding control of their industry to the invaders, they liked watching their industry being spoiled even less. So they tried to share their secrets – the knowledge and folk wisdom collected through lifetimes of experience. Unfortunately, most Outsiders simply refused to believe the Insiders' opinions were valuable.

The furniture rules changed little over time. Many of the same principles held for 50 years and a civil war, no matter how explosive or damaging, was not going to change that reality. True, the rules needed to be updated, but the principles remained constant. The Outsiders' invasions only served to underscore them. The industry has certain realities that had to be recognized, certain sins that had to be avoided, and certain transgressions that were simply unforgivable. To survive the Furniture Wars – much less to succeed – you must never lose sight of the Seven Realities, you must not commit the Seven Deadly Sins, and you must obey the Seven Commandments. Ignorance of the rules is no excuse.

SEVEN FURNITURE REALITIES

Furniture businesses operate within their own set of realities shaped largely by the industry structure. These realities include the following:

REALITY NO. 1: *The Industry Is Intensely Competitive*

The top 10 furniture companies comprise only 40 percent of total sales. The balance is divided among 5,000 companies. The fragmentation exists even after numerous mergers and acquisitions.

The largest companies tend to manage like holding companies rather than monolithic corporations. Often the divisions compete fiercely with each other to the dismay of the parent. Synergy has simply not happened.

Other industries are more consolidated, and competition is more orderly in an oligopoly. The General Mills cereal division, for example, has intimate knowledge of its four key competitors: Kellogg, Post, Quaker, and Nabisco. "Cereal Barons" know exactly where they stand in the "Breakfast Wars," even to the level of having precise market share statistics every week. Upon entering the Furniture Wars, General Mills executives were baffled by an industry where everybody competes with everybody else and no company really knows its market share. The distribution channel, which was infinitely more complex than grocery stores, also puzzled General Mills. In an example of this complexity, one furniture analyst regularly tracks 13 separate distribution channels.[1] The publisher of *Furniture Today* lists 69 distinct furniture channels.[2] In grocery stores, it would be unthinkable *not* to carry Wheaties or Cheerios, but furniture stores have no "must-have" brands and retailers have countless vendor options. Gabbert's, a disciplined furniture store, typically carries 20 upholstery suppliers and 50 casegoods suppliers. Any one of them can be moved into any floor space slot quickly and easily; any one can be removed just as easily. Even so-called dedicated space, reserved for key suppliers in return for concessions, can be converted to a competitor's product in a few hours.

Unlike the cereal business or the plumbing fixture business, the furniture business comes close to the economic model of Perfect Competition. Combatants freely jockey for position, new entrants appear frequently, and no one holds a sustainable competitive advantage. Moreover, no one has any proprietary product or even features. Painstakingly developed innovations are quickly replicated. Designs are blatantly copied. Programs are duplicated. Concepts are stolen. The only elements that seem to be safe are reputations and relationships, which is why they are so important. To succeed, a furniture company must be keenly aware of its direct competition – the rivals close to its segment – as well as indirect competitors who are vying with it for floor space and ad dollars. A company must scrupulously establish and constantly enhance its reputation, making sure it can substantively back up a reputation that is in tune with current needs.

Properly positioning a company requires a keen understanding of the subtleties of this competitive atmosphere. Successful furniture executives have a feel for the marketplace. They are adept at managing the image of their company and are hyper-sensitive to changes in the competitive landscape. Dealing with competition in these circumstances is not easy, and all the right-brain aspects of the furniture formula drive Outsiders crazy. Since Outsiders usually have not developed a sixth sense for the mood of the market and have built few relationships, they tend to dismiss these factors and demean their significance. Frustrated by their inability to make the industry fit their preconceived point of view, they respond in one of two ways. They either take the industry seriously and give it the respect it deserves, or they treat it disdainfully and give it the contempt typically reserved for things difficult to understand. All too often, Outsiders chose the latter course.

Successfully coping with competition requires the discovery and exploitation of market niches. The leaders study the market and develop a keen sense of these niches, their potential, and how to attack. They look for the openings, *cherchez le creneau*, and swiftly exploit previously underserved market segments.[3]

Weak companies follow the crowd and copy the leaders, usually arriving too late to make a big difference yet diluting the efforts of the leaders. The cheap copies confuse the consumer and undermine the efforts of the innovator. But such is life in the Furniture Wars, where combatants are nearly always surrounded, and both enemy fire and friendly fire come from all directions.

REALITY NO. 2: *The Sharper the Focus, the Better the Picture*

The analogy of a camera explains another of the realities of the furniture business. At times one needs a wide-angle lens to see the context. At other times one needs a telephoto lens to zoom in on the details and fine points. Regardless of the lens, however, one always needs to be focused so that the image is sharp, clear, and realistic.

The most successful companies are able to sustain a sharp focus on their niche for prolonged periods. A good example is the Woodmark Chair Co. As conceived by Elliot Wood, it made upholstered chairs only – no sofas, loveseats, ottomans or accent items – just chairs, and it was better at it than anybody else. Some have developed and sustained an effective presence in more than one niche, but it is rare because a broad assortment usually leads to a loss of focus. Any activity that draws attention away from the primary focus will increase the chance of failure. The more distractions, the harder to maintain focus.

When furniture companies are put in play and ownership

changes, these companies lose focus and leave themselves open to competitors. When companies grow and expand into new categories, they tend to lose focus on their original niche. When companies stretch their key people and ask them to take on special projects, focus is easily lost. Invariably there is a competitor who only cares about that niche and is intently focused on it. The minute your concentration is broken, the competitor is poised to grab your market share.

By definition, being focused on one segment means you will not be focused on something else. All too often, manufacturers put too much focus on the retailer and not enough on the consumer. It would be more effective if the focus were on selling to the consumer through the retailer. The successful firms know what they have chosen not to concentrate on, making sure those deliberately neglected areas will not come back to haunt them. Resisting the temptation to set impossible goals like "doing everything better" and "being an expert at all things" frees up time to be very good at a few things.

REALITY NO. 3: *The Closer the Alignment, the Better the Results*

Newcomers to the Furniture Zone frequently come from industries where production is only loosely connected with merchandising and marketing. A Procter & Gamble brand manager does not need to spend time in the plant to understand how they squeeze Crest into the toothpaste tubes. Nor does the General Mills product manager need to know how each tiny little "O" ends up in a Cheerios box. The manufacturing process is a constant in those industries, not a variable.

But each furniture plant has its own range of capabilities, its own DNA. Merchandisers who develop a deep understanding of this plant signature will get the most out of it. Developing products on the plus side of the range makes sense, but it is risky to force a plant outside of its "comfort zone." In the pursuit of focus, it is not sufficient to have only part of the business unit zeroed in. The entire organization must be engaged. Hence, successful companies link plant functions closely with field activities and vice versa. Results will come up short without an element of trust between operations and merchandising.

Success in the furniture business also demands symbiosis between the production and the marketing functions. How this will be impacted by the move to offshore manufacturing remains to be seen. The separation of production from merchandising could well result in a misfire. Many Outsiders see the industry as a marketing play with the plants being relatively unimportant. What they fail to grasp is that those wonderful marketing opportunities cannot be exploited without closely coordinated factory support. The challenges associated with sourcing from third-party plants are formidable, but the marketer who meets them has an advantage.

This reality also requires precise alignment among the management, the factory, the product line, the sales force, and the retailer network, just as there is with a properly sighted-in rifle. The gun will not be accurate if a single bead is out of line. Fixing one element without realigning the other elements means missing the target. On a different level, successful companies coordinate their efforts for a high degree of convergence, just as high-caliber armaments are aligned in fighter planes so the ammunition fired from both wings converges at a preset point in front of the plane for maximum impact. Unless all the weapons are armed and aimed properly, they will not attain their full potential against opponents trying to shoot you down.

REALITY NO. 4: *Product Really Is King*

Nutritionists say, "You are what you eat." Furniture people say, "You are what you introduce." Product, the right product, is so crucial to furniture success that nothing comes remotely close in importance. A company's relative strength is a direct result of its product introductions over the previous five years, and there is no getting around it. This frustrates Outsiders, because the product development process is very imprecise and ultimately depends on someone's gut feel. But it works when the right people are in place. This art must be accepted and dealt with, not disputed.

Packaged goods marketers are taught to treat the product as just one of four variables they must control – product, price, place, and promotion. Deep down, they tend to think of all products as merely commodities. Unable to sense the subtle but critical differences between furniture products, they dismiss the industry's entire output of casegoods as "just a sea of brown." Sadly, the battlefield is littered with the corpses of would-be warriors whose battle cry was, "It's not the product; it's the program that counts."

In furniture, victory goes to the troops with the best product. The reason this is true lies deep in the psyche of the consumer, who invariably strips away all the hype and decides whether she likes or doesn't like the product. She responds to the visual stimuli emitted by the item and quickly calculates what the piece would say about her if she owned it. Her visceral reaction determines whether the sale is made or not, and all the fancy marketing in the world can do little to alter or even shape this fact. This process is different from buying packaged goods, where she can be inordinately influenced by brand positioning, packaging, and advertising. Very little research has been done to support this contention, but the empirical evidence is overwhelmingly convincing. To deny it is to set oneself up to fail.

Furniture products are made from non-proprietary materials. The forms and the functions are non-exclusive and not protected by patents. Brand recognition is low. Dealer loyalty is limited. Consumer tastes are fickle. Yet, mysteriously, some products sell. This is the "X Factor" of design – the "look," as the furniture mavens call it – which drives the business. Of course, good marketing programs can surround a good product and enhance its appeal, but product is the Once and Future King. To survive, furniture companies must be able to produce one winner after another – and doing that requires companies to attract and nurture the best product development talent available. A sure sign of trouble is when an organization decides that its creative people are no longer worthwhile. When hard-to-swallow justifications are proffered for their dismissal and talent from another industry is brought in to replace them, it is a clear sign that the end is near.

REALITY NO. 5: *The Retail Channel
Has More Land Mines than Gold Mines*

Arguably, the most important factor beyond product is the distribution channel. A furniture company's destiny is irretrievably linked to the dealers who carry its line. The retail segment is also fragmented and also not very profitable. The two deserve each other. Having failed to reach détente with suppliers, the retail channel tends to drive down prices. Retailers demand better service and quality but are not willing to pay for it, and play suppliers against each another in the nasty game. This usually leads to a price war during which many of their products are sold, at least for a short while. But then, forced to sell at low margins, the retailer must cut services or discontinue the line.

The goal of Emptors, those intrepid defenders of the sacred Floor Space, is to capture as many lines as possible and keep Vendors from grabbing all their floor space. Strategically, Emptors win when they manage to tie up many lines for the whole city without devoting floor space to any of them. Not having any competition, they then can support heavy overhead costs. The problem with this game is that regardless of the victor, the consumer loses because service deteriorates and prices rise.

As much as the manufacturers try to differentiate their products, retailers tend to think of their lines as fungible commodities and assume they can easily substitute one supplier for another. As hard as manufacturers try to improve their brand recognition and enhance consumer appeal, retailers essentially denude the product at the point of sale by removing all identification – sometimes even sanding off the brand stamped inside the drawer. The manufacturers' ability to find substitute outlets is limited, because many markets have a dominant retailer who controls access to that trading area. These "gatekeepers" use their clout with vendors. The road to Michigan, for example, goes through Art Van, a powerful retailer who has a 40 percent share of the state's market.

It's bad enough that the retailer has the upper hand, but sadly, he often does not know what to do with it. The industry could benefit from strong retailers that generate large volume, but such is not the case. Embarrassingly, one powerful retailer after another has stumbled and fallen in battle. Levitz, Sears HomeLife, JC Penney, Heilig-Myers, Rhodes, Montgomery Ward, and countless other regional firms have all gone bankrupt in recent years. During the 1990s, 22 different "Top 100 Retailers" went under.[4] In the meantime, upstarts such as IKEA, Crate and Barrel, Pottery Barn, and Restoration Hardware have captured the consumers' imagination and disposable cash.

For some inexplicable reason, the industry has lacked the courage to establish more vertically integrated models with manufacturer-controlled presentations, such as Ethan Allen has. Year after year, Ethan Allen stands tall by all financial measurements, yet no other manufacturer has been able or willing to match its superb retail format.

REALITY NO. 6: *Furniture Demand Is Highly Cyclical*

Furniture purchases are easy to postpone and the products hardly ever wear out, so consumers quickly stop buying when the economy slows. This makes the category a leading indicator of an economic downturn. Unfortunately, furniture also is a lagging indicator when the economy turns up. As a result, downturns are frequent and prolonged. This makes furniture a high-risk environment for leveraged buyouts and puts unusual pressure on management. The ability to anticipate changes in the economic cycle takes on added importance, and many functions are unusually difficult to manage, such as budgeting, bonus plans, demand forecasting, and promotion planning.

Smart operators cultivate two distinct "battle formations" – an offense for good times and a defense for tough times. Less-savvy operators never make the necessary adjustments and issue the wrong commands. In either formation, costs must be assiduously controlled. For many reasons, furniture margins are not large enough to cover the costs needed to earn large margins. This paradox means most furniture makers cannot do everything that seems logical to deal with economic cycles.

REALITY NO. 7: *Companies Have Die-Hard Cultures*

The industry is so competitive that companies need very strong identities to survive. Firms without vigorous cultures can easily be destroyed by rival cultures. The culture is originally infused by the founder and is then shaped and strengthened by later owners, managers, workers, and events. Gradually it becomes imbedded and takes on a life of its own as it becomes nearly indelible. When corporations or new owners tamper with organizational DNA, they should expect severe resistance. Time and again, new owners try to reposition companies only to meet severe resistance from workers and dealers. It can be done, but newcomers must take care or the old culture will reassert itself.

SEVEN DEADLY FURNITURE SINS

It is nearly impossible for a person to change furniture reality, but blatantly violating the industry's unwritten commandments can be avoided. Maneuvering in the industry's unique environment requires that one must avoid temptation. In Dante's *Inferno*, sinners are assigned to the various levels of hell based on the severity of their sins. The length of one's stay in the furniture business is determined by the ability to avoid the following transgressions:

SIN NO. 1: *Lust*

The industry is seductive. To the newcomer, it looks like easy money. Not only do profits seem simple to increase, Outsiders expect to have fun in the process. They can relate to furniture. After all, they use it daily and assume they will enjoy running a business of products that are easy to understand. And why not? Insiders claim they love the furniture industry and seem to have fun. Outsiders expect to do the same.

The problem comes when Outsiders allow their vision to be clouded by lust. Persons consumed with lust become irrational and lose their perspicacity. This leads to costly mistakes. It's best not to confuse passion for acute mental vision or to mistake lust for love. Love connotes respect; lust connotes exploitation. When you love the business, you embrace it for what it is and work in synch with it, rather than build plans on a premise that is non-existent.

SIN NO. 2: *Sloth*

It is tempting to be lazy when entering the furniture business. Since the product seems easy to understand, outsiders incorrectly think that making and distributing furniture must be equally straightforward. They complain that current methods are overly complex and cumbersome. They correctly call them outmoded but fail to understand that what works in other industries won't work in the furniture business. Bad things happen when Outsiders try to force new, improved methods onto furniture plants or furniture retailers. The old methods have endured because they accommodate the realities of the business. Sometimes what appears to be a backward practice is actually a resourceful way to cope with an industry quirk.

SIN NO. 3: *Avarice*

Being greedy when it comes to setting profit objectives has killed many unsuspecting leaders. Furniture is too competitive to be a high-margin business. Live with it, and the fact that that some unexpected costs will occur. Chasing unrealistic margins only leads to frustration. Learn to live with thin margins or find some other industry.

SIN NO. 4: *Anger*

It is easy to become angry when things start going badly or simply do not live up to the Outsider's expectations. Directing anger at the furniture people and replacing them with non-furniture types only accelerates the company's decline. No matter the level of frustration, a boss cannot run a furniture company without furniture people any more than they can run a football team without football players. It's better to upgrade the team with better furniture people than to hire outsiders who do not know the business.

SIN NO. 5: *Pride*

Outsiders seem to bristle at the suggestion that product is the most important determinant of success or failure. Being too proud to acknowledge this fact is folly. Outsiders find it hard to grasp the product development function, and it is maddening to think that the execution of some designer's hunch will lead to huge expenditures on an untested collection. But that's the furniture business. Rather than trying to reinvent this process, the leader should hire the best designers possible, support them, and pray that their next hunch will be a great one. When they make money, you make money.

SIN NO. 6: *Gluttony*

With so many high hopes propelling them, Outsiders are prone to bite off more than they can chew. They want change, and they want a lot of it in a hurry. The furniture industry needs change and will accept it, but rushing it too much will cause it to collapse around you. Being a glutton when it comes to managing the pace of change will backfire. Seeing the need for change and prescribing the right solutions is easy; implementing it effectively is difficult. Show restraint, not gluttony.

SIN NO. 7: *Envy*

The skill positions in furniture are usually filled with merchandising and sales people who seem to have it made. Sales associates and merchandisers can make a lot of money, but they do it only by making a lot of money for the company. They are the warriors you need in battle. Being envious of their lifestyles is pointless. Their jobs are not at all easy, and your survival is threatened without real talent in the field and in the product war room. As with designers, the smart leader will hire the best talents available and hope they earn a lot of money for themselves and the company.

SEVEN COMMANDMENTS OF FURNITURE

Temptations are everywhere in the furniture business. The industry provides no warning signs to tell you when you move close to the edge of sin, but you will pay a price when you cross a line. This is true whether you are an Outsider or an Insider.

To avoid this misery, approach the industry with eyes wide open. See it for what it really is, and take the time to learn it. There is money to be made in furniture, but before you can claim it you must first accept the irrefutable fact that the industry is unlike any other. Outsiders often misread the competitive landscape and find themselves caught in a special set of strategic traps. It starts when their patience is tested with marginal profitability. Then their skills are tested when a series of seemingly sensible courses of action leads to destruction. Only when Outsiders find themselves irrevocably committed do they suspect they are headed for disaster. Again, Michael Porter identifies these traps in his book *Competitive Strategy*.

Obeying these Seven Commandments of Furniture will help avoid the traps:

COMMANDMENT NO. 1:

Thou Shalt Not Seek Market Dominance

The fragmented structure of the furniture industry means that it cannot be dominated by a single player. Attempts to dominate will fail without fundamental changes to the industry's structure. Consumers resist "one-size-fits-all" pitches from big companies while retailers resist large suppliers. Trying to be "all things to all people" will only result in being "very few things to very few people." Touting one-stop shopping to retailers ends up turning them away. Because this is a niche business, dealers instinctively favor suppliers who are focused specialists instead of large, awkward generalists. Transplants from other industries, accustomed to the accoutrements of dominant roles, have a hard time resisting the temptation to recreate that feeling in furniture. As we will see, Masco and Kohler – the respective King of Faucets and Queen of Toilets – stumbled into the furniture quagmire and never quite found their balance, much less positions of dominance.

COMMANDMENT NO. 2:

Thou Shalt Honor Strategic Discipline

Industry players need strategic discipline to compete in a fragmented industry. The "helter skelter" nature of the business can easily lead to the conclusion that an opportunistic, "get all you can" approach will work. This leads to strategic promiscuity, a recipe for disaster. Precisely because the industry is fast moving and competitive battlefields change constantly, discipline and the vision to see *through* the changes and focus on the constants are necessary. Otherwise you chase the wrong quarry. Successful practitioners of the art of furniture stick close to their original vision and do not become distracted by the turmoil that occurs every day. Henredon's focus on the upper end is an example. When the company tried to break out into mid-market pricing with Marimont, it failed. This does not mean one cannot go against the industry's conventional wisdom. In fact, one should, but only in the context of a carefully wrought strategic plan. Without this plan, you are engaging in mortal combat with few weapons.

COMMANDMENT NO. 3:
Thou Shalt Avoid Over-Centralizing

Competitive advantage in the furniture industry is based on personal relationships, reputations, reacting quickly to change, close control over operations, and an eye for fashion. These elements are not enhanced by centralized organizations. Quite the opposite is true.

Time and again, nimble organizations outperform the lumbering central headquarters that has carefully protected itself from being exposed to the realities of the battlefield. Instead of being responsive, the centralized organization actually slows the response time. Instead of attracting the skilled individuals needed to compete, it drives them away. And instead of setting an example for the divisions, it lowers the incentives at the local level. The resulting disconnects between headquarters and the field produce monumental blunders, and the competition feasts on the increasingly vulnerable divisions. This, in turn, convinces the corporate chieftains that the culprits are in the divisions, not at headquarters. Dismissals of highly skilled people often follow, and these people usually end up joining the competition, where they can punish their alma mater for years to come.

COMMANDMENT NO. 4:
Thou Shalt Not Misread the Competition

In fragmented industries, many privately held firms often have non-economic reasons for being in business. Assuming that these competitors have a cost structure and objectives similar to your own is a major mistake. Executives accustomed to competing with publicly held corporations struggle with private companies whose owners only wish to provide a nice lifestyle for their close relatives. These seemingly "irrational" competitors – who tend to underprice their wares – have a devastating impact on the margins of those companies who must compete with them.

COMMANDMENT NO. 5:
Thou Shalt Not Worship the False God of Synergy

The niche aspect of the furniture industry means there are few opportunities to realize synergy between operating units. Seemingly similar companies are actually quite dissimilar, and companies that are too close together cannot share for competitive reasons. When some measure of synergy is attained, a tradeoff somewhere else usually erases the gain.

COMMANDMENT NO. 6:

Thou Shalt Avoid the Hot Line Syndrome

The elation that accompanies a hot new product introduction can make you forget how fast competitors will respond. As sales take off, resist the temptation to expand production with costly investments. Just as the new capacity comes on-line, you may find that the competitor knock-offs are reducing sales of your top seller. You then find your break-even point has risen and your margins have slipped as overall supplies catch up with demand. It is smarter to invest your energies in the next hot line.

COMMANDMENT NO. 7:

Thou Shalt Not Ignore the Semi-Annual "Market" Madness

Combatants in the furniture business all are subject to the vagaries of the "Six-Month Year" as they undertake frantic efforts to be ready for "the Market," the twice-a-year major trade show. The stakes are high as new products are launched and dealers are enticed to commit to buy the new goods. New lines typically require at least eight months to develop, yet work starts on them only six months before the next Market. Many companies bring lots of new products that are not fully developed, and they focus on short-run tactics instead of long-run strategies. The next ever-looming Market narrows the focus of the key people who should be taking a broader view, and it contributes to much of the scrambling nature of the business. It is exceptionally difficult to take a broad view of one's business when the whole organization is continually faced with preparing for the next major trade show.

The Markets also level the field, because retailers can check out all suppliers regardless of size. Word-of-mouth helps the small start-up companies compete quite well against the large firms. This is free enterprise at its best, but it also works against consolidation.

THE NET RESULT

Cursing the realities or mocking the sins only serves to hasten one's demise. Insiders are skilled at setting traps for the unwary. Often the most talented transplants with highly sophisticated backgrounds cannot resist the chance to point out how "backward" the industry is. This triggers resentment in the furniture person's heart and sets the stage for retaliation. Frequently this is exacerbated by latent North/South emotions; God help the Yankee who even hints that he might be smarter than his Southern furniture friends. Predictably, this executive will encounter some wickedly passive resistance to his ideas, become frustrated with the lack of results, and either leave the industry in disgust or get tossed out in disrepute. In short, the more arrogant the Outsider, the more likely he or she will fail.

As we will see in the chapters that follow, Outsiders who suit up to fight in the Furniture Wars often lack the passion held by Insiders. To them, it is just a job or just another industry. To the furniture person, it is a way of life. Then the Outsider ignores the Insider and, rather than taking advantage of his wealth of knowledge, he or she simply discards it. In turn, the Insider all too willingly sets up the newcomers to fail. But in the end, such attitudes mean both Insiders and Outsiders are destined to fail – especially when they both face the threats from Asia. Let us take a closer look at some of the more notable battles in the Furniture Wars.

COLIN CARPI DIEM:

EARLY OUTSIDER INCURSIONS

CAPTURE A PAIR OF CHAIRS

A MERICAN BUSINESS EXPANDED at a feverish pace during the 1960s, a decade called "the years of the growth and performance concepts, the gunslingers, the youth revolution, the mutual funds; the years of the new-issue stocks, synergism, creative accounting, Chinese money, and the conglomerates."[1] Of all the corporate fads in the twentieth century, the conglomerate concept was the most insidious. Its proponents espoused the questionable wisdom of moving away from industries in which you had some knowledge in order to make acquisitions in industries about which you had no knowledge. A good manager can manage anything, so no experience was needed. The word *conglomerate* comes from the Latin *glomus*, which means "wax." Why anyone would want to model a corporation on a ball of wax is puzzling, but Wall Street loved the concept.

Predictably, the insular furniture industry resisted this craziness by launching its vaunted Invisible Briar Patch Defense. This strategy sought to disguise the industry so anyone who noticed it would be turned off by all the thorns.

COLIN CARPI COMES CALLING

At least one outsider was not deterred by the formidable furniture defense. Colin Caton Carpi III, a Wall Streeter, was actually attracted to it. "Meticulous study of the financial pages, bolstered by his own research, had convinced him that the home furniture market was an area sorely overlooked by venture capitalists. Unloved and untapped, it offered the potential for huge profits."[2] He pursued his dreams of becoming a furniture magnate by traveling from his home in Princeton to Lewisburg, Pennsylvania. Carpi had a plan. He hoped to buy a few family-owned furniture factories, leveraging their assets to pay off the debt needed to buy them in the first place. But that was only the first step. Once he took control, he would improve management and link the companies to form a powerful competitor in an otherwise fragmented industry. His dream was to acquire many small- and medium-sized furniture makers and create a collection of furniture companies that would meet consumer needs like no other. His prototype was General Motors, which offered vehicles aimed at every segment of the consumer market – from the baseline Chevy to the top-of-the-line Cadillac. He had Wall Street backing. All he needed was the right target.

"The Chair Factory," as the locals called it, looked promising. Known in the trade as Pennsylvania House, the company actually was incorporated as the Lewisburg Chair Co. Situated in the picturesque Susquehanna River Valley, the pleasant, provincial college town of Lewisburg is not near anything but isn't too far away, either. It is less than three hours from suburban Philadelphia, where Carpi grew up, about four hours from Princeton, where he studied engineering, and just over three hours from New York City, where he worked as a consultant for Booz, Allen, and Hamilton.

Trim and fit, the 35-year-old worked out regularly and played a lot of racquet sports, although it was hard to imagine how he found the time. He had a young, almost boyish face, but his high forehead and thinning hair gave him a maturity that offset his youthful looks. He dressed in the standard Brooks Brothers/J Press formula but never gave the impression that clothes mattered to him. He was quick to remove his jacket when he got to the office as if to say, "I'm here to work. Let's get to it." His only affectation was a pair of rounded, "owlish" horn-rimmed glasses that seemed a bit off key but still acceptable in an Ivy League sort of way. He was very intelligent and very "Princeton." He came across as self-confident, calculating, self-assured, and engaging, but not vain or self-important. He was all business, but you got the feeling he might even be fun were he not so obsessed with his dream. That side of him was closely guarded.

Carpi was fascinated with the furniture industry. In earning his MBA at Harvard, he studied the twentieth century management techniques needed to facilitate robust growth in the industry. Compared to the other industries Carpi had seen while working as a consultant, furniture seemed easy. The manufacturing process was ripe for modernization, and the barebones marketing practices were begging to be replaced by more meaningful and expansive ones. He saw weak, family-held competition combined with exceptionally favorable demographic projections. It was a classic case study: a highly fragmented industry waiting for the right person to consolidate it.

What did it matter that he had no background in this particular business? Had he not excelled at The Business School, solving case after case, competing against the best and the brightest young businessmen of his generation? Was he not a quick study who could grasp the particulars of complicated issues and pare them down to their very essence? Besides, the furniture business seemed simple compared to the 150 industries he had methodically analyzed while working at Booz, Allen and Hamilton. "I was dumbfounded," he exclaimed. "Here was a mammoth industry that was almost dormant and yet it had tremendous potential."[3] All you had to do was look at the players to see that the industry had no charismatic leaders. They acted more like entrepreneurs than corporate executives. Other than Ethan Allen's Nat Ancell and maybe one or two others, these furniture types seemed provincial compared to the businessmen he had dealt with in school. Many of the furniture companies were located in the South, and their leaders did not impress the urbane Carpi.

Any of Carpi's lingering doubts were overcome by the highly favorable demographic projections for the industry – the Baby Boomers were coming, and they needed furniture. And it looked like fun. Furniture was interesting. Even his wife, Laura, was fascinated with it, frequently sharing her impressions of the shopping experience with him. She came from an established Philadelphia Main Line family and had been a White House aide during the Eisenhower administration. They met when she was a student at Smith College and married in 1957. With four young children at home, she had little time for other interests, but she held genuine enthusiasm for the furniture business, especially product design.

Carpi's father, Fred, worked for the Pennsylvania Railroad, where he came up through the ranks to a high-enough level in management to be able to send his son to Princeton. The son had an eye for design details and was fascinated with product styling. He correctly perceived it to be one of the keys to success in the furniture business, and he wondered why furniture companies had few "fine" designs but instead favored gaudier styles. Laura agreed, and the two of them frequently asked their friends and neighbors in Princeton to take part in informal design focus groups. This led him to conclude that product design was extremely important to the consumer and that the industry needed "cleaner" designs. Carpi liked to go back to the original, pure forms for design inspiration. Two of his favorite sources were the American Wing of the New York Metropolitan Museum and Historic Williamsburg. He also sensed that the entire shopping process was inadequate, and he had many ideas about fixing that as well. He could hardly wait to apply these ideas to his newly discovered, backward industry. To crank up his plans build the General Motors of furniture, he needed an acquisition. What he found was Pennsylvania House.

LEWISBURG LANDING

The Lewisburg Chair Co. was a profitable producer of solid wood furniture and upholstery owned for two generations by the Parker family. The original company was started in 1877 and operated continuously until it foundered in the Great Depression. R. N.

Parker, a seasoned furniture man from West Virginia, purchased the assets in 1934 and reopened the facility. He built a solid business with a product line that featured basic country designs made from the native timber harvested nearby. The name "Pennsylvania House" emphasized the local nature of the designs and materials, and it capitalized on the state's reputation for craftsmanship. The business flourished in the Post War period, and Parker held to true furniture tradition by bringing his son, Greg, into the business.

The factory continued to prosper as Greg took control, but as is so often the case, the son did not share the same passion for the business as the father. Greg Parker's two sisters liked cash more than the chair factory, and he preferred the sailboat he kept at his home in Beverly, Massachusetts. Realizing that the company needed an infusion of capital to keep growing, the family was susceptible to the suggestion to sell out. Three serious buyers emerged – a coal company, a furniture company, and Carpi. The conscientious and upstart entrepreneur, Carpi, had arranged ahead of time for investment capital from the Wall Street firm of Laird & Co. While the coal company dragged its feet and competitor Ethan Allen offered stock to the Parker family, Carpi won the deal by offering $4.5 million in cash. The man with no furniture experience – who had never even run a company – joined Laird as proud owners of Pennsylvania House in January 1964. The Parker sisters got their cash, Greg sailed away in his boat, and Carpi took the first bold step by forming General Interiors Corp. Nine months later, it filed for its Initial Public Offering of stock. In October the shares were successfully sold at an opening price of $8.50. Carpi had the capital to start his bold assault on the conventional thinking of the furniture industry.

Frequently in sales of this nature, the acquired company suffers from the absence of the previous leader and has no one qualified to step in. But Pennsylvania House was fortunate to have a competent No. 2 person already in place, sales manager Richard F. McClure. Carpi made him president, and he proved to be a capable manager who led the company for the next five years. McClure was a Lewisburg native from a prominent family who had graduated from the University of Pennsylvania and obtained an MBA from the Wharton School. Trained as an engineer, he was very adept at keeping track of the detail side of the furniture business and comfortable on the sales side. He had a presence about him and he made sure you knew he was in the room. His slight frame and finely drawn features were offset by a tendency to pontificate in a deep voice that he used to assert himself. The voice, in combination with his prematurely graying hair, created an aura of maturity that belied his age. He seemed a bit aloof at first glance, but he was very well liked by those who knew him and he loved to have fun. He, too, favored an Ivy League wardrobe, but it was less preppy than Carpi's and more reflective of his Pennsylvania background. He was a highly effective divisional CEO, relating well to the local constituency, yet managing to maintain a good relationship with Carpi. He usually kept Carpi satisfied while avoiding some of the impractical suggestions coming from corporate. This invaluable political skill, combined with his love of good design and his capacity for detail, made him a competent, hands-on furniture person quite capable of running the Lewisburg Division, while Colin Carpi directed the parent corporation.

Carpi's thoughtfulness and reflection meant he brought much more to the table than money and ambition. As opposed to most of the furniture players we will meet in this book, Colin Carpi had both a dream and a plan to make his vision come true. And he could articulate that vision in a way that captivated the listener. While others seemed to follow a strategy of "attack and occupy" or "buy and run," Carpi had everything mapped out.

The View From 215 Lexington Avenue

To create the General Motors of Furniture, Carpi concluded he would need a strong corporate staff devoted to the centralization of functions such as product design, graphic design, research and engineering, timber cultivating, trucking and warehousing, data processing, dealer financing, and export sales. He needed the divisions to prosper in order to support the overhead required to staff these functions, which he figured would in turn make the divisions even more prosperous. To reflect the sophisticated, urbane image he envisioned for the company, Carpi set up headquarters not in the provinces where the divisions would reside, but in New York City. And not just anywhere in New York: he took the entire first floor of a building at 215 Lexington Avenue, facing the New York Furniture Exchange. A nice plus were the window displays stretching between 32nd and 33rd Streets. Here he would recruit and direct his officers, working late into the nights, planning his moves, and commuting to and from Princeton.

The Three-Dimensional Grid

These were heady times. It was easy to become excited about Carpi's vision because of his enthusiasm and the contagious energy he created. General Interiors was not just a furniture company. It had almost cult-like qualities, at least for some of the members. As part of his dream it was easy to see that you could make a difference in an industry that cried out for change.

Carpi's plan for General Interiors was ambitious. On countless occasions, Carpi sketched a furniture industry segmentation grid with price points on the vertical axis and style segments on the horizontal. Then he would shade the top 60 percent of the cells to indicate those he planned to target. The bottom 40 percent would be left for others. Pennsylvania House was just one cell, and his plan was to add more companies until the grid was filled with brands. But that was only part of it. With contagious enthusiasm, he would say the grid was three dimensional, with more layers. He envisioned other grids for related product categories such as fabrics, wall coverings, bedspreads, draperies, bedding, lamps, accessories, carpets, and even home entertainment. Layering on more and more grids, he would end up with an impressive matrix of his potential empire.

In 1968 he directed an executive to spend six months studying the tabletop and the carpet industry. This led to an offer to acquire Philadelphia Carpets Inc. The attempt failed but did not diminish Carpi's appetite. In each of these categories, he planned to dominate the conventional channels of distribution and to create new channels. Long before Jack Welch of GE began to talk about the "boundaryless corporation," Carpi knew no bounds. His ego was strong and he was certain his vision was right. As such, he did not see the need to devote much time listening to others. He figured most people did not "get it" the way he did, and hearing their concerns was a distraction he did not need. He was much too busy seeing to it that the divisions were designing the right kind of furniture, telling retailers how to run their stores, and proofreading catalog pages. Describing the potential was fun. Actualizing it was hard. Keeping your feet on the ground and facing reality were no fun at all.

The Consumer Vision

Combining his Harvard Business School education with keen observation skills, Carpi's starting point was an understanding of the consumer. This was in sharp contrast with traditional furniture companies whose starting point was the factory. Everything in his vision flowed from the consumer. In his view, the consumers were women who wanted individualize their furniture choices to reflect their personalities and lifestyles. He often compared the furniture selection process to the way a woman applied makeup or selected her wardrobe. Her choices were intended to enhance her appearance and to reflect her mood. Here is how he described it in an internal memo:

> Oriented toward the consumer's desires and needs, General Interiors' strategy is aimed at assisting the consumer to make his or her life more exciting. The company views its products and services as having cosmetic values as well as functional values, and seeks to make interior designing as attractive and rewarding as possible. It believes that the greatest opportunities for exciting consumer interest lie in cultivating virtuosity in design, craftsmanship, and technology, and in so organizing product planning and marketing activities as to make successful interior designing easier.

He also strongly believed that consumers wanted "better" designs, different from the "commercial" designs favored by the furniture veterans. He could hardly wait to become more involved with this part of the business. But before he could devote time to that task, there was work to be done.

The Carpi vision was based on his own instincts and his observations of the industry from the consumer's perspective more so than from the producer's perspective. To his credit, this was a significant departure from the traditional industry attitude. Most owners and CEOs were focused on the production side of the business, leaving the consumer focus in the hands of the retailer and the customer focus in the hands of the company's sales representatives. This paradigm allowed the furniture leader to concentrate on the part of the business where 70 percent of the costs were incurred without getting distracted by the annoying idiosyncrasies of the distribution channel. It was myopic as a marketing approach, but it kept selling costs low and so far had worked pretty well.

Carpi sensed that the shopping experience turned off consumers, and he planned to structure his manufacturing company to remove many of the impediments. For starters, he would produce outstanding catalogs and point-of-purchase materials (to make shopping easier), custom finish options (for personalization), broad collections (to fit different lifestyles), open stock (to facilitate add-on purchases), and quick delivery of customer sold orders (for instant gratification). These notions strike us today as basic, but they were unheard of in the late 1960s, except as espoused by the feisty, iconoclastic Nat Ancell of Ethan Allen. As Carpi put it in an annual report, "Our basic objective is more than to make and market fine home furnishings. Rather, we will provide the finest possible assistance to the consumer in achieving her plans for the home, helping her to create a warm, stimulating environment for her family, to express her own individuality and creativity, to represent her family with good taste, and to make sound long-range home furnishings investments."

Years later, Ethan Allen carried this concept to its logical conclusion by asserting control over the retailer, first by virtue of a quasi-franchise program and ultimately by owning many of the stores outright. Ancell, the company founder, sensed the only way to realize his vision was to maintain control at the point of sale. As a result of this philosophy, Ethan Allen today is one of the nation's largest furniture retailers, enjoys the highest profit margins, and has the highest brand recognition. Carpi originally opted to let the retailer handle the point of sale. He wanted his own retail stores down the road and had prototype plans drawn up, but that would have to come later. For now there was not enough money to fund a retail venture, and it would have been difficult to handle so many brands under one roof.

Carpi planned to spend heavily on national advertising to establish his consumer-based platform. Otherwise, he would not be able to position his brands in consumers' minds. In his view, the buying process was similar to that of packaged goods, especially cosmetics, and he wanted his advertising to reflect this belief. Brand imagery was another area where he had strong opinions. Photography was very important to him, and he spent a great deal of time in the details of advertising and catalog production. The exquisite GI logo speaks for itself. He had skill in this area, combining his perceptive eye for visual arts with his intimate knowledge of the precise position he wanted the various brands to occupy.

The Retail Vision

In addition to improving the approach to the consumer, Carpi saw the need for better methods of working with retailers. Most furniture companies were factory-oriented and left dealer relations in the hands of their independent manufacturer's representatives. Carpi was interested in the production side of the business, too, but his real love was the distribution side, where he saw countless opportunities to try new approaches. His dealer support programs were to include elements such as:

+ Creating interrelated product collections to help consumers furnish their whole houses.

+ Limiting the number of dealers to make it worthwhile for them to support marketing efforts.

+ Offering display planning assistance to improve sales productivity.

+ Listing dealers in national advertising to generate traffic.

+ Providing extensive sales support materials to assist in local advertising.

+ Setting a year-round sales promotion calendar to increase store traffic.

+ Hiring talented sales reps to make the programs work.

✝   Delivering sold orders rapidly to reduce the need for inventory.

✝   Offering extended payment terms to finance growth.

To provide his customers with a better retailing formula, the company had a major home furnishings Franchise Store Program under development. This was a touchy area with retailers, but this could provide a platform for Carpi to show his customers how they could improve how they ran their businesses. To go one step further, he planned to open a chain of specialty stores that would not compete with dealers to help them dispose of obsolete items and to offer consumers the chance to trade in used goods for new. Code named UFB, the Used Furniture Business might have been a worthwhile solution to a problem that plagues the industry to this day.

THE VISION MISSIONARIES

Carpi knew he needed help in converting people to his vision, especially the marketing elements. To overcome the furniture industry's disdain for marketing he packed his organization with marketing-oriented MBA types. Each year he visited Harvard and used his charm to recruit top graduates. This was unusual in an industry where the only young people hired for top management were sons of the owners, but it had a lot to do with reshaping the company.

His vision was a source of inspiration to many within the company. Only the most skeptical at headquarters were not taken in. Many at the division level had doubts, but this was largely set aside in the hopes that the "New World Order" would be worth the effort. Articulating the vision was one thing; making it work was something else altogether. To help make this happen and to carry the "gospel according to Colin" out to the provinces, Carpi hired two young graduates of the Harvard Business School – Will Somers and Tony Leonard. Still in their twenties, these exceptionally bright and highly motivated men had no furniture experience but were quick learners and loyal to Carpi. They worked tirelessly to make the dream come true. Their energy and earnestness went a long way to offset what they lacked in hands-on knowledge. Because they openly acknowledged their desire to learn the business, the in-house furniture people accepted them and they, in turn, respected and learned from the "locals."

Next he hired Bob Young, a Baker Scholar from the Harvard Class of '67. Young helped recruit Bob Zimmerman, Harvard '68. The following year, Joe Pugliese was recruited from Harvard along with a graduate of the Wharton MBA program and a still another from Syracuse. This meant there were seven MBAS under 30 working for the company, and none had a single day of experience in the furniture industry when hired. Like the Jesuit missionaries who risked their lives to convert the Native Americans, the MBAS sometimes received a hostile reception from the furniture natives and frequently encountered language difficulties, but they also made some conversions.

Correctly sensing a need to strengthen the operational side of the enterprise also, Carpi encouraged Pennsylvania House to recruit engineering graduates from schools such as Penn State and North Carolina State. These manufacturing technicians, as well the MBA types, made a big contribution to the transformation at the company. They also had an impact on Lewisburg, bringing their young families with them and tending to hang out together and to party constantly. With little to do in Lewisburg outside of work, they arranged house parties at the drop of a hint. Their spouses were curious about the goings on at work, and the MBAS and technicians were more than happy to bring office and plant home with them. This brought the families closer together as they shared victories and defeats as one group. The downside was the rivalries and jealousies that eventually spilled into neighborhoods and even to schools. But in the beginning, it was just plain fun.

Significantly, these people were still at the start of their careers. They were not Outsiders brought in to transplant concepts from other industries. They were still learning and had natural curiosity and a willingness to try fresh solutions to old problems – something the industry badly needed. Nearly each one went on to have successful business careers. Not all remained in furniture, but in those halcyon years they had an impact that transformed Pennsylvania House and, in turn, an industry badly in need of new ideas. They brought with them an enthusiasm and a natural curiosity that led them to ask "why?" and "why not?" Pennsylvania House alumni went on to become the respective heads of Henredon, Drexel Heritage, Kittinger, Brodart, and Mersman Waldron to name a few.

INDUSTRY REACTION

The key to Carpi's master plan was time. Everything would work as long as the earnings and the price-to-earnings multiple held up for GI stock. Observers on the periphery – publishers, suppliers, advertising agencies – were quite taken with his insights, but people at the core of the industry thought he was insane. They resented the newcomers' assertions that radical changes were warranted and stiffly defended their tried-and-true methods. His competitors understandably wanted to see him fail, and retailers resented his implied criticism of their performance.

This conflict would have to be resolved, even if it meant an outbreak of civil war. Carpi refused to listen to the nattering nabobs who attacked his ideas, but sometimes he also stopped listening to his friends who urged him to adjust and to learn from experience. Meanwhile, Armstrong Cork, a linoleum floor producer headquartered in Lancaster, had been using Thomasville furniture products in its advertising. When Armstrong learned that Thomasville President Tom A. Finch had health problems, Armstrong offered to buy the whole company. The deal was completed in 1968.

Finch was a prominent member of the Southern furniture establishment, and his family business was one of the industry's top brands. Word spread quickly through the country clubs in the Piedmont area of North Carolina that "Old Tom A." had sold out to an Outsider – and a Yankee no less. More than a few eyebrows were raised at his choice of a buyer, but the price was good. Armstrong executives, meanwhile, were quiet about what they intended to do with their acquired property . . . other than keep using Thomasville furniture in its flooring ads.

APPLYING THE VISION AT PENNSYLVANIA HOUSE

Pennsylvania House accelerated Carpi's "Program Selling" by changing how retail customers were treated. Rather than peddling the line to anybody and everybody, Pennsylvania House steered it toward a limited number of dealers to gain more floor space with fewer accounts. This opened up other opportunities and led to the creation of retail presentations called "Galleries" that featured contiguous displays of lifelike room settings. This resulted in more emphasis on the brand, more advertising, and a closer relationship between the factory and the retailer. It was a difficult story to get across, because retailers were reluctant to devote large space to one supplier and independent sales reps were apprehensive about creating ill feelings with the discontinued dealers. Used properly, it produced remarkable results. It helped that Pennsylvania House happened to have a pretty hot line of cherry products that dealers wanted to carry.

Pennsylvania House selectively adopted Carpi's ideas. At times, division president Dick McClure found himself caught between the reality of the furniture business and the idealism of Carpi. How he resolved these conflicts was a major key to his division's results. McClure had to navigate his ship between two perilous threats. And just as Odysseus faced Scylla – the six-headed monster that killed those who came too close to its rock – McClure would risk his division if he followed Carpi's suggestions too literally. And just as Odysseus faced Charybdis – the whirlpool directly opposite Scylla – McClure's company would sink if he followed the conventional thinking of his furniture mavens too closely. Odysseus survived by steering clear of the whirlpool's certain destruction, but he lost men by sailing too close to the monster. McClure used similar tactics, sacrificing a few men on occasion but avoiding the division's destruction by deftly avoiding the most impractical corporate suggestions. Countless division executives found themselves in similar straits in later years, particularly when reporting to an executive with little or no understanding of the furniture business. They and their divisions either made it through or were destroyed, depending on the course the navigator pursued.

McClure and Carpi worked well together as they geared up to convert "The Chair Factory" into a growth vehicle. Richard Steffenson, a young, in-house designer, developed sketches that the company said reflected "a countrified feeling and an informal expression of formal design." One of the concepts given a close look was a relaxed interpretation of the formal Queen Anne shapes normally associated with Williamsburg reproductions. Instead of using dark mahogany like the originals, Steffenson's were crafted in native Pennsylvania Cherry and given a casual finish, called "Collector's Cherry." Another small group of designs was done in an updated traditional look, again crafted in solid cherry. This subtle shift in styling emphasis began slowly before becoming the heart of the line. The appeal to dealers and consumers resulted from the fact that the forms, or silhouettes, were familiar, but the cherry finish was unexpected yet appropriate. When the Queen Anne designs were coordinated with traditional looks in later years, the American Traditional style category was born. Customers who wanted to go beyond Early American style by adding more elegance and a bit more formality flocked to it. The antiques that inspired some of these designs were indigenous to the Connecticut River Valley rather than the Susquehanna River Valley, but few people cared.

Another young designer, Jack Slear, was encouraged to add zip to the company's trade showrooms and retail displays. Although he had no formal training in interior design, he used his wonderful imagination and his display techniques to begin the process of differentiating the company from its competitors. When given more attention in later years, this would become a powerful marketing tool that led to the company's successful Gallery Program. In tandem with this marketing initiative, the plants were directed to improve quality, especially in the finishing area. These efforts paid off when the company figured out how to offer the previously premium-priced Collector's Cherry finish at regular price. To cap it off, Carpi selected a New York ad agency to craft the message he wanted to convey.

CUSHMAN IS ACQUIRED

General Interiors in early 1965 acquired the H. T. Cushman Co. of North Bennington, Vermont, for $1.4 million, or about $9.3 million when adjusted for inflation. Some were surprised that it did not extend Carpi's grid, because this solid wood producer overlapped Pennsylvania House. Strategically, it made more sense to add a company that would extend the grid, as a later purchase would do. But Cushman was available, and Carpi was anxious to cut a deal. He explained the move by pointing out that key dealers often expected to have limited distribution, if not an exclusive, so having two brands in the same niche would let the company sell "both sides of the street."

Cushman was one of the oldest family-held furniture companies in the country, with ownership dating back to 1866. Upon returning from the Civil War, Henry T. Cushman began a successful career inventing and making a series of novelty items and gradually

moved into the production of coat hangers, hat racks, telephone
stands, and smoker's stands. In the 1930s, the company hit on the
unique idea of "distressing" new furniture to make it look old.
These "Cushman Colonial Creations" were extremely popular,
and sales grew sharply. The company added more designs, and the
line flourished through the 1950s. By the mid-60s, the company
had lost its product development edge but not its reputation for
making a good product. Sales had stalled, but profits were good
enough to provide a nice lifestyle for the owners. What this company needed was a new product appropriate for its niche. Carpi
was anxious to try his hand at rejuvenating it.

With the capture of Cushman, Carpi convinced the American
Stock Exchange to list General Interiors under the symbol GIT.
Both Cushman and Pennsylvania House made a profit that year,
with the Lewisburg unit far outpacing Bennington. More progress was made in reshaping the product lines at both companies
with the introduction of several collections, though they didn't
sell well and veered from their defined style niches. But they reflected Carpi's belief in the need for "cleaner," more sophisticated
designs. Pennsylvania House tried to expand its niche by launching a French-styled Lafayette Cherry Collection, a departure
from its typical Colonial look. Cushman took a similar tack by
launching the Stone House Collection, a departure from its Early
American look. Neither of these groups was a big sales success,
but they served notice that both companies were willing to try
new avenues to growth. Some felt that the companies had made
ill-advised moves away from their defined style niches. But Carpi
kept pushing them.

REALIGNMENT LESSON

Cushman's business for years was based on a collection anchored by a legendary dining room featuring a cross-based "sawbuck" table and a high-back farm chair. Many consumers loved it. To them, it had substance. It was sturdy. It had a lot of look for the money. The table was deliberately designed to seem heavier than it was, and the chair was so sturdy that retail salesmen closed sales by inviting customers to lift it. The wood was solid Yellow Birch, which competed with "Hard Rock" Maple. It looked like maple but was denser, harder, and more figured than its rival. The chair leg posts were driven all the way through the seat, and wedges were driven into the posts to secure them firmly. The thick seat was contoured deeply, giving it a saddle shape for added comfort. Finally, it was given a unique finish, called Deep Grain Antique that enhanced the birch wood. This was furniture truly built to last, furniture by the pound, and it looked it.

Laura Carpi and her friends saw it as clunky, contrived, and commercial. It lacked style. Their preference was more refined, more graceful designs. Rather than developing a successor to the now-dated "sawbuck" table, Carpi directed Cushman to use the Pennsylvania House designer to draw a new group with more sophisticated lines. Christened the "Stone House Collection" after a beautiful family home across from the factory, the group featured clean lines based on authentic designs found in the American Wing of the New York Metropolitan Museum. Carpi took a personal role in this process, even convincing Barbara D'Arcy, the legendary curator of Bloomingdale's famous Model Rooms, to collaborate.

The resulting collection reflected the talents and the taste levels of the team. It was sophisticated and uniquely "New York," combining elegant forms with a casual wood, solid oak. The finish chosen for it, Spiced Oak, was a dark chestnut brown that disguised the typical oak grain. Many of the antiques that inspired the designs had been crafted in mahogany or figured maple, and by switching to an unexpected medium, the overall impression created was quite forward looking. This gave Cushman a fresh product line far removed from the old Bennington Collection. Magazine editors and retail fashion coordinators lavished praise on the designs, and the group sold very well at Bloomingdale's. Carpi felt he had made his point about clean designs. Unfortunately, the core Cushman dealers reacted differently and steered clear of the group because they felt it had little appeal to their clientele. And, besides, they did not look to Cushman for sophisticated designs.

As noted, success in the marketing of furniture requires a reasonably close alignment of four variables in order to hit the right consumer target – the factory, the product, the sales force, and the dealer. When all elements are in line, like a properly "sighted-in" rifle, sales usually result. If one or more variable is out of alignment, there will be trouble reaching the consumer. In the case of the Stone House Collection, the alignment was good with Bloomingdale's and Cushman's veteran New York sales rep. For the rest of the nation, however, the product was misaligned with the sales reps and the dealer network. They would have been more comfortable with a middle-of-the-road style. Carpi was more comfortable with a sophisticated style.

Have It Your Way . . .

Always on the lookout for more innovative programs to increase consumer appeal, Carpi loved the Pennsylvania House method of offering multiple finishes on wood pieces. He directed Cushman to pursue a similar course. At Cushman, however, the move could be made only after extensive changes to the plant and to production processes. To make this part of the vision work, the plant had to be re-engineered to store inventory after it was assembled, but before it was finished and packed. The plants were designed to move product quickly from the Cabinet Room, where it was assembled, into the Finish Room, where the product was stained, polished, and packed. From there it was sent to the Warehouse/ Shipping area. To alter this time-honored, tried-and-true industry practice meant major capital expenditures on new Finish Rooms, tying up more money in inventory, higher labor costs, more repairs, and more returns. Geographic limitations meant that a multi-million dollar finishing facility would have to be built across the road from the main plant. Every piece of furniture had to be put on a truck and hauled to the new finish room. Since wood is subject to atmospheric conditions and the Vermont climate can be extreme, this short journey let consumers choose from 27 finishes but led to some serious quality problems. The Cushman management thought the application of such advanced concepts would never work at the Bennington plant, but they went along anyway. Carpi was certain the concepts would work.

Pennsylvania House had better results rolling out the vision. "Have it your way," trumpeted Pennsylvania House advertisements long before Burger King. At the same time, Carpi told

Pennsylvania House to eliminate the premium it charged for its best finish and to make sure deliveries were rapid regardless of the finish chosen. Pennsylvania House had pioneered this mass-customization process years earlier and could meet Carpi's challenge. They also made some real progress in sales and marketing. Combining sound marketing principles with his retail experience as a "surf shop" owner while in school, Will Somers applied "Program Selling" techniques to the furniture business. This meant doing more volume with fewer dealers. While it seems tame by today's standards, the program was radically different from the conventional approaches used at the time.

Moving beyond the company's regional base, Somers recruited new sales representatives in other parts of the country. These new reps gave the company a burst of energy and motivated the strong veterans in the Northeast to take it up a notch. The product line remained strong, but there were rumblings about quality and service problems. As long as the capable reps could get the line placed in stores, and as long as it sold through to the consumer, these distractions were manageable and little was done to correct them.

KITTINGER IS ACQUIRED

In June 1966, General Interiors completed the acquisition of the Kittinger Co., one of the finest, most respected names in the business. This old-line cabinetmaker was started in Buffalo in 1866 and acquired by the Kittinger brothers in 1913. In 1937 the company obtained the license to reproduce the prestigious Colonial Williamsburg designs. Its impeccable reputation for quality was matched by its consistently high profit margins. Though small, the company had excellent management, a skilled work force, and a presence in the design trade with prominent showrooms in New York, Chicago, and Atlanta. Carpi was able to buy this gem because President Spencer Kittinger was seriously ill and no one in the family could take over. Carpi seized the opportunity and acquired the venerable company for $3.6 million and financed it with the issue $3.8 million in convertible debentures – about $23 million in current dollars.

These were heady times. The Carpi vision was exciting, and its charismatic architect and chief spokesman had to be pleased with the rapid progress. In 1966, sales increased 20 percent, and net earnings were up 17 percent. Earnings per share hit $1.22. Even though the share price had dropped to $11 at year-end after hitting a high of $27 earlier in the year, Colin Carpi was not overly concerned. He knew it would bounce back – and it did, reaching $26.50 by the end of 1967. The industry was proving to be more resistant to change than he wished, but he was not easily discouraged as he rolled into the new year. He was certain his ideas would prevail because they made so much sense.

COMPETITIVE RESPONSE: THE BATTLE OF SOLID WOODS

Industry veterans saw flaws in Carpi's vision because it did not match with the exigencies of the furniture business. The competitive fraternity closed ranks in rejecting Carpi the Invader, who threatened to upset their cozy existence. According to the skeptics, Pennsylvania House's "program selling" ran counter to the accepted norms and would face stiff opposition from their own sales force along with a suspicious reaction from dealers. Many sales reps would have to be replaced, and the disruption would be costly. The changes needed in the Cushman plant to accommodate the custom finish option would aggravate a touchy labor situation and stir up the union. The additional factory costs, when added to the higher selling costs, would raise prices and make the line less competitive. The new product initiatives, like the Lafayette Collection, were not connecting with consumers, and the Pennsylvania House upholstery line was simply not competitive. Furthermore, industry mavens predicted Cushman's tradition-bound culture would have a very tough time accepting the changes to the plant, and its independent Yankee spirit would resist the new owner's efforts to modernize the office. Predictably, the labor union would exploit the situation. Again, the increased costs would mean higher prices, and the new "sophisticated" product lines were not compatible with the company's sales force, dealer base, and image. This sniping did not seem to bother Carpi; in many ways, it heightened the enjoyment. The opportunity to succeed in a major way remained clearly within his sights.

Standing in the way were a host of competitors determined to defend their respective neighborhoods from this curious newcomer. More ominously, they were prepared to attack quickly if General Interiors stumbled. Every move would be scrutinized to see what kind of response was needed. Any sign of weakness or vulnerability would be quickly exploited, and intelligence networks would be put on high alert. Before long, Carpi's every move would be predicted before he made it, and competitors would pounce on the inexperienced newcomer.

The segment where Pennsylvania House and Cushman operated

was dominated by Ethan Allen, which held about one-third of the market. Ethan Allen had developed its own version of "Program Selling" and was several years ahead of Pennsylvania House in its implementation. Ethan Allen's program was extensive, and it was poised to preempt the Pennsylvania House position in the consumer's mind. Lewisburg's response was the classic aikido move of turning the opponent's momentum against him. Ethan Allen's strength was embodied in the indomitable will and genius of its leader, Nat Ancell, who was the toughest and smartest gunfighter in town. He was also capable of being a mean-spirited bully. By reminding dealers of this "basic flaw in his personality," Pennsylvania House attracted plenty of dealers who had no desire to surrender their independence to Ancell. Pennsylvania House was able to hold its own by studying Ancell's playbook and striving to out-execute him. Oftentimes, the more independent dealer was the more effective one, and Pennsylvania House ended up as the key line in the best store in town whereas Ancell ended up with the second best store in town. Pennsylvania House had the advantage in the short run, but Ethan Allen controlled the whole store while Pennsylvania House only had a part of it.

Even so, in the mid-'60s, Ethan Allen was preparing to storm the mid-to-upper solid wood category. Pennsylvania House held second place with 10 percent, followed by Temple Stuart at 4 percent and a host of small companies, including Cushman, each hanging on to 1 to 3 percent of the market. These 20-some competitors comprised only one segment of the industry, and only five would survive the Battle of Solid Woods. In battle each would fight to protect their family-held companies. The closer they came to extinction, the harder they fought – even to the point of selling product below cost as long as they could meet their payrolls. Even when one finally went out of business, a newcomer would buy the plant and restart the cycle. Like the Eagles' Hotel California, "You can check out any time you like, but you can never leave."

Added to this crowded battlefield was the host of Southern companies who made some perfectly fine furniture that just happened to be made of veneered construction. Add the fact that dealers had very little vendor loyalty and consumers had virtually no brand recognition, and you have a map of one part of the Furniture Battlefield. Like armed tribal warriors, furniture companies subsist by staking out their territorial niches, defending against enemy incursions, and being ever alert for signs of weakness in neighboring territories.

Managing to stay alive in this hostile environment was not difficult, but managing to grow and to be profitable was tough. Low price became the principal weapon in most battles. Some tried to differentiate their product as a defense against cost-cutting competitors, but this was not easy because everyone bought their materials from the same suppliers, paid similar wages, and used similar machines to build them. The most important point of differentiation was the distinctive appearance of the product line, usually referred to as "the look." Each company had its own look, and often the differences were subtle. Those in the business who "had an eye" could identify the distinctions among product lines, but outsiders had a tough time with the concept and the skill. This also had its limitations, because the stronger your look the harder it was to break out of your niche and the more vulnerable you were if your look went out of favor. Of course, in the final reckoning, the people in the companies were the real points of differentiation, especially the creative types who came up with the right looks and the skilled craftsmen who could execute those looks. Furniture was not an easy game to play, but Carpi was confident that he would emerge as a winner.

GENERAL INTERIORS'
ADVANCE STALLS

G ENERAL INTERIORS EXPECTED 1967 to be a breakout
year. The synergy resulting from the association with Kittinger was expected to be a plus. Things were going well in Lewisburg. Cushman's rebirth was supposed to be underway, and Carpi's
enthusiasm ran high. But the plans did not work out. Instead, some
important areas did not produce as hoped and began to slow the
realization of Carpi's dream. The cost controls he thought were
in place proved ineffective, and factory margins slipped while the
many programs he had installed drove up selling and general and
administrative costs. It was not a good combination.

Sales grew 19 percent, but profits declined 40 percent. The annual report dutifully told shareholders that 1967 "was a difficult
year for your company, characterized by severe changes in the expected environment on which our plans were based, and by the
heaviest investments in our history aimed toward enhancing future earnings potential." The sales growth was strictly a result of
adding Kittinger. The other companies all had declines. It was a
tough year for the characteristically cyclical furniture industry. To

make matters worse, the one major area that Carpi had not scrutinized – operations – let him down because of production problems at both Lewisburg and Bennington. These resulted in quality problems, heavy rework costs, missed ship dates to customers, and plunging employee morale.

In spite of his legendary intellect and enormous effort, Carpi could not stay on top of all the things he had started. Some felt that his miscalculation of the furniture business would catch up with him. To the Outsider, industry practices appeared to be in need of a major marketing overhaul, and that was what he attempted. In truth, the bulk of the money was spent on the production side where 70 percent to 75 percent of the costs are. What appears to be a marketing-driven industry is actually production-driven, and you cannot pay for badly needed marketing plans unless you figure out how to make more money in the plants. Some Insiders have a saying: "You make or lose money at the saws." That is to say, the first machine operation determines your profitability because lumber yield is so important. If you don't cut it right, you can't build it right.

Carpi spent little time at the saws, and he did not engage or listen to the "factory guys" very often. Had he done so, they would have told him some of his ideas "just wouldn't work in furniture." Factory guys usually said things like that when shown something new, and they were usually right. The 1967 conversion of the traditional rough mill in Bennington, for example, was attempted years ahead of other companies. According to the wizened woodworking veterans, the result actually reduced lumber yield instead of increasing it. And the disruption caused by its installation was crippling.

Yet Carpi was inclined to dismiss reports that went counter

to his expectations. It was more fun to apply his genius to other, more visible areas than to apply it to the mundane details of operations. For example, he found time to establish another facet of the vision – the chance to go global. Carpi rightly sensed that American styled and American-made furniture had worldwide appeal, and he made sure the General Interiors European Operations was "substantially augmented" by setting up a fancy office in Paris under the direction of a skilled Frenchman, Jacques Trocme.[1]

Not Enough Fuel

Conditions worsened in 1968. Sales rose 22 percent, but net income fell 14 percent from 1967. Earnings per share dropped to 56 cents, down from 73 cents the prior year. Pennsylvania House and Cushman suffered continuing "under-productivity" problems as start-up expenses and cost pressures, including inflationary wage settlements affected all divisions.[2] A two-week strike at Lewisburg and a six-day strike at Bennington hurt employee/management relations, and related quality and shipping problems contributed to a further decline in dealer relations. Also contributing to the earnings slide were costs associated with the European operation, which was not doing well. Carpi was discovering painfully that the furniture business was not as easy as it seemed.

Nevertheless, with the stock ending the year at $34, Carpi extended the vision and the workload, by acquiring Shaw Manufacturing, a custom upholstery producer located in Charlotte, North Carolina, and the Dunbar Furniture Corp, a prestigious producer of modern office furniture. Shaw would be paired with Cushman to create a mirror image of Pennsylvania House. Dunbar would fit next to Kittinger in the matrix to combine a high-end contemporary specialist with a high-end traditional one.

Shaw, a 30-year-old family business, produced a top quality line of conservatively designed products and had settled into its own niche by appealing to interior designers and designer-oriented retailers. The sales force prided itself on having a number of low handicap golfers in its ranks, and their alignment with upper-end decorators was better than their alignment with retailers. The workforce was skilled, but the plant suffered from high turnover since it was in the rapidly growing Charlotte area where higher-paying jobs were plentiful.

Just as taking prisoners will slow an advancing army, a company is often slowed when it makes acquisitions. This was the case at General Interiors, where Carpi's acquisitive style made it harder to execute his vision.

THE CUSHMAN SHAW GROUP

Carpi thought the combination of Shaw and Cushman was perfect. The ancient Vermont cabinetmaker, armed with a new product line, would mate with the quiet North Carolina upholstery maker to create incredible synergy. To make it happen, he hired street-wise industry veteran Charles Shaughnessy Jr. as president of the Cushman Shaw Group. Charlie had a furniture background but at a lower price point and he, too, had an MBA from Harvard. His pedigree was impressive. His father, Charles Sr., was a highly regarded furniture man who had demonstrated remarkable skill and resiliency during his long career, finding success in retail as president of Macy's and in manufacturing with Drexel. To round out the team, Will Somers was transferred to the group from Lewisburg, and Harry Shaw, a former owner of the upholstery company, was expected to play a major role. All the pieces were in place to create another Pennsylvania House, which was the star performer in the GI camp.

Carpi's plan was compelling on paper but did not work. Instead of adjusting it based on real world feedback, he held firmly to his idealistic views. Retailers already had one Pennsylvania House and did not need another. What they needed, along with the rest of the industry, was a fusion of "new thinking" from the outsiders with the "old pragmatism" of the insiders. What they got was a classic "disconnect" from top to bottom. Decisions were made at the top without benefit of reality checks, and programs were attempted at the bottom without the slightest chance of success. Just like the ongoing Vietnam War, as the results worsened, more resources were committed and more good people were enlisted, yet no one acknowledged the reality of the situation.

Carpi thought Cushman's product line shortcomings had been fixed, but something was amiss. The "alignment" was off, and the plants struggled with quality while the field sales were disappointing. All he had to do was listen to workers on the shop floors or listen to a few sales reps and he could have learned that something was wrong. Instead of candidly acknowledging that Cushman's pristine new product collections were not selling and restarting the process of fixing the lineup, he pumped more energy into the sales efforts. The reps were pressured to sell more of what customers did not want and the plants could not make. Had Cushman developed a pine line rather than oak, or a cherry line rather than more birch, they could well have prospered. But Pennsylvania

House already had staked out these popular wood species, and headquarters did not want to see Cushman move too close to the flagship. So, like a decoy that draws enemy fire away from the main army, Cushman management bravely tried to make a doomed campaign successful. The people were capable. Each of Cushman's top five executives later became owner/presidents of much larger companies. The strategy was ill-conceived.

In retrospect, the acquisitions of Cushman and Shaw should never have been made. They would have been better off remaining separate and focusing on their respective niches. Retailers had no compelling need to buy upholstery and casegoods from the same source. Bennington and Charlotte had nothing in common, and the North/South polarity still meant something. The sales forces were totally different, as were the dealer bases and the respective market niches. The cultures were so diametrically opposed to one another that they had extreme difficulty working together. To make matters worse, the dynamic and personable Harry Shaw, the man counted on to make the upholstery part work, was killed in a plane crash while flying home from a dealer visit. Shaw, the company, would never be the same.

THE KITTINGER BIGGS DUNBAR DUX GROUP

Meanwhile, attempts to blend the upper-end companies fared no better. Once again, the differing corporate cultures resisted the arranged marriages. Capturing prisoners was easier than changing their hearts and minds. In Carpi's mind, the combination of Kittinger with Dunbar also made perfect sense, and in 1969 he cobbled them together along with two new acquisitions, the Biggs

Antique Co. and DUX Inc. Biggs was a small reproduction cabinet maker with two retail stores in Richmond, and DUX was the North American licensee for a prominent Swedish company. The chief executive of the group was Bill Nolan, an industry veteran who had been the executive vice president of Knoll International.

The harmony of this quartet was atonal. Kittinger was known for its outstanding quality and craftsmanship more than for its design leadership. Dunbar was known for award-winning designs and little else. Kittinger was ultra conservative and fiercely proud of its long history of making money. Dunbar, a cabinetmaker based in Berne, Indiana, was quite progressive and proud of its reputation for advanced styling. Originally started as a carriage maker in the 1890s, Dunbar had proven itself to be resourceful enough to survive the demise of the market for buggies. It started making sofas and then graduated to executive desks and credenzas. Dunbar had experienced its ups and downs as a purveyor of top-quality modern designs aimed at a narrow audience. Design ruled at Dunbar, which meant that the factory was routinely expected to make products that were extremely difficult. This led to a high rate of rework and repair and a low profit margin. Not surprisingly, the company had a history of problems with its highly skilled cabinetmakers.

In the 1950s, Dunbar formed an alliance with a brilliant designer named Edward Wormley and produced a series of stunning designs which defined American Fifties Modern as much as anyone. These designs were dated by the mid-'60s, as is the case with the "modern" idiom where there is little longevity. Wormley was no longer there to work his magic, and Nolan knew that his designers desperately needed more modern styles to replace the 5- to

10-year-old models and get the company moving again. Kittinger designers were more concerned with which reproductions to select from the Williamsburg archives from the early 18th century. Carpi grew frustrated with Dunbar and in 1970 abruptly dismissed the sales force and turned the sales and marketing functions over to Kittinger.

The forced union of Kittinger and Dunbar worked no better than the Cushman-Shaw duet, mixing about as well as engineers do with English majors. The predictable clash of cultures resulted in a dysfunctional organization and a loss of focus for Kittinger, which was ill-equipped to carry this added burden. Dunbar never recovered from this corporate lobotomy, and multiple attempts to revive it over the next five years were to no avail. Pairing a weak division with a strong one may have looked good on paper, but it invariably fails. The strong unit typically needs a great effort by its management team to remain strong and cannot afford any management dilution. The weaker unit resents the involvement by the other, and hostility lurks just beneath the surface.

Compounding the problem for Kittinger was that it also had to absorb the Biggs Antique Co. that Carpi acquired for $1.5 million in 1969. With annual sales of only slightly more than that, one wonders what he had in mind for it. Within a year it ended up as another distraction for Kittinger, which was finding it increasingly hard to remain focused on its own niche.

Imports are Meaningless

DUX, in the meantime, was so small and insignificant that nobody knew what to do with it, and the corporate waif never found a home. Carpi had the foresight to envision General Interiors as a global company and saw DUX as a step in that direction. Scandinavian contemporary furniture was quite popular in metropolitan markets and most of the goods were imported. Just the same, the myopic American furniture men refused to take the idea seriously. Instead they treated it as an annoying anomaly. The very thought of some foreigners making furniture for the American market was amusing. The Avanti wall system by DUX was certainly innovative and wonderfully engineered, but it required metric tools to assemble it. How inconvenient.

HIGH WATER MARK: THE BAKER ACQUISITION

Pennsylvania House may have been the fastest horse in the General Interiors stable, but Kittinger was far and away the most prestigious. Only one company in the industry was comparable, Baker Furniture of Grand Rapids, Michigan. Founded in the 1920s, Baker embodied cabinetmaking excellence and tradition. The brand well known and well regarded, it was a must-have for upper-end retailers. Offering superb products, the company had a powerful presence in the designer showroom channel as well. Baker, at a time when this comparison meant something, was truly the Cadillac of the furniture industry.

Colin Carpi stunned the furniture world in March 1969 by announcing that General Interiors had reached an agreement in principle to acquire Baker and two other companies. An office was readied for Hollis Baker Jr. in the General Interiors headquarters at 215 Lexington Avenue. With appropriate fanfare, a Kittinger desk was built with a Baker finish to be used by Hollis, and a Baker desk with a Kittinger finish was presented to Colin. In another move with wonderful symbolic significance, the new Baker catalog was pulled off press to be given a special cover with the General Interiors logo on the spine. The dream of a General Motors of the home moved one giant step closer, at least for the high-end, and the industry had to admit that the young man with the big plans was more than a flash in the pan. Carpi could hardly contain his glee. Hollis Baker seemed dazed but pleased by the flurry of activity as he kept a wary eye on the price of the GI stock, which was trading in the $26 range in late May, down from $35 in the early part of the year.

The agreement to buy Baker was for $14 million in cash plus 60,000 shares of GI stock. Carpi had come a long way from the day when he had to pay cash for the "Chair Factory." Sure, Baker had an escape clause in the event the stock dropped too far before the deal closed, but General Interiors had been trading at 30 times earnings for years, and this deal was a blockbuster. The leverage was wonderful. Admittedly, Pennsylvania House and Kittinger were not generating the cash GI needed to prop up the weak divisions, but the debt structure could be rearranged and new bonds issued now that Baker was on board. Baker was not only big; it was very profitable. In 1968, sales exceeded $10 million, and pretax profit margins reached 16 percent. The combination of Baker and Kittinger meant that Carpi would dominate the upper-end traditional segment for residential and office furniture. When linked with a revived Dunbar, the lineup would be unbeatable. Carpi could not help but feel good about the future when contemplating the completion of this acquisition along with the three small ones already in the hopper, DUX, Biggs, and Salterini. He was moving closer to the realization of his dream.

General Interiors had to restructure its balance sheet to finance the deal, and CFO Bob McGill was ready and eager to move while the stock price remained high. In March, plans were announced to make an SEC filing of a proposed public offering of securities valued at $21 million. Of the total, $12.5 million would be raised through convertible debentures and the balance with additional common shares. General Interiors' shares closed that week at $24.125. In spite of this, things looked good for the company. The successful issuance of these debentures would mean a huge improvement in the balance sheet.

WALL STREET STUMBLES, CARPI WOUNDED

Carpi had faced many challenges during the 1960s, but financing had not been one of them. Banks and investors had been tolerant and supportive. However, the go-go '60s were coming to a close, and conditions were about to change for both the stock market and for General Interiors. The stock market tumbled in the early summer of 1969, and GIT took an unusually hard hit. The *Wall Street Journal* reported in late June that the debenture offering had been delayed because of unfavorable market conditions. GI shares by this time had dropped to $20.875, down 40 percent from the end of 1968. On July 9, the offering was canceled and the Baker deal was terminated.

After Baker exercised its right to pull out of the deal, the spurned Carpi could only watch forlornly as his share price continued to fall. Hollis Baker Jr., having gone this far, quickly agreed to a cash deal with Magnavox. Not long after the sale, he resigned abruptly following a corporate meeting when Magnavox executives challenged some of his decisions. Although Magnavox tried to leave Baker alone, the company was never quite the same after that. Carpi, meanwhile, was left standing at the altar of a collapsed wedding. Even though the bride stood him up, he still was obligated to pay for the bridesmaids. DUX, Biggs, and Salterini did not look nearly as attractive without Baker, but they now were all his.

Despite the trouble with the Baker deal, this looked like the year when the divisions would finally hit their stride. Sales climbed 42 percent, but pre-tax income rose only 28 percent. The balance sheet was not as impressive as the growth rate with the current ratio dropping below 2 to 1. Without the inflated stock price, Carpi could no longer make acquisitions. Without the acquisitions, the growth rate would slow and the grand scheme would be severely tested.

Morale was turning sour at the operating division level, and people openly questioned the corporate strategy. Most alarming was the sharp rise in selling, general, and administrative costs. Fueled by increases in headquarters staff, these already-high expenses shot up by 34 percent in '68 and another 55 percent in '69. One by one, key managers tried to convince Carpi that things were not working and that major changes were badly needed. They got nowhere. Kittinger's Batson, Pennsylvania House's McClure, Cushman's Shaughnessy, and others tried but could not convince him to act. Chief Financial Officer McGill kept sounding alarms regarding cash needs, yet Carpi refused to approve the issuance of some critically needed convertible debentures. From that point forward, the company had to scrape by financially.

His personal life was in trouble as well. He and his wife, Laura, separated in March 1970, and their relationship turned particularly acrimonious regarding custody arrangements for their four children. Before he could turn his attention to the divisions and before he could take care of the Laura matter, however, he had to contend with a more pressing matter involving the Board of Directors.

WALL STREET DISTRACTIONS, MARSHALL AND THE INDIANS

The original General Interiors board was comprised of mature investors who knew Carpi well, including fellow Princetonians Sid Staunton and Jamie Fentress. Staunton was the respected head of Laird and Co., a venture capital firm that bankrolled the original General Interiors deal. Fentress was a private investor with excellent credentials. Both were "white shoe" types, a Wall Street designation for old guard, old money, Princeton, Yale, Harvard alumni. The remaining seats were held by two more private investors plus Dick McClure, giving Carpi an extremely supportive and friendly group. Since they lacked real world furniture experience, they were in no position to challenge his concepts. They believed in him and had placed their bets on him. Carpi, in turn, had sold a piece of his soul to them. All he had to do to get it back was take part in more deals that they might bring to him. After all, they made their money on deals and there were plenty of acquisition deals out there.

Carpi's plan to consolidate the furniture industry had not gone unnoticed on Wall Street and had become the envy of several other investors. One of the interested observers was Marshall S. Cogan. He was a partner in the brokerage house of Cogan, Berlind, Weill and Levitt, which had made its reputation by buying and fixing several troubled brokerage houses. In Pac-Man-like fashion, they gobbled up Hayden Stone and then Shearson. Although initially regarded as small-time brokers – CBWL was sneeringly referred to as "corn beef with lettuce" – their appetite for challenges was substantial. Sandy Weill would become president of American Express, then Travelers, and ultimately CEO of the huge Citicorp juggernaut. Arthur Levitt would become the respected head of the Securities and Exchange Commission. Berlind would become a major theatrical producer. And Cogan would seek his fortune as a conglomerateur with some focus on home furnishings. These were years of turmoil on Wall Street as old ways gave way to new, and Carpi's overreaching attempt at restructuring an entire industry was nothing compared to what was happening on The Street. Somehow, in the midst of all this, General Interiors caught Marshall Cogan's eye.

Cogan was not a "white shoe" banker, but he was a Harvard grad with a fondness for the arts and a well-developed aesthetic sense. He too claimed to have the vision of a collection of luxury brands aimed at an increasingly sophisticated consumer. He furnished his office with Dunbar contemporary products, and his wife was reputed to be an avid Kittinger collector. After buying a sizable number of General Interiors shares in the open market, he asked Carpi for a seat on the board. Although it may have been smarter to circle the wagons to keep him out, Carpi reluctantly acceded and Cogan joined the board in June 1968. Carpi felt that the CBWL connection would be helpful in sustaining a market for General

Interiors' stock. Cogan supported Carpi at first, but by 1969 he began to question some of his ideas. Some said Cogan merely wanted to be able to buy a new Dunbar desk and a few Kittinger chairs at wholesale, but he ended up wanting the whole company.

Cogan reportedly had urged Carpi to shed a few losing divisions and openly criticized the Salterini acquisition, which, as an outdoor furniture maker, did not fit the General Interiors picture. The two clashed when Carpi refused to budge. When the debenture offering fell through, Carpi had harsh words with Cogan. People close to the company at the time remain convinced that, behind the scenes, Cogan lined up an equity partner, Iroquois Industries, to raid General Interiors. Now 30 years later, Cogan denies any recollection of any involvement with Iroquois, a company with a less-than-sterling reputation. The firm owned a brewery in Buffalo and had acquired the company that made the Champale brand of malt liquor. It's anyone's guess what CEO Terry Fox had for a vision and what it had to do with furniture. But Fox had the one thing General Interiors needed most: money. In October 1969, Iroquois offered to acquire a majority of the GI stock for stock, cash, and warrants. Carpi and his board were caught off guard by the $10 million offer. Accustomed to the role of the fast-moving buyer, they were uncomfortable as the prey. The *Wall Street Journal* reported Carpi's guarded response. "The offer will receive consideration" he said, "but it raised a number of questions" that included the merit of merging concerns with widely divergent business interests. Where Champale might fit into the matrix was anyone's guess.

Some say Cogan orchestrated a classic "Bear Raid" designed to drive down the stock price in order to wrest control away from

Carpi. Others say he was just trying to save the company. Either way, the stock dropped to $16 and Carpi fought back, rejecting the offer in a Nov. 10 announcement that said the company planned "to take all steps it deems appropriate to resist the Iroquois bid." One of these steps was to retain legendary anti-takeover attorney Joe Flom of Skadden Arps. Rumor had it that Flom negotiated a fat fee before making one phone call to General Interiors CFO Bob McGill, claiming he was in the lobby of the SEC building and that Terry Fox was going to him and say the offer had been withdrawn. He advised McGill to be gracious about it. Whatever Flom did, whomever he called, it worked. Iroquois withdrew the offer six days later. Cogan gave up his seat on the board, and Carpi celebrated the victory over what he disdainfully called "the Iroquois Indians." Cogan fulfilled his desire to be involved with "fine furniture" when he bought the Knoll Co.

THE GREAT FALL

The experience of nearly losing his company made Carpi more isolated and even less trusting of those around him. He managed to complete the purchases of DUX, Biggs Antique, and Salterini, but these companies had few assets or market position and none made money. Still reeling from the events of 1969, Carpi watched in horror as the operating divisions stumbled badly in 1970. Sales declined, and the lack of controls caught up with him. Unwilling to bite the bullet and bring expenses in line with sales, he let Selling, General & Administrative expenses reach an incredible 30 percent of sales. By mid-summer, the stock had plunged to $4. It was clear something had to be done. The divisions blamed corporate by citing the bloated headquarters expenses. Corporate blamed the divisions, citing the decline in gross margins. Fingers pointed in all directions, and rightly so.

Cogan, meanwhile, had touched a nerve with his challenge to Carpi, and he found that other board members shared his feelings. One by one they agreed that Carpi must go. His behavior went from charming to odd, and he often complained about serious sleep deprivation. His stubborn refusal to admit that not all of his moves had worked led to his downfall. As his business empire suffered setbacks, his personal life deteriorated as well. Each fed off the other in a self-destructive spiral until even his closest supporters turned against him. In August 1970 the board voted 4–1 to dismiss him as president. The founder, architect, and chief executive officer of General Interiors Corp. had been deposed by his own hand-picked board. Fred Batson Sr. was named chairman, and Dick McClure was made president. At 39, in the prime of his working years, Colin Carpi's ambitious crusade to transform and consolidate the furniture industry was over.

ADMIRABLE IDEAS, STRATEGIC BLUNDERS

Carpi earned high marks for many of his ideas. To his credit, he studied the industry and at least tried to comprehend its subtleties. His vision of what the industry could become was brilliant, and his marketing instincts were superb. By bringing in so many bright young people, he strengthened some of the divisions for years to come, and his emphasis on the product development function was correct. Had he been able to implement his retail vision as Ethan Allen did, the company probably would have been a resounding success. Several furniture insiders were smart enough to pick up on this. On the other hand, Carpi made some costly blunders that can serve as valuable lessons for other Furniture Warriors. His mistakes included:

TRYING TO DO TOO MUCH TOO FAST AND NOT LISTEN-ING WHEN THINGS BECAME HECTIC: This resulted in a loss of direction at corporate, frequent breakdowns in communication between the plants and marketing, and a failure to cope with the relentless incursions from competitors. This also was evident in Carpi's hunger for making acquisitions of small, troubled companies. His insistence on pairing them with his "horses" meant the good divisions also lost focus.

IGNORING THE CULTURE OF INDIVIDUAL DIVISIONS: Carpi failed to account for the impact of company cultures. To survive in the competitive world of furniture, a company must develop a deeply rooted culture, the essence that allows it to exist. Trying to alter this essence or, worse still, ignoring it, leads to trouble. Pennsylvania House and Kittinger lived to fight another day. Cushman, Shaw, Salterini, DUX, Dunbar and Biggs were all missing in action after being acquired by General Interiors.

TAKING ON TOO MUCH DEBT: Normal business cycles can have an impact on any business, but General Interiors was victimized by the exaggerated cycles of the furniture industry. General Interiors could not support its level of debt service costs.

LOSING FOCUS ON THE BIG PICTURE: Instead of concentrating on the critical issues, Carpi was distracted by extraneous matters such as Biggs and DUX. By getting caught up in time-consuming activities such as proof reading catalog layouts, he avoided paying enough attention to what was happening in the factories. He worked day and night in the pursuit of his dream, but there were just not enough hours for him to focus on both the inside and the outside of the business. Progress is slow in the furniture business, and gluttony regarding the pace of change can be counterproductive. The retail channel is particularly resistant to changes and quick to reject new ideas that originate with suppliers.

Carpi deserved commendations for bravery, ingenuity, and intensity as a Furniture Warrior, but he fell short in his strategic execution and decision-making during combat. His legacy as a field commander or as a headquarters general does not hold up under close scrutiny. His Pennsylvania House and Kittinger divisions won nearly all their battles, but the army he led lost the war. In his defense, he was handicapped by some cruel twists of fate, and luck certainly plays a role in The Furniture Wars. He might have survived had the stock market not tanked in the summer of 1969 and the Baker deal been completed.

An important measure of his contribution is to see how his creation performed without him. He conceived it, built it, and led it to many initial victories. Was it constructed well enough to continue to survive without him, or was it merely an extension of his own personality that would fade without his constant attention? Rarely in business does the same person find success in the role of creative founder as well as administrative builder. Next, we will explore how his army did without his generalship.

CASUALTIES OF WAR

COLIN CARPI'S ABRUPT DISMISSAL from General Interiors in August 1970 came as a shock. His challenge to the
Furniture Gods achieved some notable results, but he ultimately
failed. The ancient Greek dramatists taught that whenever mere
mortals upset the natural order of things, if they have too much
hubris, or pride, the gods invariably respond with *nemesis*, or retri-
bution. Not only had his business dreams turned to nightmares, he
now had to contend with his failing marriage. His wife Laura had
moved out of their Princeton home, filed for divorce, and made it
clear she expected custody of the children.

It is hard to measure the toll that business difficulties take on
personal lives, and vice versa, but clearly it can be formidable.
Because General Interiors contained the promise of being more
than just another furniture company, the people associated with it
worked long hours, talked about it when they weren't at work, and
paid a personal toll when it fell apart. The key players, especially
the younger ones, sincerely cared about the company and believed
in the promise it offered. Some even lived in the dream. As Dick
McClure put it years later, "Colin built his castle in the sky – and
then he tried to move into it." Having come so close to realizing

the vision, it was very hard to accept the fact that it might not be realizable, and the stress caused by its failure was enormous.

Carpi was not the only one to see his marriage fall apart. The wife of one division executive announced that she could no longer tolerate Lewisburg and walked out, leaving him with two small children. Another highly placed corporate executive experienced emotional problems. A Lewisburg manager hit bottom the day he came to work and was fired from his office job. "There might be a position open in the plant," his supervisor told him. "Check with the plant manager." Close to exhaustion after working all night as a volunteer fireman fighting a blaze at his favorite tavern, The Bull Run Inn, he headed home to tell his wife the bad news. He explained the painful choice to her: "If I want to stay in my field, we'll have to relocate, but if we want to stay in Lewisburg, I'll have to change fields." Her matter-of-fact response was, "Well, it really doesn't matter to me what you do, because this morning I filed for a divorce." In one hellish day, he had managed to lose his wife, his job, and his pub.

But this was nothing compared to the ordeal facing Laura and Colin Carpi. After separating in March 1970, they had a hard time working out the terms of their divorce settlement. She wanted a generous allowance for child support. He did not agree. If she were to get her way, he felt he would be ruined financially. It was too much for him to suffer the indignity of losing a large portion of his greatly diminished net worth after all he had been through. Gone from General Interiors in August 1970, he could devote his considerable energy to the home front. He was determined to somehow make things right.

McClure Tries to Rally the Troops

Back at General Interiors, new president Richard F. McClure was left to cope with the remnants of Carpi's broken dream. He was less than pleased with the mess he inherited. Kittinger and Pennsylvania House remained profitable, but margins had eroded and the cash had been siphoned off. The Cushman-Shaw venture had failed, and Charley Shaughnessy had resigned in disgust. Salterini was bleeding. Dunbar and DUX were in trouble. The corporate office was overloaded with expensive talent unsure of their duties. The debt service load was a killer, and the equity market was closed off as the stock market continued to fall.

Following in the time-honored tradition of "take-a-bath" accounting, General Interiors wrote off all its losses and set a new course. The financial results were horrendous. The year ended with an operating loss, as the gross margin dropped to 21 percent of sales while Selling & Administrative expenses ballooned to 31 percent of sales. Additional losses were recorded as a result of reserves for plant shutdowns and termination expenses, making the total loss amount to 17 percent of sales. By getting it all out of the way, McClure hoped he could quickly return the company to profitability. He figured General Interiors' finances would improve dramatically simply by stopping the wretched excesses.

Moving cautiously, perhaps a bit unsure in his new role, he made moves he felt would preserve the top line while reducing costs. The Cushman plants were sold, and the brand name and product line were moved to Lewisburg, where he believed they could be marketed along with Pennsylvania House. The entrepreneurs who bought the Cushman facilities announced they had reached an agreement to sell their entire output to rival Ethan Allen. Nat Ancell had, in effect, driven a competitor to close its doors and then taken over its capacity. McClure arranged to out-source production of the Cushman line to a subcontractor with a small factory near Lewisburg, figuring that its output could be sold by the combined Pennsylvania House/Cushman sales force. Others disagreed. The concept of subcontracting a specialty line like Cushman was a long shot. If it were that easy to replicate the Cushman "look," it would have been done before. The customers were rightly skeptical, and it soon became obvious that the subcontractor could not recreate the "look" or the quality, could not meet the scheduled ship dates, and had to raise prices. Cushman suffered mortal wounds, but no one wanted to admit it at first.

In a parallel move, McClure sold the Salterini facility and made arrangements to have the product line produced by Vecta, an auditorium seating company in Michigan. The brand name was to be kept by General Interiors, but the plan was flawed. The supplier failed to make the product properly and the wrought iron rusted on its way to stores. Massive return goods resulted, and the Salterini name was tarnished beyond redemption. The supplier then announced it had to raise prices. Again, mortal wounds were inflicted, but the body kept fighting.

The Shaw facility and product line survived, but the brand was abandoned later when the company decided to build a premier line of Pennsylvania House upholstery in the Charlotte plant and to move the Shaw promotional line to Lewisburg. These moves weakened the linkage between merchandisers and builders, and neither of the relocated product lines proved to be successful. The severed linkage caused problems, and the alignment between the merchandisers and the builders was not in place. Retail customers were skeptical. Quality slipped. Service was unreliable. Shaw suffered terminal wounds, but Pennsylvania House managed to survive. Deprived of their dedicated factories, Cushman and Salterini disappeared along with Shaw.

To save money, McClure closed the New York office and dismissed much of the staff. Bob McGill, the beleaguered CFO, tried to refinance the company to get out from under the staggering debt load, as the debt-to-equity ratio soared. While in 1968 and 1969 the debt to equity ratio had been better than 1:1, it shot up to 4.4:1 at the end of 1970 and hit 9:1 in 1971. The leverage that had allowed Carpi to grow quickly was now dangerously high, and cash flow was a serious concern.

THE CASE OF THE MISSING RUG

Carpi's personal struggles continued after he was forced out of General Interiors. On the morning of Feb. 8, 1971, he dropped off a support check at the rented house where Laura and the four children lived in suburban Princeton. After returning to his own house and making several phone calls, he drove to Manhattan to conduct some banking. Instead of driving to Philadelphia to see his parents, as he had planned, he returned to Princeton in the afternoon, met with his attorneys at their office and went home. Mid afternoon, school called to say that Mrs. Carpi had not picked up the children, so he went to retrieve them. As the day wore on into night, nothing was heard from Laura Carpi. She had missed her regular appointment with her psychiatrist and an 11:00 AM appointment with a friend. She had disappeared.

Police could not locate her, either. Her house showed no signs of a forced entry, the silverware in plain sight, and her clothes hung undisturbed in her closet. Investigators thought no other valuables were missing either, until a neighbor pointed out that an oriental rug had been removed from the dining room. Investigators found traces of blood in the dining room and in the kitchen, where a mop was found with similar traces. These facts seemed to rule out burglary and made it improbable that she just ran away. Officers questioned Colin but filed no charges. Regardless of their suspicions, without more evidence of violent activity – a murder weapon, the corpus delicti – there was nothing they could do. The children moved to Colin's house while the search continued for Laura. Her parents hired private investigators to look into the matter, and one of her close friends offered a $10,000 reward for her safe return. Still she did not return.

A few months after Laura Carpi disappeared, The *New York Times* printed results of its investigation of the New York City Medical Examiner's Office that uncovered questionable practices and procedures, including a number of misidentified bodies. The shocking story broke in the *Times* under the headline, "Severed Head Brings City into Jersey Murder Case." Quite the scandal unfolded, replete with accusations of misconduct, denials, and a call by Mayor John Lindsey for an official inquiry. In one lurid instance, an employee had allegedly used a skull as a paperweight. The *Times* reporter determined that the partially decomposed body of an unidentified woman had been recovered from the East

River at 22nd Street on June 9, 1972. No autopsy was performed, but the cause of death was recorded as drowning and the body was buried June 29 in a "potter's field" on Hart Island. For some reason, the head became separated from the torso and ended up on a desk. Someone found a bullet in the skull, prompting the Medical Examiner to exhume the body on July 8 for an autopsy.

The autopsy revealed that death had been caused by a "bullet wound of the head, base of skull and spine – homicidal." The law enforcement agencies in the area were informed, and the message was eventually delivered to the Princeton police. On a hunch, Princeton detectives took Laura's dentist to the Medical Examiner's Office on July 22 and identified the body as being that of Laura Carpi. Had the head not been on the desk, the bullet probably would not have been discovered. Had the newspaper not become involved, it is possible that the body would have gone unidentified. But now the police had what they needed and, after two days of intense interrogation, they arrested Colin Carpi and charged him with murder.

ZIMMERMAN & KENNEDY

Back in Lewisburg, the organization was struggling. In making the transition from divisional head to corporate chieftain, McClure decided not to replace himself at Pennsylvania House. Instead, he split the work between marketing/sales chief Bob Zimmerman and operations chief Tom Kennedy.

In a company filled with bright, ambitious MBAs, Zimmerman was the acknowledged leader, the one who stood tall, and at age 33 seemed destined for greatness. The nickname, Zim, fit him perfectly. He was formidable yet friendly, calculating yet caring, powerful yet personable. "Bob" did not really fit – it seemed too common. "Mr. Zimmerman" seemed too pretentious. He was "Zim" – a dynamic force who could either carry you or knock you down, depending on whether you were on his team or in his way. The other MBA's *wanted* to be successful. Zim *had* to be successful, and his lack of furniture experience did not hold him back. He was a marketing type. And he had no "eye" for furniture; in fact, he was color-blind. When he traveled, his wife had to preselect his ties. Yet none of this mattered, because Zimmerman was a quick study who listened better than anyone. He became a "furniture type" almost overnight and could wing it with the old pros as if he were born to the business.

Kennedy, on the other hand, was a "trophy executive" blessed with impeccable furniture credentials. He was a graduate of the furniture program at North Carolina State University and later worked for the highly regarded Heritage Furniture Co. He was well liked and respected by peers as well as his staff. He knew furniture, especially quality furniture, and he was the possessor of a great deal of Southern charm. He was the perfect manufacturing compliment to Zimmerman's marketing skills.

Both men were exceptionally competent and became close friends, so it was logical to assume they would work together cooperatively and set aside the normal differences between their respective functions. They even took vacations together, but both wanted to be the head of Pennsylvania House. While McClure was off trying to straighten out the mess at GI headquarters, Kennedy and Zimmerman were supposed to be working together to generate profits in Lewisburg. Instead they tore into each other, and earnings at the division suffered.

Instead of being a turnaround year with new management, 1971 showed another hefty loss. Gross margins improved to a respectable 25 percent, but SG&A expenses remained embarrassingly high at 27 percent as McClure's cost-cutting moves failed to get the desired results.

McClure redoubled his efforts in 1972 to fix the problems and again hoped for a breakout year. To remind everyone to concentrate on Profit Improvement Programs, he insisted that "PIP '72" be put on all memos. But turning the company around required considerably more than slogans. The troublesome Dunbar "fix" never materialized, and Kittinger could not make up for it. Salterini's convoluted joint venture with Vecta continued to drain management time and cash. Pennsylvania House continued to miss its profit forecasts. As a result, Bob McGill's ingenious plan to raise money through a combination of privately placed and publicly offered preferred stock never got off the ground.

The Zimmerman/Kennedy skirmish continued in Lewisburg, but Zimmerman's marketing team took the upper hand and began to bury the operations side. Zimmerman unleashed his "dogs of war" during a two-day general marketing meeting in February 1972. The group introduced an array of powerful new products, increased advertising expenditures, strengthened a direct-mail program, beefed up sales promotions, added new sales reps, went after new accounts, and expanded floor space at existing accounts. By the summer, year-to-date incoming orders rose an astonishing 41 percent.

The plants could not handle this surge in business, and backlogs doubled over 1971. Deliveries were slow. Dealers became upset, and margins suffered as a result of the promotions and plant variances. Zimmerman actually issued a memo entitled "Selective De-Marketing" to put the brakes on. Politics became more important than results. Teamwork disappeared. Morale plummeted and rumors circulated of impending collapse. Much of this could have been avoided had there been an on-site general manager to coordinate the making and selling functions.

TRIAL BY JURY

When the Carpi case went before a grand jury, the state prosecutor's evidence included some convincing results from lie detector tests. Since polygraph tests were inadmissible as evidence in New Jersey, the judge quashed the indictment and released Carpi. But prosecutors did not abandon the case, and the murder indictment was reinstated.

Carpi's lawyers fought to have the indictment dismissed again. They filed a motion on Jan. 4, 1974, claiming prosecutors had suppressed evidence. The judge denied the motion, and the trial began. The defense counsel argued that Carpi could not possibly have had time to kill his wife considering his busy schedule that day. But prosecutors built a fairly strong case against Carpi, claiming that he stopped by the house, shot Laura, wrapped her in the Oriental rug and drove the body to New York City, where he dumped it in the East River. The motive – his anger over her plans to divorce him – was clear. Prosecutors chipped away at his alibi with phone records contradicting his statements. He told police his calls lasted from 80 to 105 minutes, but records showed they lasted only 20 minutes. This would have given him more time to be at the house. Witnesses testified that Laura had stated that she feared for her life because of threats he had made to her in the presence of lawyers. A detective stated that Carpi had a bruise on his right hand and scratches on his face the day after the disappearance. One of Laura's lawyers gave confirming testimony.

Most significantly, witnesses stated that the support check was on the top of the mail pile, which cast doubt on his testimony, since the regular mail was delivered at noon and Carpi claimed he slid the check through the slot at 9:30 that morning. Finally, a legal secretary testified that Carpi tried to call her at 3:30, saying he had to pick up the kids at school. But both the daughter and Carpi said the call from the school came at close to 4:00 PM. How could he have known at 3:30 that Laura could not pick up the children, when the daughter did not call until 20 minutes later?

One by one, Carpi's lawyer neutralized the damage from the prosecutor's evidence. The phone call times were not material. Another witness, a schoolmate of Carpi's, testified that Laura had no bruises or scratches. The alleged threats were "fabrications." As for the check ending up on top of the mail pile, the explanation was simple. Carpi's daughter, 11 years old at the time her mother disappeared, testified that she had handled the mail when she came home and probably resorted it. Finally, in a dramatic moment, after being shown a log of incoming calls, the legal secretary revised her testimony about the time of Carpi's call and said he probably called twice that day. And throughout the trial, the jury was not allowed to hear that Carpi had failed multiple lie detector tests.

During the summation, the prosecution claimed the evidence

was overwhelming and that Carpi's own testimony amounted to perjury. But defense attorney Gerald Stockman was brilliant in his closing statement, essentially introducing enough doubt to make the jury deliberate very carefully. "How could he have gone to her house in broad daylight, killed her, taken 170 pounds or so (body and rug) to his car with nobody seeing a thing, then return, clean it up with a mop, ring it out so well the state police could not even detect that the drop of blood remaining on the mop was human, and drive off?"

After nearly two full days, jurors found themselves still sharply divided, particularly over the testimony relating to the timing of calls related to picking up the children. The division was cleared up only after the testimony was read to them a second time. At 4:03 PM on Jan. 30, 1974, the jury announced a verdict of not guilty. "There just wasn't enough evidence to pin it on him," juror Louis Stanziale said. "There were things that pointed to him, but nothing that really established (his guilt.)" Another juror said, "There was too much reliance on the timing of things people did three years ago."

At a press conference following the verdict, Carpi lashed out at the justice system, the police, the press, the grand jury, the judges, and prosecutors. "They had no case against me to begin with," Carpi said. "The indictment was a sham. In three years of this case, the state violated basic human rights, distorted and lied about facts and concealed important evidence that now leads me to believe I have a pretty good idea what happened." What that idea was, he never revealed. In response, the acting prosecutor said, "I want everyone to know, I want the jury to know, that he flunked a lie detector test three times."

The following day, in an interview with a reporter from the *New York Times*, Carpi said he hoped to take time to write articles and eventually a book on the country's judicial system. "The cumulative effect of the improvements I propose would be to shorten trials, unburden our courts, and help citizens who can't afford long, expensive litigation," he said. In a parting shot, he attacked the Mercer County prosecutor's office, claiming it "lied about the facts, concealed important evidence, and (engaged in running) a massive, prejudicial publicity campaign."

Carpi was free to seek changes in the judicial system, to rebuild his business, and to spend time with his children. He married the former secretary who stood by him throughout the trial. He was not heard from again in the furniture business. One could only hope that others would learn from his innovative ideas and from his mistakes.

THE GREAT FLOOD

The easiest way for The Furniture Gods to dole out punishment is by fire. Furniture plants are susceptible to fast-spreading fires because of the sawdust and lacquer elements, and it did not take much to wipe out whole structures before firefighters could set up their hoses. But just to be different, Hurricane Agnes stalled over Virginia in June 1972 and dumped rains of biblical proportions from New York State through Pennsylvania, Maryland and Virginia. Lewisburg was hit particularly hard. Overnight flash flooding in streams and small rivers wiped out the Pennsylvania House showroom and many employee homes. Then, the mighty Susquehanna River overflowed its banks, eventually flooding the area. Pennsylvania Governor Milton Shapp estimated the flooding costs at more than $1 billion in his state alone.

Pennsylvania House's main wood plant suffered damage, and the three-story upholstery plant along the river was wiped out. Countless homes, including McClure's stately residence, were flooded. Production was disrupted and inventory was destroyed. McClure could scarcely believe the company had to contend with this on top of everything else. In July, he returned to Lewisburg from New York to get a handle on the mess. In addition to two feet of muddy water on the first floor of his home, he had a mess on his hands at the office. The Residential Retail Group – consisting of Pennsylvania House, Cushman, Shaw, DUX, Biggs, and Salterini – had let gross margins drop to a pathetic level of below 20 percent. Net profits were close to zero.

The company's marketers felt they had done everything asked of them, and more. If only the plants had been able to respond with higher shipments, they said, the company would have been fine. But the corporation was in serious trouble. Something had to be done to improve earnings, and McClure chose to reorganize the sales and marketing function. In an Aug. 8, 1972, memo to the sales force, he detailed far-reaching actions he hoped would right the company. These included cutting corporate and manufacturing overhead, a drastic reorganizing of the Marketing Team, firing many people, closing showrooms in Chicago and High Point, canceling sales promotions, folding Cushman into Pennsylvania House, slicing sales commission rates, and selling the company plane. He had little choice but to gut the organization and dismantle the strategy he had encouraged his staff to pursue. The impact was devastating. Some said he should have made these moves a year earlier. Others said they were the wrong moves.

The dismissed people were distraught, and the resulting wounds took many years to heal. It wasn't necessarily easier for staffers who held their jobs, either. Quality had suffered badly, customer service was a disaster, and dealers were furious. Many survivors felt an irrational sense of guilt and vowed to leave the company as soon as they could. Gallows humor helped keep things going. Zimmerman distributed posters of a cat frantically holding on to a chinning bar with the caption, "Hang in there, Baby." The motto of the marketing crew became "Protect your ass; they're coming in the windows." Whenever production people mentioned high backlogs, sales people would respond, "Just ship it!" quoting Zimmerman, who had shouted this at Kennedy during a production meeting. And now, the company was running out of cash. A new owner was highly likely; bankruptcy loomed. The tension and the sense of impending doom seemed unbearable, but Zimmerman held the remains of the marketing crew together. Taking the name of the successful Lewisburg High School football team, they defiantly proclaimed, "Don't Mess with the Green Dragons."

RUMORS OF SURRENDER

As many rumors flew about more layoffs and potential buyers, another indignity occurred when it was reported in August that Ethan Allen head Nat Ancell was in Lewisburg to tour the Pennsylvania House plants. The marketing and sales group panicked, assuming Ancell would immediately dismiss the entire crew were he to buy the company. They had harassed him so effectively in the past; it would be just like him to buy the company so that he could get even. Then someone said he was going to buy it so he could shut the whole company down. Before people could react to this unsettling rumor, word went out that Ancell had rejected the deal after touring the plants and reviewing the numbers. According to the rumor mill, Ancell said the plants were so poorly run and the union so resistant to change that the company was doomed to fail and he wanted nothing to do with it. This was the ultimate competitive indignity.

From Baker to Candlestick Maker

In September, McClure knew that an outside infusion of capital was needed. He continued his frantic search for a financial partner and worked up a complicated plan whereby General Interiors would buy a small brass accent producer called Virginia Metalcrafters from Sprigg Lane Investment Corp. As part of the deal, Sprigg Lane and Euclid Partners, reputedly a Hanna family trust fund, would put cash into General Interiors by purchasing some GI notes. Kittinger and Virginia Metalcrafters both made licensed reproductions of Williamsburg designs, but no other synergy could be seen. The deal fell through within two weeks, and rumors claimed that Carpi somehow had killed the deal, although no one could explain how. Clearly, McClure was running out of options.

Morale reached an all-time low in October, when the marketing and sales contingent headed South to the semi-annual Furniture Market in North Carolina. They went with heavy hearts, wondering whether the company would still be there when they returned. Like scouts leaving their home base as it was about to be captured, they planned to hold down expenses because reimbursement was unlikely.

The Lewisburg troops were proud of their performance and embarrassed by the corporate collapse. The thought of competitors possibly buying the company was humiliating. As each rumor surfaced, they would dismiss the reputed buyer as being unworthy. "What makes them think they can buy *us*?" Then, as the deals collapsed, they would worry even more. "Wonder why they don't want to buy us?" There were no desertions, partially because no one wanted to leave and partially because there were no offers. Meetings with dealers were painful because the service and quality had deteriorated so badly.

The deconstruction of the Carpi vision was extensive. Not only was he gone, but Tony Leonard and Will Somers also were gone. Bob Young and Joe Pugliese were gone. Cushman was gone. Shaw had been folded into Pennsylvania House. Salterini should have been gone. Biggs had disappeared into Kittinger. The New York office was closed, and the cash was gone. The once proud House of Carpi had turned out to be a house of cards. It would not take much of a breeze to collapse it into bankruptcy.

LESSONS LEARNED

The eight-year history of General Interiors, from the Chair Factory to the Flood, provides the student of the furniture industry with some valuable lessons:

YOU ARE NOT INVISIBLE: When a company struggles, retail customers can read the warning signs and instinctively reduce their commitment to factories that they feel are headed for trouble. Factories may think they can conceal these problems, but dealers and the sales representatives invariably detect them and react quickly. Competitors exploit the situation overnight.

YOU NEED A FIRST AMONG EQUALS: The Mr. Inside/Mr. Outside model of top management works best if one person is the designated "first among equals." Zimmerman and Kennedy were capable and dedicated, but they worked against one another instead of pulling together. Had McClure designated an "acting president" when he took over the corporation, the results in Lewisburg might have been different and the purge of the marketing department may not have been needed.

DISCARD YOUR WEAKEST BRANDS: Trying to sustain multiple brands was a needless distraction, especially once the factories had been sold. This made it difficult for the management team to focus. Carpi enjoyed collecting brands while Nat Ancell of Ethan Allen kept his focus on one brand.

THE MYTH OF SYNERGY: Synergy by combining companies is rare in furniture. Kittinger and Pennsylvania House had a lot in common and tried to help each other, but they served different niches and find absolutely no common ground. On paper, it always looks like consolidations will result in more profitability. Reality is different.

TURNAROUNDS ARE RARE: True turnarounds in furniture companies are hard to accomplish. The internal resistance to change is formidable, and external forces can be devastating when the dealers pull back from a wounded supplier and make matters worse. Trying to push the pace of change only worsens the problem.

A great deal of waste and heartache would have been avoided had people heeded the lessons of the General Interiors saga. But as later chapters will show, Santayana was right when he pronounced, "Those who cannot remember the past are condemned to repeat it." But General Interiors was not dead yet, and we need to remember how difficult it is to leave the furniture business. Will the banks step in and dismantle the remaining assets or will the company avoid the dreaded Chapter 11 that seems to be only a few pages away?

FOGARTY TO THE RESCUE

THE LONG ORDEAL at General Interiors was about to end. Like a sparkler that burns brightly, but flames out quickly, Colin Carpi's cobbled-together army had won many early skirmishes but now was in full retreat and needing leadership to avoid a rout. New chief Dick McClure felt trapped. The divisions were not performing well; banks and suppliers were unsympathetic; and prospective buyers had come and gone. What General Interiors needed was a miracle worker.

On Thursday, September 5, 1972, a visitor showed up at General Interiors headquarters. He introduced himself as Robert Sherman Fogarty Jr., and he announced that he was willing to pay $1.70 per share for control of the company. McClure was insulted and reacted with all the indignation he could muster. A mere two years earlier, the shares had traded above $30. Who was this Fogarty guy, and what made him think he could run these companies? He claimed to be the president of Mode, an upholstery company in California, but McClure had never heard of it. His partner was California investor William H. B. Chan, who had made his money in the unrelated field of health care. McClure had plenty of questions, but Fogarty had done his homework and was prepared for combat.

Kittens do not Devour Lions

McClure had never dealt with anyone like Fogarty. Reminiscent of a Clint Eastwood character, Fogarty was implacable, indomitable, fearless, and cunning. Fiercely focused on his goal, he was not to be denied. He had a remarkable ability to project himself into the middle of a business transaction and then predict the outcome with uncanny accuracy. It was as if he were forecasting an entire chess game. First, he would outline what he was going to say and then predict the most likely responses by the other party. Then, he would lay out, word for word, how he would respond to each possible move by the other side.

Fogarty's position was enhanced by being the proverbial "last man in the room" when it came to doing a deal with General Interiors. Every other suitor had passed on the opportunity to buy the company, not so much because the price was wrong, but because potential buyers did not know how to fix GI's problems. The assets, most notably the brand names, were swamped by the liabilities in more ways than one. The strong divisions had been decimated, and the weak were on life support systems. Leadership was lacking, and the plants were not running well. The information systems were ineffective, and the marketing teams were undisciplined. It made more sense to liquidate than to continue the struggle, and major lenders wanted their money back. The General Interiors army, nearly out of ammunition and suffering from battle fatigue, was ready to surrender.

Fogarty knew this and never wavered from his "take-it-or-leave-it" offer. The General Interiors board may have been insulted by the offer, but they did not have to deliberate long in deciding between certain bankruptcy or selling out to the strangers from California. The board took the offer on October 20, 1972, and Fogarty was elected chairman and chief executive. In the midst of final negotiations, he flew to High Point to tour the Pennsylvania House showroom during the Furniture Market. Although the executive selected to escort him was understandably nervous, the tour went well until they came upon a special room that contained a mix of furniture from each of the General Interiors divisions. It was one of those foolish corporate moves that embarrasses the divisions but makes headquarters happy. Fogarty's reaction was caustic. "And exactly *what* are you trying to sell here?" he sneered. His body language and his tone made it clear that the new chief had no use for meaningless gestures. The effect he had on those who came in contact with him at the Market was electrifying. He knew the industry. He knew what he was doing, he knew what he wanted, and he expressed himself perfectly clearly. He struck fear in the hearts of people who met him, but this was not unwelcome after months of aimless drifting. Besides, if his staff feared him, just think how competitors would react. The mood of the marketing team as it returned to Lewisburg from the market was decidedly different from the depressing trip down. A popular song at the time, Johnny Nash's "I Can See Clearly Now, The Rain is Gone," kept playing on the radio, bringing smiles to the Pennsylvania House faces.

Fogarty Assumes Command

Fogarty wasted no time in taking control. Zeroing in on the troubled Lewisburg flagship, he moved McClure aside and appointed

Bob Zimmerman president of the Pennsylvania House Division. Tom Kennedy was let go. He then called together the key managers and made it clear that he expected to make a profit and would not tolerate any politics, or "foolishness," as he termed it.

He was born in the Hudson River Valley and became a Phi Beta Kappa graduate of Wofford College in Spartanburg, South Carolina. His career path took him first to Burlington Industries and later to Schlumberger, where he was involved with a successful turnaround of the Daystrom Dinette Co. From there he went to Virtue Brothers in California, another dinette company in need of a turnaround. As president, he quickly reversed five years of losses. In 1970, he invested his life savings and bought a broken-down upholstery producer, Mode of California, and after avoiding bankruptcy managed to triple sales and generate healthy profits in two years.

Tall and distinguished with a serious expression and tone, Fogarty was blessed with an extraordinary intellect that he constantly augmented with a great deal of reading and thinking. His "senatorial" demeanor was enhanced by his preference for dark wool suits. The brand he preferred was Oxxford, a very expensive label, and he treated his wardrobe accordingly, always careful to remove his jacket when sitting down to avoid wrinkling. His days of playing basketball took a toll on his knees, and it showed in his stiff walk. On meeting him, you could sense he was sizing you up, always calculating, looking for an edge, thinking, and planning, not his next move, but several moves down the line. His tough, intimidating presence was accented by a sharp sense of humor that was always close to the surface. He saw the humor in people and events, but never let his guard down, saving his rare relaxed moments for when he was with family. At work, he was all work. He was a true furniture insider capable of operating behind enemy lines. The man clearly knew how to revive sick companies, but whether he could handle one that was near death remained to be seen.

Accustomed to losses, the Lewisburg accountants prepared to take another accounting bath in fiscal 1972. But Fogarty directed them to close the books in a normal fashion with no special write-offs or reserves. The results, it was revealed later, were so bad they required no additional embellishments. Sales in fiscal 1972 rose 12 percent, but the company lost $1.37 a share. Obviously, the post-Carpi turnaround had not taken hold after two full years.

Many observers were convinced the company was too far gone and that Fogarty would soon meet his Waterloo. These people did not know Robert Sherman Fogarty Jr. His management style was intimidating and uplifting at the same time. You wanted to be on his team but lived in constant fear that he would fire you if you let him down. He made few organization changes, but the ones he made were right. Next, he set reasonable goals and promised not to interfere as long as you "kept it on the road." Then, he stated he would be there, if needed, to remove impediments. Finally, he made it clear that if you did not meet the agreed-upon goals, he would see to it that you could never get a job in the furniture industry again and, if you betrayed him, he would bury you.

Beneath it all, he understood the furniture business as an Insider. This had a remarkable impact on the company, which had long been directed by people who only thought they knew the business. Carpi was a brilliant conceptualizer, but he had trouble executing his plans. Fogarty was skilled conceptually, and enormously effective at getting results.

CHAPTER SIX

THE BERNE SPEECH

In June 1973, he convened a special conference at the Dunbar office in Berne, Indiana. Virtually all managers from all divisions were included, and there was much speculation as to the purpose. The company was beginning to improve and Fogarty had to be pleased, but nearly everyone was fearful of his razor-sharp mind and stiletto-sharp tendency to be vindictive when crossed. The audience was very much an organization in transition. Many managers had not seen the new leader up close and, having been accustomed to weak leadership for many years, the group tended to be disrespectful and cynical. At Lewisburg, the rank-and-file attitude more closely resembled the mindset of the inmates at the Lewisburg prison than a business. Many of the younger managers thought they knew "the score" far better than top management, and for good reason. They also tended to give what loyalty they had to the "warlord-like" leader of their function. The marketing types paid allegiance to Zimmerman, while Kennedy received support from the manufacturing types. More importantly, there was a deeply rooted cynicism that bordered on defeatism. The attitude was not that of a losing team, but more that of a talented team that was prevented from winning by countless outside distractions.

The Berne meeting afforded Fogarty the opportunity to change all this, which is exactly what he did by enunciating, in remarkably clear prose, what he demanded of the organization. In capsule form, his message was this:

✝   Management is expected to produce results or be dismissed.

In the first minute of the speech, he vowed that he would "prune laggards quickly, just as a surgeon cuts a cancer."

✝   There is only one leader of the company and he knows exactly what he is doing. Office politics would not be tolerated.

✝   His business philosophy was based on four qualities – integrity, discipline, ability, and loyalty.

✝   The budget was the inviolable test of performance. God help the manager who missed his numbers.

✝   The "Cost of Goods Sold Control" concept would guide the company. This meant profit must be made on the inherited sales base, not on expected increases. The key is rigid cost control, a radical departure from previous regimes. "Increased volume at reduced prices tends to make the breakeven point rise even faster than sales . . . and serious losses are generated," he said.

✝   Budgets were to be determined by a method that first required the division to attain its historical averages – surely a reasonable goal that no one could challenge. Then, the division would be expected to recapture its historic best numbers and, finally, the goal would be to match the industry's best numbers. In scaling costs back to the level of the historical best year, the division would simply be recapturing what it had once attained. In the process, the company would be invoking what Fogarty called "The Safety of Principle Rule," which dictated that the "avoidance of loss was the first step to profitability."

✝ The real marketing challenge was to increase profits, not sales. Eliminating money-losing products and programs was an essential first step. "We must commit ourselves never to sell an unprofitable item."

✝ Product development is crucially important, but care must be taken to ensure that products are not only in tune with the market, but also in tune with the plant's capabilities. Marketing and production must be aligned.

✝ A deeply held sense of commitment across all levels of the company is required to be successful. People must feel that the numbers are "doable" and sign on to their "rightness."

✝ Finally, "good numbers, swiftly delivered, are our early warning system," and the job is to anticipate problems and react immediately.

The Berne Speech re-energized the majority of the managers, inspiring them to work harder and more effectively than ever. It scared the others. Working for Fogarty was not for the faint of heart. He demanded much of his troops, and he expected them to win. Managers who went into battle could count on him providing the needed support and didn't have to worry about headquarters screwing up the battle plan. For most, it was a welcome and dramatic change.

FOGARTY'S FOUR QUALITIES

Of particular interest were the four qualities he listed. To help remember them, some wag suggested that Fogarty wanted everyone "to get LAID" – Loyalty, Ability, Integrity, and Discipline. The ability and integrity qualities were present before Fogarty arrived, and Carpi certainly engendered loyalty. Discipline, however, was sorely lacking. For some, the most difficult to swallow was the loyalty issue, and he made it very clear there was to be no compromise. "If what the company stands for does not mesh with your world-view, then find a company that does," was his message. "This is the fabric of greatness, and I will not have that fabric torn." Ability was a given but only a starting point. Fogarty demanded that his managers be very good at their jobs. "It's in the order of things. Kittens do not devour lions . . . and ability is measured by the dramatic test of performance under pressure." Integrity involves basic honesty to self and to the organization, which leads to credibility and trust. It is concerned with *what* is right rather than *who* is right. Discipline involves the harnessing of human energy toward the attainment of company objectives. He had no use for the democratization of business, "for in business there is no room for failure, and the greatest insurance against failure is discipline."

A STUNNING TURNAROUND IN 1973

Fogarty closed his speech by showing a slide of the General Interiors sales and earnings history. In the first six years of Carpi's ascendancy, from 1964 through 1969, the company earned about $3 million. In the three years between 1970 and 1972, the company lost nearly twice that much. In the first year of Fogarty's reign, the company made more than it had in the first six years. And that was just the beginning. You could argue with the strictures Fogarty imposed on the group, but you could not argue with the results.

In the 1973 annual report, Fogarty's letter to shareholders made it clear that he was not responsible for the pitiful results generated in 1972. As he put it, "There is nothing we can do to correct yesterday. Our purpose is to build tomorrow. We, as professional furniture people . . . prefer to let our performance speak for itself." The bottom line results in his first year spoke eloquently indeed. Sales went up 16 percent, and net income reached $3.2 million, a $4.4 million turnaround. General Interiors earned $1.37 per share in 1973, the opposite of 1972's loss of $1.37 per share.

The philosophy outlined in Berne was implemented precisely, and the results were exactly as he predicted. First, Fogarty stripped the corporate staff down to the bare necessities, leaving a head-quarters group of a controller, a secretary, and himself as chairman of the board. Then he streamlined the division structure. DUX was discontinued. Biggs was folded into Kittinger, but Dunbar was separated to stand on its own. New presidents were appointed to each division, and the company bought Brown Saltman, a Califor-nia based case goods producer. Skeptics noted that Brown Saltman was purchased for $3.2 million, considerably more than the entire General Interiors acquisition, and that the principal stockholder was William H. B. Chan. Was this a payback for funding the ear-lier purchase, or was it a strategic move designed to strengthen the presence of Pennsylvania House in California? At the time, Brown Saltman had a very hot line called Ponderosa Pine and a capable president named David Fields. It did not seem so bad that some of General Interiors' cash found its way to California. At least it had cash.

DIVISION RESULTS

At the division level, Kittinger quickly returned to steady profitability. Pennsylvania House, with Bob Zimmerman at the helm, produced some amazing results. The Pennsylvania House management team responded to Fogarty's leadership and Zimmerman's exuberant style with an intense focus on results. The brand and the team always had plenty of horsepower but had been held back by too many distractions. Spurred by the challenge to show what it could do and given clear direction, the Lewisburg Green Dragons tore into the competition with a vengeance. The chronic service problems were addressed head-on with a marketing strategy called The Good Turn Program. The goal was to direct sales efforts to the company's proven best sellers, which had the effect of channeling more volume though fewer items. That let the plant run larger, more efficient, and more profitable production runs.

The Good Turn Program also meant faster shipments and better service for the customers, who had become disgusted with erratic shipping performance. Pennsylvania House had a terrible reputation for "split-shipping" – delivering tables to customers without chairs or beds without nightstands. This meant that retailers had to carry extra inventory, which slowed growth. Whenever management discussed how to solve the problem, it always concluded that there was no solution. Fogarty basically said, "Solve it, or else." And it was solved.

Analysis of sales patterns revealed that even though the consumer could buy one piece at a time, certain items tended to sell together – the Queen Anne oval table with the Queen Anne chairs, for example. By scheduling production runs so these logical groupings were made at the same time, the factory could ship more "complete orders" without having to hold inventory. The dealers were urged to set up their displays accordingly and to make sure they kept the best sellers on display.

To increase production, it was suggested that the company eliminate the custom finish options. This meant abandoning the "Have it your way" feature so cherished by Carpi. In practice, it was a big contributor to the split shipping dilemma and raised production costs. Production begged to have it eliminated; marketing insisted it must stay; Zimmerman made the tough call. It was dropped shortly after New Year's Day 1973, and the plant people rejoiced. Sales of the best sellers increased almost immediately, and production went up also. Productivity and quality rose, costs fell and no one shed a tear. By the end of March, wood shipments were running 24 percent ahead of the previous year, and upholstery shipments were up 18 percent. For the first time in five years, the company expanded plant capacity with a large addition.

Then Marketing decided to drop the multiple brand strategy by giving up the ghosts of Cushman and Shaw. This One Brand Strategy would propel the Pennsylvania House brand into the forefront of furniture marquees and take it far ahead of the also-rans. The decisions to focus the company were long overdue, but at last they were made. The management team now was free to concentrate on the most important tasks at hand, and concentrate they did.

After losing $1 million in 1972, the new management team at Pennsylvania House produced profits of $2.7 million in 1973 on a sales increase of 18 percent. Promotional discounts were cut in half. Gross margins jumped from the teens to the mid twenties, while selling and general and administrative costs as a percentage of sales fell by a third. Divisional operating income actually hit 20 percent as a percentage of sales in several months.

The Money Keeps Rolling In

Fogarty demanded even more in 1974. The Pennsylvania House Divisional operating income budget was set at 15 percent of sales, a level seemingly beyond reason. To make matters worse, January started slowly at Pennsylvania House and management fretted over how to make sense out of the Brown Saltman acquisition. An attempt was made to produce the Stone House Oak Collection at Brown Saltman's California plant, and the Pennsylvania House sales force was told to carry Brown Saltman's Ponderosa Pine Collection. Neither initiative produced much. Fogarty was hard to please even when things were going well, and no one wanted to find out what he would be like if the results came up short. The divisions knew they simply had to hit their numbers and could make up Brown Saltman's shortfall with more from Pennsylvania House. That was what happened.

During the Carpi era, Pennsylvania House had sustained a strong marketing orientation that was not always supported by equally strong manufacturing. Under Fogarty, the plants slowly became more efficient and better able to meet the needs of the marketplace. This played to the strength of the company. Since office politics had been banished by executive order, the organization began to function smoothly, and results were held in higher regard than titles. An important factor was that the top management trusted each other. The vice presidents of marketing and manufacturing got along well and avoided the battles that Zimmerman and Kennedy enjoyed so much. These managers were not long on furniture experience, but they respected the industry and made sure they had access to the counsel of more experienced people. This helped them learn the idiosyncrasies of the business and avoid the mistakes caused by misreading those quirks. The added benefit is that they also avoided some of the myopic thinking that too often comes with a lot of furniture experience. Pennsylvania House was fortunate to have a balance of outside and inside thinking.

The marketing emphasis, when added to the strong product line, pushed up sales levels sharply. Zimmerman's "full-speed-ahead" style resembled that of his hero, General George S. Patton. And like a rapidly advancing army that neglects to secure its supply lines, the company paid little attention to its customer service function. Management kept ignoring the warning signs that flashed repeatedly as dealers complained about quality and shipping problems. The line was so hot, and the marketing support was so powerful, that it was easy to shrug off the warning signs. Besides, sales management and sales reps were good at deflecting complaints.

A Few Clouds

Not everything went according to Fogarty's plan, and his insistence on ever-higher earnings put tremendous pressure on management. Kittinger and Pennsylvania House rose to the challenge, but Dunbar continued to founder. Then, in the summer of 1974, the National Home Furnishings Association published a report that ranked all suppliers for dependability, quality, and complaint handling. The interviews included responses from dealers with an ax to grind, and Pennsylvania House had hundreds of discontinued dealers eager to get back at the company. The Pennsylvania House management knew they had legitimate problems with quality and service from the turbulent years before Fogarty, but they felt they had been addressed after the survey was taken but before the results were published. They hoped their scores would be above average.

The published results were devastating. Out of 45 companies rated, Pennsylvania House ranked 42nd in dependability, 37th in quality, and 43rd in complaint handling. There ensued a mad scramble to explain and defend the results, but the facts were there for all to see. All the dealers that management talked to insisted they had not been critical of the company. Largely because of strong relationships with the sales representatives and partially because the line was so "hot," the company's glaring performance deficiencies were tolerated.

The report did not derail the Lewisburg Express, and neither did a slowing economy. By year-end, sales had increased by 21 percent, profits were up by 40 percent, and net margins hit 17.3 percent. In his 1974 letter to the stockholders, Fogarty sounded philosophical as he again let the results speak for themselves. Overall, General Interiors sales climbed 24 percent, and pre-tax income rose 39 percent. Fogarty's company had made so much money that it had used up its tax benefits from the operating loss carry forward "earned" during the Carpi/McClure era. It would be a remarkable story were it to end here, but the momentum continued.

GENERAL INTERIORS CORPORATION
Net Income (Loss)

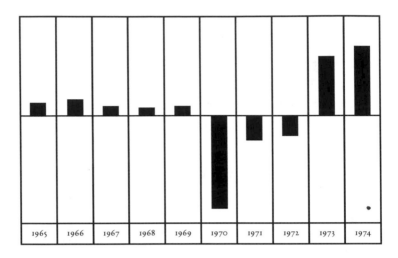

| 1965 | 1966 | 1967 | 1968 | 1969 | 1970 | 1971 | 1972 | 1973 | 1974 |

LESSONS LEARNED

The most valuable lessons from the Fogarty Era at General Interiors are contained in his Berne speech, which spells out his guiding management philosophy with remarkable clarity and economy. Loyalty, ability, integrity, and discipline are the qualities he demands of his team, and Safety of Principle is his cardinal rule. This is, in turn, based on rigid cost controls, full margin pricing, and a budgeting system with serious accountability.

In Fogarty's hands, it produced remarkable results. Before Fogarty, the company had three good years with profits of $1.4 million (about $7.6 million after accounting for inflation), followed by three bad years with losses of $7.9 million – or $44 million in current dollars. With Fogarty, GI made profits of $7 million (about $33 million today) in the first two years.

Beyond Berne, there are two other lessons worth noting. The revival of General Interiors taught that experience can't hurt. Outsiders bring new ideas, but even better is a professional manager who also happens to be an experienced furniture person. With Fogarty's reign came fewer distractions and little wasted effort. When divisional executives have to spend time explaining things or answering "dumb" questions to inept bosses, it erodes their instincts and makes them tentative when they need to be bold. And finally it showed how little love Wall Street has for furniture. So many Outsiders have failed to survive the Furniture Wars that any new combatant will be treated with skepticism. The investment banking mentality operates at a much faster frequency than the furniture industry's frequency, which is first into a recession and last out like a bad house guest who arrives early and stays late. The cyclicality of the furniture business works against the need to leverage assets and make debt payments. They cannot count on the cycle being favorable when it needs to be. For public companies, the variability of earnings works against the management of quarterly earnings reports, and the dependence on creative product development frustrates the analysts.

In spite of all this, investment bankers are drawn to the furniture business. Its superficial simplicity is alluring, but once they get into it they see similarities with unlikely industries. Surprisingly, the dependence on creative product development and the hit-or-miss nature of product introductions reminds them of the entertainment business, another unpredictable "industry" they are not crazy about.

Nevertheless, Fogarty and Chan showed that furniture makers can make money, too.

GENERAL MILLS MEETS GENERAL INTERIORS

ALTHOUGH THERE WAS NO Fort Sumter-like declaration of war, the furniture industry by 1975 was engaged in its own form of civil war when the Outsiders took on the Insiders. A number of outside companies sensed weakness in the furniture industry and launched full-bore offensives through corporate takeovers. Mead Paper acquired Stanley Furniture of Stanleytown, Virginia; Georgia Pacific acquired Williams Furniture of Sumter, South Carolina; Singer and Magnavox jumped into the fray. One by one, Insiders threw down their arms and sold out, like warriors exchanging their weapons for land.

General Interiors was not exempt from this battle. It drew a considerable number of suitors because of its attractive earnings and the Pennsylvania House brand appeal. In late 1974 discussions were started with a giant from another industry far removed from furniture. Robert Fogarty was wary, but his partner, William Chan, needed cash to cover other ventures. The negotiations continued, and Fogarty was told he would remain at the helm of the company after its sale. Besides, the prospective owners had impeccable credentials and the price was right – very right.

HELLO, BETTY CROCKER

The suitor was the estimable General Mills Corp., the highly respected Minneapolis-based owner of brands such as Wheaties, Cheerios, Betty Crocker, Bisquick, and Slim Jims. For several years, management had been pursuing a diversification strategy as it moved to reduce its dependency on breakfast foods and snacks. These products seemed mundane when compared to other consumer goods like toys, games, jewelry, ready to wear, and, yes, furniture. General Mills had noticed the performance at General Interiors and expressed serious interest.

General Mills' orderly, profitable, non-fragmented, non-cyclical food businesses were doing fine, but the company kept with the spirit of the times by plunging into the ownership and management of companies such as Monet jewelry, Parker Brothers board games, Izod sportswear, David Crystal women's-wear, Kenner toys, and more. In each case, General Mills bought top-notch brands with first-rate management and vowed to leave them alone. What did it matter that the Cereal Barons knew nothing about these industries? They couldn't be that difficult. They thought they could handle them as long as they stuck with branded consumer goods companies with favorable demographic outlooks.

On Jan. 29, 1975, General Mills signed a definitive agreement to buy General Interiors. The exchange rate meant that each GI share would be worth $27, a 16-fold increase over the $1.70 that Fogarty paid two years earlier.

The announcement stunned the organization. Fogarty had a knack for shielding the divisions from distraction, so no one had an inkling of an impending sale. Rumors circulated from time to time, but the organization ignored them.

The sale made sense to Fogarty. He respected General Mills' CEO James McFarland, and General Mills had a long-standing reputation for integrity. The sale also would provide the working capital needed to grow the furniture group and make Fogarty a very rich man. It appeared to be a marriage made in heaven.

The pressure to perform just before the final signing, with so much money at stake, was unlike anything that General Interiors' managers had ever experienced. Fogarty had a threatening demeanor even when things were going well. When a lot was at stake, his demeanor was scary. As the closing of the sale approached, the economy sputtered and incoming orders dipped. Fogarty was so focused on closing the sale that he nearly demolished a few managers. His threat to fire managers – or worse – had the desired effect. Sales and earnings continued to grow, and the deal finally went through. Fogarty became the owner of a large pile of General Mills' common stock. And for people who had gone through the humiliations between 1970 and 1972, this was a proud time.

Interestingly, Fogarty seemed oddly restrained when he called management together to announce the sale and to tell them that he had successfully convinced General Mills to honor the employee stock options. He somehow sensed that the honeymoon would end soon and he would no longer be able to lead the company purely how he wanted to. "Don't worry about the chiefs," he advised, "but watch out for the Indians."

The Green Dragons Strive
to Impress the Big General

Business continued to go according to plan after the sale. Over the next three years, Pennsylvania House and Kittinger still performed well by furniture industry standards, and the relationship with General Mills was cordial. Fogarty had the support of CEO McFarland, who was furniture's most ardent fan and made sure Fogarty reported at the highest level. His "boss" was a seasoned, top-level General Mills executive named Don Swanson, who treated Fogarty with great respect. Even so, Fogarty chafed under this scrutiny and was clearly frustrated. He could not stand having a boss of any sort. And he suspected that when McFarland retired, his successor would not pursue the furniture venture as aggressively as Fogarty wanted.

Gradually, Fogarty grew bored by the corporate role he was called upon to play. In June 1977, he shocked the organization by abruptly resigning. Instead of deploying his talents on the battlefield, he took his General Mills stock and withdrew to his estate in the horse country of central New Jersey.

General Mills appointed Bob Zimmerman to assume Fogarty's role, but instead of reporting to Swanson, he was slotted at a "group level." This lumped the furniture business with several other divisions that were not directly related. Even worse: The group executive knew nothing about the furniture business. Zimmerman's new boss, Jim Ruben, was a classic Outsider who neither understood nor cared about the furniture business. He and Zimmerman clashed the first day. Ruben's experience was in retailing discount liquors in northern Wisconsin. He acted as though the people who understood furniture were not as bright as him, so he saw no reason to listen to them. Showing no respect for the Green Dragons and insisting they do things his way, Ruben went on the attack. Zimmerman fought back, but he did so while Ruben was still in the honeymoon phase with General Mills. He should have waited for Ruben to make a mistake or two and lose favor in Minneapolis. Ruben grew tired of Zimmerman's independence and before long, "Zim," the seemingly invincible warrior, was gone.

Ruben did not last long at General Mills because his heavy-handed style was not their style, but he was around long enough to run off Zimmerman and thoroughly alienate the Green Dragons. The relationship between Lewisburg and Minneapolis had been superb with Swanson, but now it was strained. When a division made good margins, the Barons fussed about the low sales growth rate. When sales grew, they fussed about the margins. During one Pennsylvania House review, a well-meaning Cake Mix Wizard compared furniture to Yoplait Yogurt, a recent acquisition, which was growing at a phenomenal rate with obscenely high profit margins. As he put it, "Even if you were to capture the entire solid wood market, you'd only be a $400 million company. Why, Yoplait can become that big in one year!" The normally cocky Green Dragons sulked through the rest of the meeting, feeling condemned to be the poor country cousins in a family of wealthy snobs and wondering what it would take to impress their owners.

The General Mills executives' sales and profit performance made them one of the world's foremost companies, and their ability to launch and market new consumer packaged goods put them on par with the vaunted Procter and Gamble. They were decent and polite for the most part and treated the furniture people well, but they gave off the feeling that the top management did not fully support the strategic move from the cereal bowl to the breakfast table. In fact, No. 2 man Bruce Atwater was against the move but was out-gunned by CEO McFarland, who was intrigued by furniture. Unfortunately for the Green Dragons, Atwater took over when McFarland retired in 1977. Furniture no longer was the favored child, and Wall Street questioned the fit. With the Wall Street analysts beginning to ask why General Mills even bothered with furniture, management predictably paid less attention to their furniture holdings. The Pennsylvania House management team was good, and they knew it. Their success within their niche was obvious and their need for recognition was high, but General Mills seemed less than impressed.

A Furniture Marketing Revolution

The Green Dragons stayed busy competing with Ethan Allen and a dozen solid wood specialists, while at the same time they were trying to win the approval of their Minneapolis bosses. Fighting for attention, the Lewisburg group stressed the one thing they were most comfortable with: marketing. This was where Pennsylvania House excelled anyway, and it made perfect sense. Besides, there was a more compelling reason to strengthen their marketing. Ethan Allen was growing stronger by the day as their store program picked up speed. As the old saying goes, "In the valley of the blind, the one-eyed man is king," and Pennsylvania House and Ethan Allen kept one eye open during the mid-to-late '70s. The competition between the two companies was good for both.

Historically, the furniture industry had shunned marketing as a strategic weapon in favor of focusing on the factory. The typical furniture company in the 1960s had no marketing strategy. The standard approach to marketing management went like this:

PRODUCT STRATEGY: At best, ask your dealers what competitive line is selling and try to copy it. At worst, ask your sales reps what they need and try to give it to them. Do not be daunted by the fact that this product already exists and another version may not be needed.

PRICE STRATEGY: When the backlog is high, raise prices to get all you can. When the backlog is low, cut prices to ensure that your margins will also be low.

DISTRIBUTION STRATEGY: When your line is hot, let your independent sales reps sell every dealer they can, regardless of what it does to the retail margins of your line. When your line is cold, be prepared for dealers to get even. Leave the big decisions in the hands of the reps and pay them a commission rate higher than your profit margin.

PROMOTION STRATEGY: Make sure your sales reps have a supply of black and white photos of your line, a price list, and cheap catalogs aimed at dealers, not consumers. If consumers contact you, send them to dealers.

ADVERTISING STRATEGY: Do nothing if possible, but if you must advertise, run a trade ad in a publication that will only reach the people who already know you. The publication will even prepare the ad for you, making sure it looks a lot like everybody else's ad.

These strategies were not effective, of course, but it didn't matter as long as everyone played by the same rules. Then Ethan Allen's Nat Ancell came along and refused to play by the rules of what he considered to be a silly game. By having the audacity to cater to the consumer while browbeating the retailer, he propelled Ethan Allen from the backwaters of New England to the forefront of the furniture industry. Since Pennsylvania House was his prime competitor, the Lewisburg outpost could easily have been wiped off the furniture map had it not been staffed with some valiant warriors.

The embryo of the Pennsylvania House Marketing Plan was in place when Fogarty arrived in 1972 but had not been given enough running room. What the Harvard types liked to call "Programmed Selling" went back to the early years. Will Somers and Bob Young had started the marketing collateral support as early as 1968. The concept stressed a careful coordination of all related elements as opposed to the scattershot approach followed by the competition. By 1972, it existed more on paper than in fact. In most cases, sales reps still called the shots. Some used the support elements. Some rejected them disdainfully.

In 1973 the sales reps were directed to follow the plan by using the collateral and by selecting the most appropriate dealers as partners. This meant the sales reps must resist the temptation to "peddle" the line to everyone.

As a group, the sales force skillfully manipulated managers as well as customers. Before the new regime, they exploited the insecurity of management. They used this to their advantage when they disagreed with anything. Two of the more defiant veterans were dismissed in 1972, and both threatened to sue the company. Rather than caving in, as might have been the case earlier, management stood firm and both reps backed down. This sent a clear message to all territories that management finally was conducting the orchestra and setting a tone based on consumers more than retailers. It would require strong reps who sold programs as well as products. It went against the reps' standard operating procedure, but it worked.

A Better Way to Do Business

Faced with the formidable competitive threat of Ethan Allen, Pennsylvania House crafted a marketing strategy different from most furniture companies. Key elements included in the new program were:

PRODUCT PLANNING: Rather than offering one product category, Pennsylvania House developed a full range of compatible styles designed to meet a variety of consumer needs. When a consumer need was detected within the company's niche, it developed a product to meet it even if the factory could not produce it. This was unique among manufacturers and meant the company routinely went outside to independent suppliers to meet market needs, thereby giving the retailer a complete assortment of goods. As before, the collections were coordinated so consumers could purchase rooms as well as items.

DISTRIBUTION: Rather than delegating distribution responsibilities solely to the reps, Pennsylvania House brought this function inside and aggressively pursued a course of limited distribution that offered the line to only a few dealers in each trading area. The company still hired and trained the most powerful exclusive reps possible, but it insisted that they follow the marketing plan. In the hands of weaker reps, it would not have worked. The result was a network of marketing-oriented sales representatives who were among the best in the industry servicing a network of dealers who considered the factory to be a "resource," not just another "vendor." Significantly, the bulk of the dealers were smaller, "Mom and Pop" type stores, not the domineering large volume retailers. This let the factory, more so than the retailer, be the "captain of the channel."

MARKETING SUPPORT: Pennsylvania House developed an array of support materials that were unheard of at the time. The keystone was a full-color "Collectors Book" published every year and put in the hands of countless consumers. A third of the people who received a book actually made a purchase, and the book was self-liquidating because the dealers paid for it. To support semi-annual sales events, the company distributed tabloid circulars to millions of consumers. These, too, were self-liquidating, and they incorporated innovative traffic builders such as sweepstakes and loss leaders. During the 1976 sale period, for example, it sold more than 12,000 Bicentennial Chests. Backing up the promotional plan at the national level was a powerful print advertising campaign that dramatically raised the brand's awareness level. According to the Gallup Furniture Index, only Ethan Allen and Drexel Heritage exceeded Pennsylvania House's brand awareness in the upper-end segment. On top of these elements, the company offered an exceptional array of the standard tools, including hang tags, brochures, dealer catalogs, ad slicks, TV commercials, in-store seminars, and factory training seminars.

The Collectors' Gallery Program

The marketing plan reached its peak when a retailer installed a "shop within a shop" called a Collectors' Gallery – a large contiguous display of product from one supplier arranged in accessorized room settings. Implemented properly, it makes the consumer's shopping easier by offering a thoughtful mix of related product. Benefits include higher sales per square foot, higher consumer satisfaction, and higher margins. The problem is that it takes a tremendous amount of effort and cooperation between manufacturer and retailer to make it work. The product line must be right, a highly skilled sales rep has to be in place, distribution in the area must be limited, service must be dependable, and, most of all, the manufacturer and retailer must trust each other. Otherwise, the efforts revert to the natural tendency of the "Vendor vs. Emptor" mentality, in which the seller treats the buyer as an "outlet" and the buyer treats the seller as a "dispenser."

No one seems to know who originated this approach, but an industry-wide study called "Profile V" had a lot to do with its acceptance by Pennsylvania House, who had been in the game since the mid 1960s. By the 1970s, Ethan Allen and Drexel Heritage were the only other companies to adopt this strategy. It was not easy to pioneer something that retailers inherently resisted, but it sure got results.

The Pennsylvania House Marketing Plan was focused on the consumer. Management worked hard to understand the changing preferences of the target consumer. Then, they served those consumers by working with the most appropriate retailers in each trading area. Finally, they supported those retailers with an arsenal of merchandising aids calculated to build brand awareness and perception.

The results speak for themselves. In the early 1970s, sales grew 130 percent while the number of accounts fell by half to 750, and the average sales per dealer rose to $40,000, up from $8,000. The company distributed 20 million advertising circulars a year, and brand recognition went from non-existent to ninth place overall in the Gallup Index of Furniture Brands. Finally, the company went from a regional "chair factory" to a nationally recognized brand. Eventually, sales of Pennsylvania House within its home state comprised only 15 percent of the total, compared to 44 percent in 1969.

Outsourcing Leads to New Model

During the late '70s, Pennsylvania House and Kittinger continued to flourish even though General Mills treated its furniture business with benign neglect. The marketing emphasis paid off as the marketing team won battles as readily as Bear Bryant's Alabama football team rolled over opponents in the 1970s. With glee, they graduated from comparisons with the Green Dragons to comparisons with the Crimson Tide.

At the same time, the manufacturing team kept getting better at supporting the full range of products needed by the marketing programs. Because of capacity limitations and General Mills' reluctance to invest more, Pennsylvania House had to rely on more outside purchases to meet demand. The manufacturing group, under the leadership of John Pastrone, learned how to outsource product from other factories – even competitors. That helped the company overcome its handicap of limited capacity, and the limitations of dealing with one factory did not prevent the marketing team from going after product segments they identified. The company's innovative approach, born of necessity, was unique within the industry where most companies insisted on making all their products in house, even if this meant stretching beyond core competencies. The conventional approach often resulted in a cumbersome, hard-to-manage facilities lineup and a high breakeven point. It also meant that some marketing opportunities were missed simply because the product could not be made inside. When Pennsylvania House's marketing team saw a product need, the manufacturing team found a production source to make it.

All the groundwork done by the pioneering Will Somers, Bob Young, and others paid off in the late 1970s. Sales nearly doubled between 1976 and 1979, and margins remained in double digits. By stressing the limited distribution approach, the number of dealers actually dropped below 500. The average sales per dealer climbed to $115,000, making the relationship between the resource and the retail account all that more important. In 1978, Pennsylvania House shifted into high gear with the introduction of The Better Way and The Best Way, successors to 1973's Good Turn Program. The new programs centered on the gallery concept, and both proved to be highly effective with consumers and dealers. Very quickly the Best Way dealers averaged 70 percent higher sales per square foot than non-program dealers. Pennsylvania House held its own against Ethan Allen and pulled away from the host of smaller competitors who had historically hounded the Green Dragons. By 1979, the company had become a fast growing, highly profitable competitor that was respected by everyone – except its owners at General Mills.

Jim Ruben's Ghost

The Wheaties types were neither impressed nor annoyed by furniture. They continued to treat the furniture companies fairly, but Pennsylvania House management hungered for more respect. Reporting to passive non-furniture types with cereal and snack backgrounds was a picnic compared to what occurred in 1983, when the furniture divisions were assigned to a new group executive – a hard charging, head banging, kick-ass type. Armed with a retail background, he not only knew nothing about furniture, he considered this to be an advantage.

Convinced that the industry and the people in it were hopelessly incompetent, he was certain he could transform the company if not the industry. In spite of his bravado, the furniture types sensed he did not know what he was doing. Worse still, he did not know what he did not know. Centralizing everything he could get his hands on and building a large corporate staff, he accomplished what the competition was incapable of doing: He slowed down Pennsylvania House. A classic Outsider with an "attitude," he substituted a pre-determined point of view for a clear understanding of the business. General Mills eventually dismissed him, but not before he caused some damage. Among other initiatives, he tried to put a new Information Technology System in place that would supposedly give him the control he desperately wanted. The only problem was that the businesses moved so fast that the system could not keep up with the real world – a typical problem when an Outsider takes over.

Reporting to an aggressive non-furniture boss is a nightmare for the experienced furniture executive. There is always the risk that the boss will fire the furniture person for refusing to comply with his dictates, but the greater risk is that the boss will allow the division be damaged by the Outsider's zealous ignorance.

1980 AND BEYOND: THE HOUSE IS NOT A HOME

Furniture was not the only division that gave General Mills trouble during this time. The extensive diversification strategy begun in the early '70s was not working out very well. Between 1950 and 1986, General Mills made 86 acquisitions in new industries; 73 percent of those made by 1975 had been divested within five years.[1]

The Wall Street analysts kept hammering the Minneapolis Cereal Barons for straying too far from their core competencies, and the bottom line results were beginning to look bad. One by one the new ventures into non-foods began to falter. The Fashion Group, for example, stunned observers by destroying the fabulous Izod brand. First, it was pumped up with growth steroids and then cheapened to the point where it became so meaningless that it all but disappeared. The Toy Group had a hard time keeping up with its fast-paced market. The Specialty Retailing Group failed to take off, and even the Restaurant Group had problems. It was clear that General Mills should have stuck to its food and snack business, and observers predicted they would come to this realization sooner or later.

That day of reckoning came in 1985, when the company began to spin off the Restaurants, Toys and Fashion Groups. Among the divisions jettisoned were such brands as Izod, Lacoste, Ship'n Shore, Monet, Red Lobster, Olive Garden, Parker Brothers, and Kenner. The Specialty Retail Group followed, dumping Eddie Bauer and Talbot's.

Attempt to Sell Kittinger

For reasons not exactly clear, General Mills held on to furniture, even turning down a management-led buyout proposal. Quite possibly, General Mills' bosses were still smarting over the experience they had with a failed 1983 effort to sell the Kittinger Co. – further evidence that it is easier to get into the furniture industry than to get out of it. The problems begin when a company is put up for sale, which leads to demoralized management and hourly employees. Rumors fly; the press snoops around; competitors attack; customers become nervous; key people are recruited; and the entire organization loses focus. Foolishly, the owners think the impending sale can be kept secret, but word always leaks out, usually by the potential buyer. Management invariably issues denials, but the rumor mill produces evidence to the contrary. All it takes is for one or two key people to leave during this time, and the organization can unravel. Recruiting good replacements becomes impossible during the uncertain times, and defectors usually end up working for a direct competitor. A weak company can be wiped out quickly, and even a successful company can be irreparably damaged by a prolonged sale.

Finding a buyer for Kittinger should have been easy in 1983. This, after all, was the company that made elegant furniture of the highest quality, the furniture of choice by countless dignitaries. Traditionally, each newly appointed member of the President's Cabinet received a Kittinger conference chair. And the company earned double-digit pre-tax margins, had a network of showrooms in the top design centers, and had been supported with prudent capital investments by General Mills. Sure, it had some problems – an aging work force and a tough union, for example – but the prognosis seemed bright.

THE SACK OF BUFFALO

Kittinger saw no shortage of tire kickers, but few serious buyers with the financial wherewithal emerged to buy the company. Lance Funston had the desire but needed more time to line up his financing. In an admirable attempt to avoid dragging the process out too long, General Mills agreed to proceed with the sale anyway. Funston was allowed to take over the operation of the company even though he had not completed his financing.

Funston's first business venture started while he was a student at the Harvard Business School, where he pioneered a computer-based investment-reporting system. He then became involved with the Houston real estate boom and supposedly made a lot of money converting rental properties into condos. He reached an agreement with General Mills in November 1983 to buy Kittinger for $15 million – about $32 million in today's dollars. Then the fun began.

The deal required Funston to pay General Mills $250,000 on signing and another $2.25 million in cash on Dec. 15, 1983. The remaining $12.5 million was to be paid in the form of a promissory note due on March 1, 1984. Lining up financing proved to be more difficult than Funston expected, and running the company was not nearly as easy as he thought. Unable to meet the agreed-upon deadlines, he began to look for a scapegoat and accused the management of conspiring with General Mills against him. The chief financial officer claimed that Funston directed him to alter the books, "to create a better financial picture for the company." Five of the top managers walked out – including former President Fred Batson Jr. and the chief designer. The whole mess ended up in court. Among other things, General Mills claimed that Funston used Kittinger money to buy a 22-room mansion in Buffalo and furnish it with Kittinger samples pulled from showrooms.

Fun with Funston

Funston's behavior and management style while at the helm was highly unusual. He was another outsider who was not deterred by his lack of furniture experience. His attraction to the industry was a result of an experience when he and his wife attended an antique auction and were amazed at the price of a block front chest. His lack of a track record did not faze him despite repeated blunders. At his first Furniture Market in High Point, he introduced a new line that he claimed could be shipped faster. "Production could be accelerated," he said, "by simplifying the finishing process."[2] This baffled sales reps and furniture buyers, who concluded that the "simpler" finishes looked cheap. In later court documents, Funston was described as stating on many occasions that he was a superior manager of businesses and fully capable of running Kittinger."

After a year of Funston's "superior" management, the Kittinger Co. was badly wounded and General Mills took it back. After sending him a Notice of Default, they changed the locks on his office and sent a Pennsylvania House truck to remove the Kittinger furniture from his house, leaving him with only a bed. The management of the company was turned over to a Pennsylvania House executive, Craig Shoemaker. Batson moved on to run a Canadian furniture company, and the chief designer went on to play a key role in the success of the Stickley Co. Shoemaker and his team tried hard to repair the damage done to Kittinger, but the incursion, on top of the on-again, off-again ownership problem, was too much to overcome.

RIDERS ON THE STORM

General Mills finally sold the entire furniture group in 1986 to Chicago Pacific for $83.5 million – about $175 million after adjusting for inflation. Having narrowly avoided being acquired by a coal company in 1964, the old Lewisburg Chair Factory was now owned by a railroad company. Chicago Pacific was a balance sheet in search of an income statement. Having liquidated its huge real estate holdings and gotten out of the railroad business, it was loaded with cash but had no core business. Furniture seemed as good a bet as anything. They also had bought the Hoover Co. and figured there might even be some synergy. After all, furniture and vacuum cleaners both belong in the home.

Business under new owners went well at first, and the furniture division was treated with respect. Then, in October 1988, Chicago Pacific announced plans to merge with Maytag Corp. After making the appropriate noises about planning to stay in the furniture business, Maytag revealed its true strategy. They wanted those vacuum cleaners, not the bedrooms and dining rooms. So in early 1989, Maytag sold the furniture group to LADD Furniture for $202.5 million. LADD was a High Point-based furniture holding company that specialized in low-priced furniture. What was left of the General Interiors properties had been peddled in six years from General Mills to Chicago Pacific to Maytag to LADD.

Lessons Learned

The experience of General Interiors' properties "after the flood" provides the student of business with valuable lessons. The industry did not consolidate to any significant degree during this time, despite intentions by some in the industry to do so. Many new Outsiders came and went. Few made an impact, as the Insiders used all their tricks to defend their positions.

Sadly, the industry suffered a great deal of collateral damage in the process of trying to improve it. Outsiders typically did not realize how temporal success was in this industry, as good results one year do not ensure more of the same next year. The fragile nature of the business means that heavy handed, bullying tactics will result in failure. Extreme care is necessary but not always sufficient. General Mills deserves credit for instinctively grasping the fact that these were relatively high maintenance companies. Here are a few lessons contained within this saga:

OUTSIDERS CAN BE VALUABLE: Transplants can make a huge contribution, as they did at Pennsylvania House, but only if they take the time to understand the nature of the business. They will cause havoc if they assume they already know all the answers. General Mills was unwise twice in appointing retailers with no furniture experience to head its furniture group. For these two men to substitute attitude and arrogance for understanding and experience was unconscionable.

PEOPLE MAKE THE DIFFERENCE: Having the right talent, especially in the "skill positions," means more than any other asset. Pennsylvania House had a remarkable number of very capable people over the years, and they remained productive because the company was a good place to work. Any activity that causes these key people to leave is anathema.

FIND APPROPRIATE STRATEGIC INITIATIVES: Strategic initiatives and programs must be "organic" and appropriate for the organization—not grafted onto it. The Pennsylvania House Gallery Program was organic. It evolved over time and was consistent with the company's culture. Most of the later copycats were not, which is why they failed. You cannot have a gallery program without pursuing limited distribution, for example. Attempts at forcing imported programs onto organizations that are not ready for them are destined to fail.

CHAPTER SEVEN

APPLYING MARKETING TECHNIQUES FROM OTHER IN-
DUSTRIES CAN BE DANGEROUS: Packaged goods marketing techniques do not work with furniture, yet many unwisely
tried to transfer their packaged goods skills to furniture. Pennsylvania House developed furniture specific marketing techniques tailored to big-ticket durable goods, and they worked.
Beware of packaged goods marketers who think they have the
answers. They are accustomed to marketing products where the
package costs more and may actually be more important than
the product itself. In furniture, only truck drivers and ware-
housemen see the package. These wizards may know all about
the products that consumers buy every week, but consumers
buy furniture only every five years or so. Ask the wizards how
they think they would market a box of cereal that lasts several
lifetimes, costs at least $5,000, is only sold in a few stores, has
the package removed before it is displayed, and has no brand
identification.

FOLLOW MICHAEL PORTER'S RULES: Professor Porter's
observations about fragmented industries and corporate diversification strategies apply in this case. General Mills was too
smart to try to consolidate the industry. Instead, it differentiated its brand names and got good results. But its overall diversification moves failed, and only when it spun off its non-food
divisions and returned to their original "food and snack" businesses did its stock multiple move up.

LEARN TO MANAGE INDUSTRY CYCLES: You cannot
predict when the environment will be favorable or brutally

indifferent. If you abandon a good strategy or break up a good team in slow times, you may ruin the company. Management is never as good as it looks in good times and never as bad as it looks in bad times. Pennsylvania House experienced phenomenal growth during the '70s, but some years were flat while others were up. As good as the management team was, it could not overcome the devastating economic impact of the oil embargo in 1973. The key is learning to cope with the cycles, rather than railing at them.

Robert Fogarty's intensity, and his amazing ability to size up situations and people quickly and accurately, resulted in a commendable turnaround for the original General Interiors properties. People intent upon entering the industry could do worse than to pay attention to his principles. It is interesting to note that after leaving General Mills he bought Kindel Furniture, a small upper-end casegoods company, rather than taking another corporate position. After seeing both sides of the business up close and being successful at each, he opted for the entrepreneurial world. Not surprisingly, Kindel was successful under Fogarty's leadership and captured a niche not too far from the position once occupied by Kittinger. Kindel's rise coincided with the decline of Kittinger – happenstance or just another example of a focused furniture warrior defeating a distracted opponent? The company's smaller size let Fogarty and his daughter, Paula, stay focused on customers while maintaining tight controls on the operations side of the business. He repeatedly turned down offers to sell out to larger corporations, knowing what that might lead to.

GREEN STAMPS
GET LICKED

GENERAL MILLS HANDLED its foray into the furniture business with relative class. It made no big mistakes, treated the properties with respect, and did not plunder the assets. The divisions earned decent profits, and countless General Mills' executives filled their homes with nice furniture at a discount. The marriage lacked passion, but at least it was polite and businesslike. Initially, General Mills executives were seduced by the potential for major earnings growth, but once they realized this was not likely, they avoided the foolish posturing adopted by so many other Outsiders. The opportunity was just not big enough to hold their attention, and they rightly sensed that furniture would not respond to the high-powered packaged goods marketing approach they loved to employ.

However, the divisions did not do as well once they were cut loose from the nurturing, marketing oriented protection of "The Big G." Pennsylvania House's management team in 1989 found itself in the hands of LADD, a company it held in contempt. The Lewisburg crowd saw its new owners as a boring collection of low-end, colorless companies, while Pennsylvania House was a marketing driven, sophisticated and irreverent organization. Meanwhile, LADD couldn't wait to improve Pennsylvania House by cutting costs. The cultural differences were huge.

THE SPERRY & HUTCHISON INVASION

LADD was an acronym for Lea, American Drew, and Daystrom, the residue of the Sperry & Hutchinson Co. incursion into the Briar Patch of the furniture industry. Founded in 1896, the New York-based S&H made a lot of money selling Green Stamps to merchants who gave them to consumers as an incentive to buy products such as groceries and gasoline. The consumer redeemed them for merchandise. It was very simple and also very lucrative – almost like printing money. Consumers felt like they were getting "free" merchandise; merchants had a low-cost promotional tool, and the stamps that S&H sold to merchants were, on average, not redeemed for seven years. S&H invested the cash it collected from merchants and made money on their customers' money.

In the mid 1970s, S&H correctly sensed that its money machine would not run forever. Tighter retail margins were eliminating the use of such incentives. The Beinecke family, the principal stockholders, decided to diversify. After an extensive study of many industries, they were impressed with the demographic projections for home goods and felt furniture would be a good bet. The research accurately identified the burgeoning consumer demand for home goods, but it stopped short of defining the complexities of the fragmented retail channel. S&H reached the same conventional conclusions the other Outsiders did – backward industry in need of modern marketing and better management, highly fragmented, easy to acquire companies, inevitable consolidations will occur, etc. This rosy vision even included horizontal connections between floor coverings, indoor furniture, outdoor furniture and other home goods creating a complete "S&H Home."

The S&H top management knew nothing about furniture, but no matter: they knew nothing about manufacturing, either. How hard could it be to make chests and tables? They knew a lot about gas stations and grocery stores, and dealing with those businesses seemed to be a lot more complicated than furniture retailers.

In a self-assessment of the company's strengths that they felt could be leveraged, S&H figured it had an edge in furniture because of its strong in-house market research capability, its skill in managing warehouses and redemption centers, and its public relations capabilities. The market research function would prove to be a true asset, but logistics and public relations rank nowhere among the most important talents needed to succeed in the Briar Patch. S&H's urge to diversify overcame common sense. The first move was to acquire the Bigelow Carpet Co., and it worked well at first. So it then formed the S&H Furnishings Group and acquired five furniture companies – Lea, American Drew, Daystrom, Pontiac Chair, Gunlocke, and Homecrest. Now, all S&H had to do was figure out what to do with them.

The moves made sense in theory, but the gap between theory and reality was perilously wide and eventually would threaten the very existence of S&H. The acquired companies had no connection with each other and had no overlapping dealer base, making consolidation unlikely. American Drew was a stolid, dependable producer of moderately priced, conservatively styled bedrooms and dining rooms. Its best-selling collection actually was a fairly close copy of the Pennsylvania House cherry group. It had carved a niche catering to "Mom & Pop" independent retailers. Lea was a fast-moving, trend-setting producer of cheap youth bedrooms and master bedrooms. Its niche was with the big-name mass merchants like Levitz and Sears. Daystrom specialized in chrome table and chair sets, called dinettes, which were mostly sold through specialty stores. Pontiac specialized in motion chairs; Homecrest made outdoor furniture; and Gunlocke made office desks and chairs. Each company had its own culture, and each was very different from the other. If S&H was expecting to build a cohesive powerhouse from this discontiguous collection of specialists, it was bound to be disappointed.

LEA AND THE BIG STORES

Lea and American Drew, the two biggest divisions, were as different as Cushman and Shaw. Based in Richmond, Virginia, Lea originally produced crates but eventually switched to making bedroom cases. When later beset with quality problems, competitors delighted in reminding customers of this legacy. Undaunted by these humble origins, Lea became an effective low-cost producer and assembled a capable and aggressive young management team led by Don Hunziger, who delighted in pinching pennies and squeezing nickels. Hunziger was an unlikely CEO. He was neither a manufacturer nor a marketer nor a manager, but he possessed an uncanny knack for being in the right place all the time. Meticulous, and gentle in appearance, he was a skilled political survivor who withstood the attacks of rivals while seeming not to notice them. Originally a plant personnel manager, the Powell family appointed him as plant manager just before the sale to S&H. Angus Powell and his brother, Supreme Court Justice Lewis Powell, were old guard Virginia gentlemen who were more comfortable with Hunziger's polite demeanor than his more flamboyant rivals. Before long, he was made president of Lea Industries. When S&H took over, they immediately placed a non-furniture manager above Hunziger, but when he was pulled off the job to take on a more pressing assignment, Hunziger again moved up.

In the 1970s, Carter V. Fox joined the company from Stanley Furniture and gave Lea a product development boost. He championed the idea of producing modular furniture that could be stacked and configured in a variety of ways depending on consumer needs. This product, coupled with a burgeoning youth bedroom line carried by a strong group of sales reps, drove volume well beyond historical levels. Much of this came from the high-profile, high-volume retailers like Levitz and Rhodes, whose buyers were close to the Lea management group.

AMERICAN DREW AND THE MOM & POP DEALERS

American Drew, on the other hand, was based in North Wilkesboro, North Carolina, where city folk were viewed with caution. The management reflected the region, and the company built the company's reputation for being honest, straightforward, and decent. They spoke with pride of the day that a dresser fell off the back of a delivery truck – and survived without a scratch. They gave away mallets as part of a sales gimmick, encouraging customers to pound on the case to demonstrate its strength. Shunning the flashy big-name stores, they built their business on the small independent retailers who appreciated the simple integrity of American Drew. They felt comfortable with the management and could count on the products. They may not be very stylish, but "dadgumit," they were well-built. To offset the small volume these accounts could generate, the sales force compensated by selling as many of them as possible. The running joke was that the line was available everywhere except Texaco stations. This strategy worked because it was uniquely fitted to this particular company, and American Drew grew to a sales level equal to Lea.

SHOTGUN WEDDING

Like medieval communities who found relative safety in walled hill towns, survivors in the furniture business have learned to occupy market segments that can be defended against marauders. Because of the competitive nature of the furniture industry, these companies become so obsessed with their own "villages" that they cannot relate to neighboring communities. Such was the case with Lea and American Drew. Both companies had strong alignments among factories, products, reps and dealers – but each alignment was unique to each company. There were no similarities between the companies, no interchangeable parts, and no synergy.

Despite the overwhelming differences between the two companies, they soon were put under one organization and under one roof. S&H decided to merge them in 1978 and to move the offices to the new First Citizens bank building in High Point, North Carolina. This kind of move looks good from the perspective of headquarters and shows significant savings on paper. But to the front-line troops, it looks like insanity. The move resulted in great expense, the loss of countless key people, and a severe disruption of customer service. The savings did not materialize, the new Management Information System did not function, service deteriorated, and morale plummeted. Competitors took away market share while Lea and American Drew lost their focus. The two cultures clashed sharply, and when the forced consolidation was complete, the more aggressive Lea mentality took the upper hand while the more genteel American Drew survivors seethed with resentment.

Hunziger Leads a Rag Tag Group

Under the stern eye of Don Hunziger, the group gradually recovered and earned decent profits, but the emphasis at the division level focused on maximizing short-run profits, and S&H kept fussing about the lack of an enlightened strategy. Hunziger tried to find one that would satisfy the Green Stamp people yet still be palatable in the highly competitive niche that the divisions occupied. His efforts were futile. No one seemed to know what the end game was supposed to be, so the Furniture Division resorted to operating in a perfectly conventional manner, by the furniture book. This is a natural reaction to having a group of people who are unfamiliar with your business constantly looking over your shoulder. You protect your job by keeping earnings up, and you avoid criticism by refusing to make any unconventional moves. Creating a vision or devising a strategy for the company is the last thing you worry about.

Lea developed some great new products but left the marketing and distribution up to the sales reps. American Drew rode the success of a blockbuster group called Cherry Grove. Here too, the reps called the shots, and there were few marketing support activities except a fairly effective small space print advertising campaign. The plants in both divisions were managed aggressively to drive out costs, and everyone was motivated to make the products cheaper. It did not matter that the process often reduced quality, because bonuses were based on cost reductions. The short-range strategy was to minimize costs while maximizing shipments for the month. The long-range strategy was to do the same for the quarter. The mission of the entire group was to ship everything you could by the end of the month. If quarterly goals were hit, a raucous beer blast would be held at the Holiday Inn across the street. On Monday, the process started over again.

The three smaller divisions were based in out-of-the-way towns and received little attention. South Boston, Virginia, Pontiac, Illinois, and Wadena, Minnesota, were hard to get to and harder still to get excited about. Since the amount of "headquarters help" given to the divisions was proportional to the proximity to headquarters, these units escaped the influence of the Green Stamp people. The problem is that when a key person leaves such a small company, recruiting someone to relocate there proves to be difficult, as S&H would discover.

In 1979, under pressure from S&H to become more marketing oriented, Hunziger recruited a top marketing executive from Pennsylvania House. It was an odd fit, because the S&H Furnishings Group's underlying philosophy was as far from the General Interiors mindset as you could get and still be in the same industry. This newcomer from Pennsylvania House went into mild culture shock when he tried to adapt to the new environment. He bailed after two years of frustration, unable to tolerate the short-term-oriented, numbers-obsessed management style. In spite of his decade working in Lewisburg, he felt like a stranger in the conventional furniture world where marketing was a curiosity, not a necessity. Like a foreign language that only a few understood, marketing was not organic to this group.

What to Do? Centralize, of Course

Growing frustrated with the perceived lack of professionalism at the division level, S&H decided to make marketing a high priority and to centralize both marketing and manufacturing at the division staff level. The best line management people were given the top positions and given full support by Hunziger and from the S&H headquarters in New York. In 1980, they held a series of meetings in a futile attempt to devise a strategy for the operating units, including an all-day session devoted to the issue of being "Cost Effective vs. Price Efficient." During the course of this discussion, it was agreed that it would make a lot of sense for S&H to acquire Pennsylvania House from General Mills. A call was made to General Mills, but the cereal company declined to pursue the matter. After five years in the furniture business, S&H still did not know what to do with its captured territories, and the leadership was still trying to come up with a vision. General Interiors had a surplus of vision but had trouble at times executing. S&H excelled at running the divisions day to day, but had no vision.

The S&H furniture companies made some improvements despite the oppressive atmosphere. The divisions used market research more effectively than anyone in the industry, thanks to the efforts of a highly talented man named Jay Shaffer. Lea developed a successful youth bedroom based on a market research project that identified an opening in the market. Lea developed a successful gallery program for youth furniture that featured realistic room scenes. American Drew developed some impressive collateral material for dealers that made their promotions stronger. And all division executives could clearly describe the demographics of their target consumers. But the research was ahead of most retailers, who responded with bored indifference.

Despite the gains, the overall organization did not function as a team. After one year, the centralization experiment was disbanded and the staff people returned to line positions. It failed because day-to-day decisions must be made on the front line, and staff people, no matter how talented, were too far removed to have a handle on the real situation. It did not work because the progressive marketing tactics were not organic and the alignment was not right. The American Drew sales force, for example, was not skilled at selling programs like advertising circulars, and selling the line to as many dealers as possible worked against the gallery concept. Forcing a gallery program into that culture was risky.

Besides, it was obvious that Hunziger would abandon the effort as soon as it missed a beat. His natural inclination was to criticize and to pick at ideas until the proponent gave up. He rarely gave full support to anything or anyone. As a consequence, innovation was stifled, the talented people became frustrated, and a general malaise spread throughout the company. There was a lack of direction coming from New York, a lack of leadership at the top of the Furniture Division, and a lack of a champion at each major division. The warrior chiefs at the time of acquisition had moved on and were not replaced, so Lea and American Drew had no presidents or even general managers. There was no one to rally around, no one to lead. The absence of leadership crippled the divisions, and no one seemed to know what to do. The talent was there – the direction was missing.

Again, at the urging of New York, a reputed financial wizard named Dick Allen was brought in from ConAgra. Highly skilled in generating numbers, Allen installed a sophisticated system of controls that delighted Hunziger but made the operators feel that their hands were tied tighter than ever. Allen was most certainly not a furniture person, but his expertise in finance and accounting were considerable. He was also instrumental in pushing the management team to face up to its strategic issues and resolve some of them. Allen was the key driver of a tightly drawn strategic plan at long last.

During this time, the relationship became more strained between Corporate, up north in New York City, and the group down south in Carolina. The Northerners felt the Southerners were too conventional and too slow to pick up on changes in the marketplace. The Southerners felt the Northerners did not understand or appreciate how tough the furniture business was. Both were right. This marriage lacked passion and a common language. When overall demand dropped in 1981, the company had no fallback position, and earnings went down as well. S&H's constant nagging at Hunziger over a lack of a division strategy stemmed from its own lack of a plan. The niche companies they bought needed entrepreneurial Warrior Chieftains to make them successful, but the S&H controlling culture ran them off. It was obvious that S&H had no corporate strategy for furniture to begin with; it was just looking for a place to invest its Green Stamp cash flow. Furniture people frequently comment, "You gotta love the business or you won't survive." When the sledding got tougher, it became obvious that, except for the S&H President Jim Mills, there was not a lot of love for the furniture business at headquarters.

Assault on the Green Stamp Fortress, and LADD is Born

The core Green Stamp revenues continued to slide, and corporate management continued to be distracted by the frustrations of the furniture venture. Suddenly, the S&H board was blindsided in the summer of 1981 by a takeover attempt by an upstart company called Baldwin United. The venerable Baldwin Piano and Organ Co. had been taken over the year before by Baldwin United Corp., an aggressive promoter of single premium annuities. Baldwin CEO Morley Thompson had no interest in pianos and organs, *per se*. What he liked were the financing opportunities afforded by the installment purchases of these products.

Thompson was not interested in the furniture companies, either. He wanted the cash flow from Green Stamps to add to the cash from the annuities, which made him like a banker but without all the regulations. The Beinecke family, known more for its generosity than its ferocity, put up only token resistance and the assault on the 90-year-old purveyors of trading stamps was over quickly. In May 1981, S&H was sold for $339 million (about $850 million in current dollars) and broken up with the spoils divided. Baldwin kept the lucrative cash generating units and set up leveraged management buyouts for Bigelow and the furniture division. Financial wizard Dick Allen astutely saw the opportunity and convinced Hunziger to take it. Due to a fortuitous set of circumstances, Hunziger and what was left of his crew were able to buy the furniture group for a mere $70 million (about $175 million in current dollars.) The name chosen was LADD Furniture – for Lea, American Drew, and Daystrom. Pontiac and Homecrest were discarded.

They wisely recruited an experienced furniture veteran, Bill Fenn, to become president and chief operating officer. Fenn, who had started his career at Thomasville and then became president of Stanley Furniture, had good sales instincts and gave the company instant credibility with retailers. He assumed the position of acting president of American Drew and inherited a great new collection based on a license from the Independence Hall Foundation. The development work and the designs were finished before he arrived, but he knew a good thing when he saw it. His presence was significant in improving the retail visibility for the line, and many new dealers joined. At Lea, Fenn installed a badly needed division president and then concentrated sales and marketing while Allen tackled reducing the debt caused by the buyout. The assets were formidable, especially since S&H was used to having tons of excess cash and never stressed tight asset management. Allen got excited when he contemplated the next opportunity. With his relentless guidance, the company drove inventories and receivables down while stretching payables. During this time, Hunziger pretty much stayed out of the way. The result was a flood of cash that was used to pay down debt and position the company for the ultimate gambit.

LADD GOES PUBLIC

Thanks to a remarkable confluence of events, LADD management struck it rich in 1983. First, the raid on S&H, which had nothing to do with furniture, put the group in play. Next, an improving economic climate made it possible to convert surplus assets into cash to reduce debt. And finally, the equity market window opened just long enough for LADD to attempt an Initial Public Offering of common stock. The company successfully went public on May 28, 1983.

The mismatched collection of assets that S&H put together but could not manage had become a hot property after two years back in the hands of furniture people. The complementary skills of the top men – Hunziger, Allen, and especially Fenn–guided the company to four consecutive years of success with reported profits in excess of $20 million in 1987 and 1988.

LADD TRIUMPHANT

The company reached its high water mark in 1989, when it concluded an agreement to acquire the General Interiors furniture group from Hoover for $202.5 million – about $350 million in current dollars. This now included Gunlocke, McGuire, and Brown Jordan in addition to Pennsylvania House and Kittinger. Like a defensive end who tackles the whole backfield in order to get to the guy with the ball, Dick Allen bought the whole group in order to get Pennsylvania House. He made it clear that he only wanted to keep Pennsylvania House and Brown Jordan. Gunlocke, Kittinger and McGuire were immediately put up for sale. Kohler,

the plumbing equipment producer that had recently acquired
Baker Furniture, scooped up McGuire, a high-end importer of
wicker and rattan furniture. HON Industries, a low-end office furniture company, grabbed Gunlocke. This marked the second time
Hunziger was involved with the sale of Gunlocke. Both were good
strategic fits for their new parents and had no place in the LADD
environment. Kittinger's sale was another story.

Kittinger's "For Sale" Sign Goes Up Again

Kittinger had its challenges, but it still had a wonderful reputation for quality and the valuable Williamsburg license. But the top
people at LADD saw no strategic fit between the regal Kittinger
and the blue-collar markets of LADD properties, so the division
was put on the block again. LADD management was warned to be
extra careful with two things that were the principal determinants
of Kittinger's viability – the labor union and the Williamsburg
license. If anything were to upset one or the other of these two
independent minded groups, the consequences would be severe.
Within two months, LADD managed to alienate both. Relations
with the Williamsburg board and the labor union soured, making
the sale considerably harder than it should have been. In a serious
blow, The Historic Williamsburg Foundation revoked the license,
which considerably lessened the value of the company.

The foundation offered the Williamsburg license to Henredon,
which turned it down. The license wound up with Baker Furniture, who mishandled it. Baker eventually lost it to Lane, who also
botched it before it moved to its fourth licensee, Stickley. When
the license was terminated, Kittinger was stuck with thousands of

work-in-process parts that became worthless, since the company was prohibited from marketing any designs similar to the licensed product.

There was no shortage of interested buyers, but financing again was an issue. Predictably, real furniture companies steered clear of the deal because of the high cost structure and narrow market niche, but the prestigious name and the desire to keep manufacturing jobs in western New York produced a host of potential suitors. Still, the numbers were not good, and arranging for suitable financing proved to be difficult. The cumulative effect of being on and off the market, and losing so many key managers, had taken its toll on Kittinger. Customers and key employees were worn down by the process. In frustration, LADD came perilously close to shutting down the whole thing. It was, after all, losing money and LADD, after all, was a publicly traded company. Shutting Kittinger would stop the losses.

Let Me Be Your Candy Man

At the eleventh hour, Pittsburgh businessman Michael Carlow made an offer. Dick Allen, who took special pride in disposing of unwanted assets, was ecstatic. Carlow, who prided himself on buying and reviving once-famous brand names, was happy as well. His claim to fame was the acquisition of the Clark Candy Bar Co., an American icon that had fallen on hard times, only to be rescued by this civic-minded businessman who later on would acquire another Pittsburgh icon, Iron City Beer. Now he was offering to rescue the Kittinger Co.

Dick Allen may have been surprised had he checked out

Carlow more closely. Furniture experience was not the only thing he lacked. He actually got his start by demolishing businesses, not building them. His father, Frank Carlow, made money tearing down failed factories – there were many in Western Pennsylvania – and selling off the machinery and reusable materials. Young Michael joined him after college and went on to other, more sophisticated ventures, but at the beginning, "demolition was the core competency of the Carlow business empire" according to the March 1, 1991, *Buffalo News*. Furniture observers wondered how a demolition expert could rebuild Kittinger.

LADD sold Kittinger to Carlow for $2.3 million, considerably below the $5 million Allen had hoped for. The deal brought a great deal of excitement at first, as the hero from Pittsburgh set out to save Buffalo's finest cabinetmaker. Carlow made all the big noises that new owners typically make when entering the Briar Patch of the furniture business. A *Buffalo News* editorial on January 12, 1991, gushed over what it called "The Comeback at Kittinger." It reported that employment had risen from 80 to 180 workers, and claimed that Carlow said the company might have more sales next year than ever. Predictably, he also suggested that the former owners, those furniture people, were not aggressive enough. The paper concluded that Carlow had "considerable entrepreneurial talent to apply to the job."

Carlow was no exception to the list of Outsiders who assumed the industry was backward and easy. Thanks to help from a furniture veteran who served as his adviser, he liquidated some inventory and recouped his purchase price within three months. Within six months, he had acquired another furniture company, Helikon, which he thought would fit with Kittinger. Its niche, style, quality, and image were different from Kittinger, but Carlow did not let that bother him. By March 1991 he brashly stated he was looking to buy still another furniture company. "You can't be a small furniture company and exist in today's world," he told the Canisius College MBA Alumni Association. "I think there is a great opportunity for me in the furniture industry because the foreigners aren't coming in. They don't understand it," he said.[1] It's unclear what he meant by "foreigners," but the amazing thing is Carlow's contention that he – still losing money after a full nine months of experience – felt that *he* understood the business. The furniture veterans just shook their heads.

But soon it became apparent that things were not panning out. Dealers steered clear of Kittinger because they, too, were skeptical of another Outsider who acted as if he knew more than the Insiders. Carlow knew that the loss of the Williamsburg license was a serious blow. This had been the most coveted of Kittinger's assets, carefully protected and nurtured by a succession of five owners until it landed in LADD's lap. It was unthinkable to mention one name without the other.

With much fanfare, Carlow launched the Historical Kittinger line that looked amazingly similar to the original Williamsburg line. One can just imagine some adviser to Carlow saying, "Just knock off the Williamsburg designs and nobody will do anything, Michael. Everybody does it." This time, the Foundation did something. It sued and won $500,000,[2] as Kittinger was "found guilty of civil contempt for illegally making and marketing furniture licensed by Colonial Williamsburg." So now the Williamsburg volume was gone, and Carlow's "entrepreneurial" management team had blown its best chance to replace it.

As cash flow lessened, the company missed some medical insurance premiums and workers' compensation payments, along with some Social Security payments to the u.s. Treasury. But that's not all. In 1995, the company was investigated for defrauding the PNC Bank by writing $31 million in checks from one company to another for funds it did not have. Formal charges were brought in March 1996. Convictions were eventually obtained, and both father and son ended up in prison. The Kittinger Co. failed to survive the Carlow rescue and closed its doors in 1995. Ironically, a demolition company razed the physical plant to make way for new construction, and Carlow's company did not get the job.

Lance Funston and Michael Carlow were like caricatures of the furniture Outsiders who cruise into the industry and unleash the dogs of war. Funston was probably sincere in his desire to buy the company, but he had no idea how to run it. Carlow was "sort of a serial swindler, it appears, who from Buffalo to Tacoma and places in between has seduced bankers and business executives, coal miners and county commissioners, lawyers and journalists as easily as if they were dewy-eyed innocents who wanted desperately to believe in princes."[3] Together, Funston and Carlow presided over the wreckage of a fine furniture company.

Lewisburg during the Occupation

Having disposed of Kittinger, LADD management turned its attention to Pennsylvania House. Almost immediately, the two cultures banged heads. LADD wanted to keep John Pastrone, who had been the head of the Chicago Pacific Furniture Group and had directed the sale of the assets, but he quickly turned down an offer to join the new owner. He knew he would be neither happy nor productive in an environment so alien to the one he had directed. LADD's way of dumping Kittinger was very revealing, and its way of managing Pennsylvania House was to do it "by the numbers." Unlike the Lea and American Drew models, Pennsylvania House had high factory margins and high selling expenses. The two went together. The brand position, the gallery program, and the promotional programs were expensive to sustain, but they also made it possible to command higher prices. Harking back to the strategic debate S&H had in 1989, Pennsylvania House was more "price effective" than "cost efficient." Hunziger and Allen could not quite grasp this, and they pushed Pennsylvania House management to cut expenses.

The division president fought the move at first, but then gave up and proceeded to give top management what they claimed they expected. He got the results – but at a price. Sales territories were divided to make room for more sales reps, but veteran reps became disillusioned. New dealers were added, but the old standby accounts felt betrayed. Advertising expenditures were cut, and the brand image suffered. Products were cheapened, and consumers felt cheated. Inexplicably, the responsibility for the merchandising and the manufacturing of the upholstery product line was taken from Lewisburg management and given to another LADD division in North Carolina. This undermined the cohesiveness of the Gallery Program. Earnings rose at first but declined as the company began a downward spiral. Having abandoned its core competency and moved away from its traditional marketing point of view, Pennsylvania House tried to be more like a conventional furniture company, and it was not particularly good at this. Like a ship that lost its engine and sails, the company drifted for a while and then foundered. Total sales climbed close to $150 million at the peak, but then quickly fell back to $90 million on their way to $50 million. The short-term profit maximization prescription was not good for Pennsylvania House, and the company lost a great deal of its vitality. It would never again recapture the mystique it still had after many years and several management changes. The other LADD divisions were not performing very well either, and the need for earnings was intense.

HE WHO LIVES BY THE NUMBERS, DIES BY THE NUMBERS

The decline and near fall of Pennsylvania House paralleled the rest of LADD's overall performance. In 1991, the earnings streak ran out and they stumbled badly, reporting a loss of $12.7 million. Hunziger and Fenn retired, and Allen took over as CEO. Under Dick Allen's numbers-oriented leadership style, without the moderating influence of Fenn, the company did not come close to its earlier successes. For all his brilliance in managing by the numbers, Allen's reign did not produce impressive results and the company never seemed to acquire an identity. Earnings picked up a bit to $5.2 million in 1992, but they fell back to the $4 million to $5 million levels in 1993 and 1994. In 1995, the company reported a staggering loss of $25.2 million. The profit margin had gone from 8.7 percent in the mid 1980s to less than 1 percent in the early '90s. The stock price tumbled from a high of $74 in 1987 to below $10 in 1996. Dick Allen's relentless focus on managing "by the numbers" ultimately resulted in bad numbers. In 1996, he was forced to step down. One of the smartest, hardest working Outsiders ever to penetrate the upper levels of the furniture industry, Dick Allen's grasp of the numeric side of the business was never matched by an understanding of the alpha side of the business. LADD's new CEO was Fred Scheurman, a furniture person who gradually returned the company to profitability. In 1999 the company was sold to La-Z-Boy for $299 million.

LESSONS LEARNED

From the Parker family to LADD, the saga of Pennsylvania House provides a rich storehouse of lessons. From benevolent family owner to brash outside investor to inside leader to cereal barons to vacuum cleaners to LADD, the "Chair Factory" had quite a ride. A great deal can be learned by studying the company's history. Here are a few important "take-aways" from the Pennsylvania House experience:

START WITH A PLAN: If S&H had a grand vision when it began buying companies, no one could articulate it. If you are considering buying a furniture company, take the time to learn all you can about it first. It most definitely is different from what you think it is. The industry can be seductive and cause temporary blindness. The sooner you recognize it for what it is, the better will be your chances of succeeding.

BEWARE OF OVER-CENTRALIZATION: Gaining control by centralizing functions does not lead to timely decisions. The situation on the battlefield changes so quickly that, unless the furniture executive is on top of things enough to have an excellent feel for the business, he will make decisions without the right information. It's better to form strategy at the corporate level and then give division-level executives the latitude to set their own course to meet those strategic objectives. Something is wrong when Corporate finds itself micromanaging the divisions and drawn into tactical proceedings.

EXPECT MARKETING RESISTANCE: Smart marketing will produce a great return on the investment, but it cannot be superimposed on an organization that is not ready for it. American Drew was not ready. Lea was close. Employing a marketing mindset calls for resetting the company's alignment, not unlike the way putting a scope on a rifle requires a re-sighting of the gun. The marketing-oriented model of a furniture company, as espoused by Ethan Allen and Pennsylvania House, can produce better profits in the long run than the conventional model as espoused by Lea and American Drew. However, you must be careful how you install it, because furniture margins are not big enough to support typical marketing ventures. Make the transition slowly or your margins will suffer.

CONSIDER SHORT-TERM VS. LONG-TERM: A short-term focus is essential, but a short-term obsession is dangerous. LADD exhibited such an obsession. The creative elements, which are so badly needed to survive, can easily perish in a "management-by-the-numbers" environment. Current earnings are not a good measure of current company health. The battlefield conditions change so fast that "intelligence reports," like operating statements, are soon out of date. Pennsylvania House earnings were excellent even as the company was being weakened under LADD's direction.

REMEMBER THE EXIT BARRIERS: The exit doors in the Briar Patch are limited, and getting out of the business can be a big problem. Going public is possible, but only rarely. Finding a buyer with financing is not easy. Ask General Mills and LADD. The best way to prepare for this is to take good care of the divisions when you own them. Nobody wants to buy a used car that has suffered abuse. If you must sell a furniture company, do it fast and do not assume that you can keep it a secret. The news always leaks out, and your competitors will seek to take advantage of the situation. The story of the Kittinger demise is a textbook case.

The lessons are there for all to see, but they go unheeded all too often. In the next chapter, we will see how an invader fared who took the time to study the Briar Patch terrain before his invasion.

THE TANGLED WEBB

THE OUTSIDER INVASION HAD RUN OUT of fighting spirit and ammunition by the late 1970s. Mounting an attack was one thing; sustaining one was another. The Insiders had absorbed a furious assault on many fronts without being defeated. Conglomerate organizations fell out of style. Diversification strategies were being questioned, and conglomerates were running away from marginally profitable industries. It was time to cut and run, but how? If they wanted to get out of furniture, to whom could they sell it? Who would want to buy into a segment that everyone else wanted to vacate?

THE MAN WHO STOOD ON HIS HEAD

Among the observers of the Baldwin United raid on Sperry & Hutchinson was a Wall Street banker named Webb W. Turner. His specialty of mergers and acquisitions required him to keep a close eye on that battle, and beyond that, he had more than a passing interest in the furniture industry. For many months, Turner had felt the time was right to move beyond the frenetic pace of his life as an investment banker. He wanted to settle down with something more tangible. His research led him to the conclusion that the furniture industry might be a logical place to stake his claim. Turner was not so much enticed by the conventional demographic projections as he was by the investment opportunity. A contrarian by nature, he saw a chance to buy furniture companies on the cheap precisely because nobody else wanted them. He was no stranger to the business, because he had been close to Bob Fogarty since being retained in 1974 as an investment adviser during the sale of General Interiors to General Mills. At that time, he was with Kuhn Loeb, a major investment-banking house. In 1980, he resigned to form Turner and Co. in order to pursue his furniture dream.

Turner, then 47, was tall, and thanks to a regular regimen of swimming for exercise, he managed to stay trim despite a fondness for desserts. The impression he created was that of an important person, one to be treated respectfully. Frequently, strangers would eye him closely as if he were a celebrity whom they just could not identify. His normal expression was studious and serious, yet he had an easy laugh. His typical approach was to engage companions intensely and question them as if he had to drain them of every ounce of information before he could disengage. His face was not particularly animated since he tried to conceal his thoughts, but his dark eyes usually gave him away. On the phone, he was quite different. Here, you always got the impression that he had one or two other calls on hold while he dealt with yours. He made up for his relatively short attention span by being a quick study, able to grasp and evaluate meaning and nuance in a heartbeat. At times, he jumped to conclusions based on sketchy, anecdotal evidence – and usually he was right – but it was very difficult to convince him to change his mind when he missed.

Plagued with a chronic sore back, Turner went to extremes to alleviate the pain. A favorite technique was to lie on the floor and, without warning, raise his legs until he was practically standing on his head. He did this during meetings, and the effect on the attendees was to distract them so much that all they could remember later was that he stood on his head. Some felt that this was his way of "erasing" meetings that did not go the way he wanted.

Turner's keen mind and vast knowledge of business in general went a long way to conceal the fact that he lacked operational experience in any industry, much less furniture. After graduating from Duke University, he sold industrial machinery for a while and then went into the investment-banking field. On occasion, he gave the appearance of being an actor playing the part of a tycoon, not unlike Walter Pidgeon or William Holden in *Executive Suite*. Real or otherwise, he deftly led people to reach desired conclusions on their own, without overtly persuading them. He never said he was wealthy, but he made sure you knew about his brownstone near the park on Manhattan's Upper West Side and his house in the prestigious Tuxedo Park. He never told you his wife was even wealthier, but he made sure you knew her maiden name was Kress, as in S. H. Kress department stores. His business address, One Wall Street, was more impressive than the small office he rented, but hardly anyone knew this. Besides, he was so disarming and enjoyable that it hardly mattered. It mattered that, in the midst of serious negotiations, the seller would often arrive at incorrect conclusions about Turner's intentions. Later, he would remind them that he never actually said what they thought he said.

The "Stitch Together" Plan

Unlike many other Outsiders, Turner had a plan. He studied the furniture business and had developed a good grasp of its quirks. He was at heart a "banker," conditioned to view manufacturing companies through the lens of the balance sheet more than the operating statement. Rationally, he concluded that the time was right for some owners, especially conglomerates, to begin dumping the furniture divisions they had rushed to buy not that long ago. His reasoning was that the industry was burdened with the baggage of what he called "The Seven Negatives"—low returns on sales, working capital, and assets, combined with high working capital needs, cyclicality, and fixed costs, plus weak cash flow.

These glaring faults are easy to ignore when the Siren Song of furniture is first heard, but eventually they overwhelm the owner. Turner's plan was to use them to his advantage when buying companies from the big corporations and to cope with them after he became the owner. The former proved to be considerably easier than the latter. By his reckoning, he could end up being the only buyer in a market filled with impatient sellers – not the "last man in the room" as Fogarty was in 1972, but the "only man in the room." His instincts were correct.

He was not carried away with Carpi-like visions of grandeur. He merely wanted to buy three or four small, high-quality producers and "stitch them together" to form one medium-sized specialist in the upper-end segment. Turner's original target list included four old-line companies, White Furniture, Unique Furniture, John Widdicomb, and Union of Batesville. Assuming the differing cultures could be melded, the plan made sense. Widdicomb had the prestigious brand name but no capacity; White and Unique had capacity but no market presence; Union had neither but was for sale; and Turner was dying to buy something.

Equipped with his instincts, armed with his checkbook, and fortified with nerve, Webb W. Turner began his single-handed assault on the Furniture Zone in 1980 by making an offer for the outstanding shares of the 120-year-old Union of Batesville Co.

An Unusual Niche Is Captured

As the local legend goes, in the 1800s a prominent cabinet-making family in Batesville, Indiana, made a lot of money building bedrooms and caskets. They could provide you with just the right box, whether you were asleep overnight or for eternity. The business grew as the family grew, with the Romweber branch making furniture and the Hillenbrand branch making caskets. Fifty years later, Hillenbrand had sales in excess of $1 billion making caskets and hospital beds, while Romweber had sales of less than $4 million making furniture. One practically owned the town; the other was close to bankruptcy along with its cross-town rival, Union Furniture.[1] In 1981, both of the furniture companies were sold to out-of-town investors. A Cincinnati banker bought the better of the two for his young son. Wall Street banker Turner bought the other.

Founded in 1860 by a handful of cabinetmakers who proudly named their company after the Union they fought to preserve during the Civil War, the Union Furniture Co. made quality furniture for the next century with the ownership remaining in the hands of the founders and their descendants. Some owners were hourly workers, and the managers were not necessarily stockholders in this worker-owned cooperative corporation. That changed in 1981, when Webb Turner and his wife, Jocelyn Kress Turner, bought controlling interest by virtue of a so-called hostile takeover.

Union of Batesville, as it was known in the trade, was an example of how a furniture company can find a niche and survive by concentrating on that niche. If the niche is small, the big companies will not bother with it, and as long as you don't lose focus and the niche does not disappear, you can continue. Union did this for 120 years. The Union niche was far removed from the mainstream of the marketplace. Their specialty was bedroom and dining room suites made for a very narrow consumer segment – the "ethnic trade." This market was comprised of recent immigrants who had prospered and wanted to buy furniture on a grand scale that would let them enjoy the fruits of their labor. Located in major cities, these consumers were largely of Southern European extraction after World War II, but the market declined as those families were assimilated into the American melting pot. By 1981 it was barely big enough to support Union and its four competitors, and it had splintered into several sub-segments, each with its own product preferences.

The company and the niche were very small and had been in decline for more than decade, and management failed to change as the market changed. It was not much of a company, but Turner saw it as a significant beachhead in the Furniture Zone. Turner's new partner, the author, the same marketing person who migrated from Pennsylvania House to LADD, was not so sure. He had now been in the industry for 12 years and had never heard of the company or its dealers. Nevertheless, he accepted the challenge of reviving Union and was appointed president in July 1981.

ROMA FURNITURE

A good place to start was for the two of them to visit the company's largest dealer, Roma Furniture, in the heart of New York's "Little Italy" section. Each major city had a retailer or two who catered to the ethnic consumer, and Union of Batesville was a valued supplier. The most prominent of these dealers was Roma. Turner and his partner toured the store one summer evening with owner Tommy Iucalano and sales manager Julio Ferrari. The operation catered to customers who had a lot of money and "wanted furniture that was like the furniture in the castles they remembered from their homeland, before coming to America," Ferrari said. "The only problem is, they never set foot in the castle, so they have no idea what the furniture should look like," he added. Their clients included big-time athletes, entertainers, and perhaps a mafia don or two. Iucalano, when asked to describe the store's typical consumers, replied in a pronounced Brooklyn accent, "Well, I'll tell you, Mister Turner, we don't get a lot of Presbyterians in here. You know what I mean?"

In a later meeting, Union's New York sales representative Lee Mandel suggested that Union could grow its business by copying the designs of a rival company owned by the Gallo family. The president got excited, thinking this could be a quick way to pump up sales. After all, knocking off your competitor's best sellers was a time-honored tradition in the Furniture Zone. Turner said he didn't know the Gallo family was in furniture manufacturing, just wine producing. Mandel replied: "Not the Gallo family from California; the Gallo family from Brooklyn. You know, Crazy Joey and his brother." Somehow, the idea of knocking off designs owned by a Brooklyn family – known as one of the "Five Families" that ran organized crime in the New York area – did not seem like a smart strategy. Besides, the possibility of the Union of Batesville niche starting to grow again was about as likely as the Dodgers returning to Brooklyn. The company was destined to go out of business unless it found a new niche. So Turner's plan was to link Union to other companies he would soon buy.

The economy intervened in 1981 and 1982, when high interest rates brought furniture industry sales to a screeching halt. The Union president went on a field trip to learn what styles were selling and learned that *nothing* was selling. In similar fashion, the owners of Widdicomb, Unique, and White Furniture decided not to sell their companies during such troubled times. Turner's incursion into the furniture industry was stymied while the economy stalled, which prevented Union from breaking out of its narrow confines. After managing to buy Union, the other three prospects turned him down and said they would never sell. All three sold within two years of rejecting Turner, and two closed within five years. During the first half of the '80s, Turner's prediction came true, and a flood of furniture companies were offered for sale. The Outsiders who had rushed into the Furniture Zone now could not wait to get out.

The marketing guy and the Wall Street banker found themselves frustrated and bored, hovering over a little company in Batesville with no place to go.

A Sterling Opportunity

In late 1982, the Sterlingworth Co. came on the market. This producer of solid wood bedroom in Jamestown, New York, was on its last legs as its owner/manager, an Outsider, had run out of cash. Since the company had already gone bankrupt twice, it might have been better just to let it go down for the third time. This was one of those smaller companies that Pennsylvania House had blown by in the '70s. But Webb Turner could still hear the Sirens' sweet song and could not resist closing the deal. With the Outsider's optimistic belief that it could be revived, he bought Sterlingworth and made his partner president. Turner then challenged the skeptical partner to make things happen, but only after they resolved their working relationship. Like most owners, Turner liked to tinker with the day-to-day, "nitty-gritty" of the business. Then he would grow tired of it and move on to the loftier activities for which he was better suited. This confused the organization and drove the partner crazy. Turner felt it was his prerogative as the principal owner to do this, and it was consistent with his Wall Street partnership mentality. Dugan met with Turner and declared, "Either you run the company or you let me run the company by myself. I do not know how to run it with someone." Turner reluctantly agreed. The partnership worked well after that.

Worthless Sterling Finds Its Opening

Sterlingworth was a mess. Its history of failure was so pervasive that Turner changed the name to Jamestown Sterling. The manufacturing plant had a leaky roof and broken-down equipment.

Its products were not selling, and the sales force was incapable of opening new accounts and stuck with third- and fourth-rate stores. Yet the hourly workers and supervisors were excellent, and the front office was more than capable. Harold Kirby, a top-notch case goods manufacturing veteran from North Carolina, was made vice president of operations with responsibility for production. Turner's instincts proved to be right and the gamble paid off.

Dugan went to work analyzing the solid wood market, paying close attention to the sub-segments within the niche. Countless dealer visits and interviews confirmed his gut feeling: There was a gap in the market below prestige lines such as Harden, Henkel Harris, and Pennsylvania House, and above the promotional lines such as Kincaid and Crawford. If a shopper wanted moderately priced, commercial-looking products, the choice was excellent. If she wanted expensive, clean-looking products, the choices were also plentiful. However, if the preference was for a clean design without spending a lot, there was nothing available in solid wood. The consumer had to settle for veneered products from American Drew or Thomasville, and research showed that the solid wood consumer would not settle for veneer. Finding a gap in the market is not easy, but it is the best way to ensure that your product will have a chance. When a new company tries to go after a niche that is already occupied, it is not unlike trying to get someone else's seat on an airplane. Even if you have the same seat number, they are not likely to move out of the way for you. In this case, Jamestown Sterling found a perfect opening. The French phrase for this is *cherchez le creneau* – "look for the opening." In architecture, *creneau* means an opening or a niche. In furniture, it means an opportunity. A brochure was printed with a graph that diagrammed the void that Jamestown Sterling attacked. The companies shown flanking the opening, Thomasville and American Drew, offered veneered products rather than solid wood. Consequently, they did not fill the gap.

The company commissioned a top-flight freelance designer with an upper-end background and challenged him to develop a line to fill this void. While waiting for the new line to be introduced at the Furniture Market, they hired a new sales force, leased a small showroom in High Point, and sold the old inventory.

FIRE IN THE MACHINE ROOM

One freezing Jamestown January morning, the president was reviewing new product designs when the plant manager burst into the office yelling that a fire had started in the machine room. Everyone in the office rushed outside. Experienced furniture people knew the dangers of a fire in an old plant loaded with volatile finishing materials and sawdust. There was a good chance of a fiery explosion. The president joined the workers outside, worrying about the fire until he realized he had left the original details of the new product designs in his office. What should he do? Risk losing his life or risk losing the designs? The decision was easy. The designs had to be preserved, so he ran back in and rescued the drawings. The fire was contained, and at the 1983 April Market the new product was launched under the new brand name Jamestown Sterling, which rose from the ashes of a the twice-bankrupt bedroom producer and an almost bankrupt "ethnic" producer. The retail response was immediately favorable as the retailers related to the product offering and liked the idea of getting in early with a potential winner.

Guerilla Tactics Get Results

The veteran sales reps placed the product well and proved to be a major element in the company's success. Because the company had no sales management, the reps reported directly to the president, and he treated them with respect. The result was a remarkable esprit de corps as the company evolved. The usual antagonism between the factory and the field was eliminated, and the reps, who carried other lines, became remarkably loyal and dedicated. This attitude of trust carried over to the dealers who also felt good about the company, and Jamestown Sterling soon had workers who liked the company, salesmen who wanted to sell its products, and customers who liked the company and wanted it to succeed. The resulting productivity was amazing. When the initial samples of the new line shipped, the quality was excellent and they sold quickly. Consequently, the dealers expanded their assortments and bought more goods. At the October Market, a compatible dining room line, made in the Batesville plant, was introduced and sales grew even faster. The "ethnic" line was gradually phased out at Batesville, and the plant was converted into a Jamestown satellite. The cultural differences were overcome by making it clear that management expected an aggressive, "can-do" Western New York approach to business. The lackadaisical Union attitude was eliminated, and Jamestown Sterling flourished. Rather than letting the two cultures slug it out on their own, management led them to the desired culture.

The hourly workers could hardly believe their eyes. They were so accustomed to watching factories shut down rather than reopen, and so used to inept management and broken promises, that they quickly realized things were different this time. They responded with a sharply increased work pace and improved quality. Word spread that this was a good place to work, despite fairly low wages, and the company had no trouble finding skilled people to meet its rapidly expanding production needs.

Strategically, the company viewed itself as a guerrilla marketer that used hit-and-run tactics against the larger, more established companies, especially Pennsylvania House. Having smart, aggressive sales reps gave Jamestown an advantage over small competitors, and having a low-cost factory helped it outfight big competitors in small battles. As Chairman Mao put it, "The enemy advances, we retreat. The enemy camps, we harass. The enemy retires, we attack. The enemy retreats, we pursue." Pennsylvania House was an easy target for the insurgent Jamestown Sterling because it treated dealers poorly and moved slowly. Orders kept rolling in for Jamestown; production kept increasing; profits kept growing; and because everything was sold before it was packed, cash flow was positive. As Steve Sealy, the company's sales rep in the South and an avid Alabama fan, used to proclaim, "Roll Tide."

Turner's Southern Tier Strategy

Buoyed by the success of Jamestown Sterling, which appeared to be easy, and tempted by the number of deals offered to him, Turner kept charging ahead. His contacts alerted him to the fact that Georgia Pacific might want to sell its Williams Furniture division. Williams made moderately priced, conservatively styled traditional casegoods, a classic example of a modestly successful company that was acquired by an Outsider who had succumbed to the Siren Song. Perhaps the giant paper company figured that since both paper and furniture come from wood, it made sense to buy a furniture company. Predictably, the usual pattern of decline followed. The line went cold, sales and earnings slumped, and the paper company decided to bail out. The price was right, and Turner could not resist. In 1983, he bought Williams Furniture Co. in Sumter, South Carolina, from Georgia Pacific for an estimated $16 million.

Williams was more of a struggle than Union and Jamestown Sterling. From the beginning, Turner did not settle on a general manager/CEO in whom he had full confidence. Instead, he used a team approach that did not work. The top line did not accelerate as planned, and the needed turnaround was slow to take hold. It was never clear who was in charge, and the company continued to struggle as it failed to settle into its proper niche. It kept improving but did not catch fire. Williams had a deep Southern culture, and the local reaction was less than enthusiastic to the new owners and managers, who were brought in from "up North." The industry has had a long history of Northern "carpetbaggers" and the furniture "good old boys" were not particularly fond of Yankees, especially when they acted "ugly" and treated the Southerners as if they were somehow inferior. As one Southerner put it one day, "You Yankees are always trying to *outsmart* the other guy. You should learn to *outdumb* him and you will be amazed at what an advantage you will have."

Shop 'Til You Drop

Turner did not slow down. Jamestown Sterling was still accelerating, and he had every reason to believe that Williams would turn out to be even bigger than Jamestown Sterling. By now, he was convinced he could leap tall buildings in a single bound and he, once again, turned his attention to acquisitions. In 1984, he bought three more companies: a waterbed producer in New Hampshire called Stone Hill, and two upholstery companies, DeVille in Hickory, North Carolina, and State of Newburgh in New York. You could hear echoes of Colin Carpi's acquisition moves if you listened carefully.

DeVille was another example of a successful furniture venture that had been acquired by an outsider briefly seduced by the Siren Song. Margins are razor thin in promotionally priced furniture, and your success is primarily based on relationships with key customers and how hot your styling is. As soon as corporate owner National Linen Service figured this out, it wisely realized it was ill-equipped to make a go of it and happily sold the division to Webb Turner. Unlike his other acquisitions, this one was making money and had a good management team, but it was operating in a very tough segment and its existence was fragile. It could fall apart quickly if the line suddenly got cold.

Turner bought State of Newburgh, an upholstery producer, practically on a whim, possibly because it was near his beautiful home in Tuxedo, New York. The company was small and in trouble, but he thought it would complement Jamestown Sterling. Like some of the General Interiors combinations, both parties resented this one. Cultural problems surfaced the first day, and State proved to be more a distraction than a benefit. The upholstery people did not take kindly to advice given by the "wood guys," and the "wood guys" resented taking time to work on upholstery. But Turner was not daunted by the obvious challenge.

The waterbed excursion was another risky purchase. Turner was impressed with the energetic entrepreneur who drove the company, and they thought the production could be moved to the Sumter plant. The idea died when it became obvious that the Williams plant could not service the waterbed trade at the prices they needed and the Williams sales force could not sell the product. Turner's furniture experts knew these things before the acquisition, but by then he was ignoring their counsel as being too conservative. People were always telling him he could not do things. It was fun to do them anyway, and Turner was having a lot of fun.

Soaring With Wings of Wax

In July 1984, Turner entered into negotiations to buy the furniture division of Burlington Industries – but not before convening a meeting with his closest advisers. In each case, they urged him to slow down, consolidate his holdings, and steer clear of Burlington, but he could not resist such an attractive deal.

Burlington showed great promise at one time. They had deep pockets. They had staying power and were from the related industry of home textiles. In 1966, on the heels of Colin Carpi, Burlington acquired two of the best companies in the business – United and Globe – and set out to extend the well-known Burlington brand into the rest of the home. They failed abjectly. Without batting an eyelash, they proceeded to make nearly every mistake in the book, including many of the Seven Deadly Sins. In the process, they converted two fine furniture companies into one pathetic division that, after 19 years of Burlington's expert guidance, was losing $1 million a month on annual sales of $120 million.

How Burlington moved from point A to point B involves a catalog of Outsider errors, but the most foolish was the systematic dismissal of experienced furniture people. The pattern works like this. First, the original leader leaves or is driven out after a falling out with the new parent. Next, his replacement, usually from the outside, alienates the executive staff and replaces them with people who have no furniture experience. Then, the front-line managers decide to leave because no one above them knows what he is doing. In the meantime, qualified people steer clear of the place. The company is left with people at the top who may be good managers but know nothing about furniture and people at the operating level who know furniture but are not good managers. Time and again, the outside invaders lose the best furniture people in the organization and then wonder why the second-best people cannot turn things around. Finally, in desperation, they try to recover by bringing in journeyman furniture people from some other companies, but by then it is too late. In the industry, this is known as the Burlington Syndrome.

While this systematic purge was going on, Burlington made one mistake after another. In an attempt to reduce labor costs, it ended up cheapening the product. It added more engineers and middle managers and ended up raising costs. To process lumber for all the plants, it installed a centralized rough mill that backfired. Each time a well-intentioned project failed, furniture types would get canned and more textile executives would be brought in. The newcomers would steer the company closer to the textile model with which they were most comfortable, and the situation would worsen.

In 1984, Burlington finally admitted defeat and started looking for a buyer. Most furniture companies shunned the opportunity to acquire this collection of assets considering it to be damaged beyond repair. A few, including Taiwan-based Universal Furniture, took a close look and passed. Webb Turner, the last man in the room, was offered the prize no one else wanted. Had he rejected it, Burlington probably would have shut the whole thing down. In retrospect, that would have been the wiser course, but Turner was not about to turn down the chance to double his volume to the $200 million level. He could not resist the temptation any more than he could pass up a good dessert. Besides, this was as much fun as he had ever had. He bought the Burlington Furniture Division on July 25, 1984, for an estimated $60 million – about $125 million today after adjusting for inflation.

Exclusive Interview & Association Speech
Stir the Pot

In August of 1984, Turner agreed to an exclusive interview with *Furniture Today*, the industry's leading business journal. His interview revealed a game plan far removed from his modest original concept. No longer a niche player focused on the upper-end, he wanted to go for it all, to attain what he called "critical mass." He said he wanted to "become large enough to play with the big boys – the Intercos, the Bassetts, and the Thomasvilles – and become important to a broad base of dealers and weather any cataclysmic changes that might occur in the industry." This was far beyond the original plan to "stitch together" three or four small companies. "Stitching up" was more the order of the day now. The thrill of the hunt and the art of the deal still coursed in his veins, and he lusted for more acquisitions. Leveraged to the teeth and the owner of seven troubled companies, he still wanted more.

"Although I am channeling the majority of my time and energies to the middle-price and promotional segments," as he put it, he would not rule out further acquisitions in the upper-end. In that segment, he "expected to buy several additional companies as they become available over the years." These would be in addition to the upholstery companies and the occasional table companies he wanted to buy.[2]

He seemed unconcerned when asked about the overlap between the Burlington and the Williams product lines, as if this question had not occurred to him before, and rather weakly resorted to a comparison with General Motors. As for the issue of how to manage the Burlington mess, he prophetically said, "Initially, there will be four or five people running Burlington. Each person involved will have six days of work. . . . We do want to strengthen this company and there's going to be more opportunities and challenges than any three or four people can handle." The Wall Street partnership mentality had not left him. He basically planned to employ all his troops except Dugan, the president of Jamestown Sterling, who told Turner he wanted nothing to do with the venture.

As for Turner himself, the experience had been most profound, like Odysseus and his men when they stopped at the land of the friendly Lotus Eaters, where they ate the lotus, forgot about their families, and wanted to stay forever. As he told the *Furniture*

Today reporter, "I'm seeing precious little of my family, which is very sad. I'm intending to hire four or five people in the next eight to 10 weeks so that I can stay in the role I've selected for myself . . . which is not to have any operating responsibility for my companies. I'm often exhilarated and often exhausted by what I'm doing. It's the most fun I've ever had. It's proven to be what I set out for it to be – a challenging way to spend the rest of my life."

The apogee of the Webb Turner Furniture Venture occurred in February 1985, when he made a presentation to the Marketing Division of the American Furniture Manufacturers Association. The guy with the big address and the small office had come a long way in five years. The intoxication level gets pretty high when the trade group's Marketing Division asks you to share your strategy with them, and you tend not to realize you may be getting set up, if only a little bit. Attendance was big. Practically the whole industry showed up to hear what Turner had to say. And did he ever say it. He stepped into the mode of the Outsider who can't resist telling the Insiders what they are doing wrong. Without intending to, he came across as another Outsider with all the answers. This was unfortunate, because he really had a great deal of respect for the Insiders and wanted to be more like them. But he came across as yet another critic, and the result was considerable competitive animosity.

WATERLOO

Buying Burlington was easy. Turning it around was nearly impossible. Turner again failed to appoint a clearly identified CEO because he could not find one he liked. He even made some public statements about the furniture industry being "backward" and said he "was going to get away from the 'personality' aspect of one absolute company leader and show how a horizontal management team could better run a company." He had a host of talented and experienced furniture veterans, but no one was ever really in charge. Admittedly, unconventional methods were required to save this terminally ill company, but a shuttle system at the top was not the answer. What Turner desperately needed was an operational leader who knew furniture but went beyond the typical furniture executive's range. He needed someone like Bob Fogarty, or Howard Haworth, who had led Drexel Heritage to greatness, or Wes Collins, who had made Bernhardt successful and then made Universal work. Some experience in turnaround situations would have helped, too, because Burlington's systematic extermination of the experienced furniture people had stripped the organization of its vitality. No such person was available. All too often, the capable furniture-type managers were not as broad in their managerial skills as they needed to be, and this frustrated Turner. He had been exposed to some top-notch executives in his Wall Street years, and he was understandably frustrated by the difficulty he had in finding similar leaders in the Furniture Zone. So, instead of finding the one key leader who could right the ship, he appointed three leaders. In August 1984, he named former Broyhill executive Jerry Dodson as president, Charlie Shaughnessy as chairman, the same Charlie Shaughnessy who resigned as president of the Cushman Shaw Group of General Interiors, and retailer Buck Thornton as special consultant.

One of the original attractions of purchasing Burlington was the tremendous amount of finished goods inventory on the books.

Turner, ever the banker, saw an opportunity to convert this to cash. What he did not see was how difficult it would be to sell these goods, because their styles were less than hot. Turner's junta resorted to deep discounts, which triggered price cuts by the competition, which depressed sales of Burlington's best groups, which forced further price cuts.

The Turner flagship now found itself in the midst of a furniture version of *The Perfect Storm* without a true captain and in a ship that would remain in troubled waters no matter which way it turned. Events moved swiftly as desperate attempts were made to save the craft. People were fired. Executives from the other Turner companies were called in to help. Cost cuts were made. Shaughnessy, the key link with the top reps and big dealers, did not like the direction and left. A plant was closed. The top executives were reorganized. Another plant was closed. Still another acquisition was made, Dunmore Furniture in Hickory. A new division, Turner Contract, was formed to go after the hospitality market. Another new division, Turner Overseas, was formed to import dining rooms. More layoffs followed. More key executives left, including some Turner had hired. Turner Contract was shut down. Still more layoffs were made. And, in November 1985, the Burlington Division sought Chapter 11 bankruptcy protection, just a little over one year from the day Turner took over.

POST WAR FALLOUT

Naturally, the impact on the other Turner companies was negative as vendors suddenly curtailed credit limits. The impact on

Webb Turner was catastrophic. He was a proud man, and unlike the image he sometimes projected, he was far removed from the cold-blooded raider who cared not a whit about bankruptcy proceedings. His psyche was deeply wounded and, to make things worse, his marriage was shattered. He had become so obsessed with his business and so determined to fix Burlington that he had no time to spend with his wife, Jocelyn, and their two young sons. At the outset of his campaign, Jocelyn was a very involved spouse. Her name meant more to the bankers than it did to the "good old boy" furniture types, unless they made the connection between the name and the "five-and-dime" stores they knew as kids. Jocelyn Kress Turner was a strong-willed, intelligent, non-conformist woman who was very much in love with and fascinated by her husband. The deeper he became involved with furniture acquisitions and the more she disagreed with his course of action, the more strained the relationship became. While he became more and more caught up in the Southern Strategy, she remained in New York to look after the children. The separation occurred, and the highly contested divorce followed, as still another Furniture Warrior returned from battle to find he had been locked out of his castle.

The shockwaves from the bankruptcy filing were enormous. More than 1,400 jobs were lost in Burlington Furniture's hometown of Lexington, North Carolina, and dozens of suppliers were caught with big money owed to them. Although astute observers saw it coming, most people were caught totally off guard. Those hurt the most were the hourly workers who had nothing to do with the decisions yet lost their jobs.

The effect was felt as far away as Sumter, South Carolina, where Williams found that key suppliers stopped extending normal terms, and in Hickory, North Carolina, where the upholstery companies started hearing lots of questions from customers, suppliers, and key managers. Working through the bankruptcy court, Burlington Furniture's key competitors pored over the bare, ruined castles of the defeated Turner Empire. They publicly shed crocodile tears over the demise of these fine companies, but privately they were delighted that the Yankee interloper, who had boasted of the "new order" he was going to bring about, was blown off the field. Had Turner been able to liquidate the massive inventories he bought from Burlington, even at a discount, he would have had a fighting chance at surviving. But the competition responded with deep price cuts that locked him out of the channel. Had he been able to start the overseas import idea rolling, he might have revolutionized the industry and trounced his competitors. But no quarter is given in the Furniture Wars, where the victors divide the loot. The best managers, sales reps, and skilled workers were picked off. Stanley Furniture bought one of the idled United Globe plants, Lexington Furniture bought another, and Universal grabbed one along with the freestanding showroom.

Williams was not able to withstand the shock of the bankruptcy, and after a deal to sell its facility to Vaughan Bassett fell through, another Turner company was forced into bankruptcy. In May 1986, Turner announced agreements to sell DeVille, Dunmore, and State of Newburgh to each respective company's management. A better description of these transactions might be to "give back" rather than sell.

Jamestown Colony Hangs On

Amazingly, Jamestown Sterling continued to grow and prosper during the rise and fall of Turner's Southern Tier Strategy. Cash flow remained positive despite the need for more working capital to keep up with sales growth, and management was able to convince vendors to keep needed supplies flowing. Miraculously, the company was able to avoid the artillery barrage triggered by the Burlington explosion, but the pressure was intense. The impact of the divorce caused another distraction as Jocelyn made a pass at taking Jamestown Sterling away from her estranged husband. That thrust was also parried, and the two plants kept producing. Incoming orders were so good that arrangements were made to contract some bedroom production to other companies. During this crisis, the intangible feelings of loyalty that so many had for the company really paid off. Key suppliers wanted the company to make it, so they continued to ship needed supplies regardless of the risk of still another Turner bankruptcy filing.

Each year, the Jamestown Sterling sales force met with the company president in what was dubbed "Summer School," when the group thoroughly reviewed the competition, the product line, the merchandising, and the marketing tactics to find ways to make the upcoming Fall Furniture Market a success. The sessions were held in a beautiful, turn-of-the-century summer home that once belonged to the Eastman family of the Kodak fortune. The reps took an active role and were encouraged to speak candidly, because management wanted to hear their perspective on the situation.

The atmosphere was highly charged because everyone took it seriously, but it was also a lot of fun because the process worked.

The company's product line became more sharply focused on three well-defined and closely related style segments, and the reps became more adept at showing dealers why the concept made so much sense. The marketing mindset was bred into the organization's core. It was organic. Following on the heels of the initial positioning statement – "We fill the gap between promotional and prestige" – Jamestown Sterling used analogies to capture dealers' attention and explain where the company fit in. A Market invitation proclaimed, "Jamestown Sterling is like a Southwick Blazer – versatile and it never goes out of style; Stag's Leap Chardonnay – the best in its category, but not everyone has heard of it; Coors Beer in the '70s – extremely popular, but not available coast to coast; an Audi 5000S – a lot of Mercedes feel, but priced more like a Volkswagen."

Many good ideas came out of these sessions, and a palpable level of bonding connected the field representatives with the company in a way seldom seen in the Furniture Zone. The company was characterized by openness, trust, and mutual respect. The formula worked.

The dealer perception of Jamestown Sterling was enhanced by the fact that the company was able to pick off one of the better showroom locations in High Point. Thanks to a close connection with the director of the main exhibit building, this small start-up line leased the highly prized Pennsylvania House showroom location after it moved to a new site. This created the impression that Jamestown Sterling was bigger and more prominent than it really was, and it strengthened the claim that Jamestown Sterling was the ideal replacement for Pennsylvania House. The classy, colorful showroom was popular with retailers, and the new product introductions continued to be well received.

The executive staff at headquarters was spartan, comprised of the CEO, a vice president of finance and administration, and a plant manager. The president operated from his home in High Point with no real office. A neighbor handled secretarial duties, and another neighbor, who freelanced out of his home, did the sales collateral materials. At the company's first Market, when it was Union of Batesville, the CEO used his home as the showroom.

In April 1987, the company celebrated the move into a new High Point showroom with a black-tie dealer party. The significance of the new location was noteworthy. It had been the Pennsylvania House showroom address for 17 years. This was the furniture business at its best, entrepreneurial driven, focused on a well-defined niche, making money, and having fun. The company was now shipping $2 million a month and poised to break away from the pack.

However, Turner was still the principal stockholder, and the uncertainty surrounding the numerous bankruptcy proceedings made everyone aware of the fact that the considerable success of the company was fragile. The company had another big Market in October, when it successfully launched a major new collection. Unfortunately, at the end of the Market, the president resigned to become president of Henredon Furniture. He hated to leave Jamestown Sterling but could not resist the offer to head the company he had always considered to be the finest in the industry. He left his heart in Jamestown Sterling.

Ed Fritz, who had previously been president of Universal Furniture's Canadian division, was named his replacement. No stranger to the Jamestown Sterling group, Fritz knew most of the people, had been a guest speaker at one Summer School session, and was well qualified to run the company. Under his direction, the company continued to do well even though the economy went into a tailspin. For some reason, Turner never quite gave Fritz his full support and, exercising his prerogative as owner, began to involve himself more and more with operations. Without his realizing it, a simple suggestion from the owner can be translated into actions that can have a big impact on the company. Neither the owner nor the president wants this to happen, but it does. In this case, a simple decision was made to open the line to a number of North Carolina dealers who sold product nationwide at a deep discount, usually over the phone. This kind of distribution had been resisted steadfastly throughout the company's short history and was one reason why dealers in other states liked the line. It was an emotionally charged issue that carried much more weight than most people realized. The consequences were severe. The non-North Carolina reps felt betrayed, as did many dealers. What the company gained in short-term orders it lost in long-term dealer relations, as the unique fabric of trust between the factory and the field was torn.

Next, the company experienced organizational problems. The vice president of finance and administration left to pursue a better opportunity, and his replacement had no furniture experience. Then, Turner hired a vice president of operations with no furniture experience. Fritz was now isolated. By this time, State of Newburgh had moved to North Carolina and was renamed State of Hickory. The Jamestown Sterling people often referred to the company by another name, "State of Confusion." In 1990, it ran into cash flow problems, and Turner re-acquired it. His hope was to put the two companies together and to rebuild around them. Gradually, he became more involved with operations and again created uncertainty as to who was in charge. At first, there was conflict between Ed Fritz and the president of State. Then, Turner hired a veteran upholstery executive, who had made his mark with a division of LADD. He was a competent industry veteran, but his experience was in upholstery, not wood. In any event, the two small companies now had no less than three CEO designates and no one was sure who the boss was. Soon the company was in trouble. Fritz resigned in 1992 and was replaced by the upholstery executive. His culture and the Jamestown Sterling culture were about as dissimilar as those of LADD and Pennsylvania House. As so often happens, he brought in one of his own men as sales manager, and he immediately clashed with the sales force and many dealers.

It wasn't long before the new management's mistakes piled up. Inventory problems began to plague the Jamestown plant as the non-furniture executive stumbled with the subtleties of plant schedules. Key dealers who sensed the worst continued to de-emphasize the line. The salesmen's commission rate was cut, a surefire way to demoralize key producers. Lumber inventories were reduced in order to stock more upholstery fabric, and the oxygen flow of successful new products dried up because no one knew where to start. Mercifully, the end came fairly quickly. On a bitter cold winter's day in February 1995, the company filed for Chapter 11 bankruptcy protection and the plant closed.

It was a sad ending to the classy little company that had defied the odds and had come so close to the Platonic Ideal of a furniture company. The final days of a failed furniture plant are not pretty, especially after earlier days that held such promise. Bill Bamberger and Cathy N. Davidson capture it well in *Closing: The Life and Death of an American Factory*:

> There was a grim logic to the layoffs. They followed production. The last piece of furniture came down the line, was worked on, and then the line closed down behind it, and the workers in that section would be let go. A few workers made one last walk-through of the plant, saying goodbye to their friends, but most just left. The layoffs started in the kiln area where the lumber was brought into the yard. After the lumber ran through the saws in the rough mill, those people would be let go. After the wood was glued together, the workers on the glue machine left. The piece was machined, and the next day the machine room was empty. The last piece of furniture was sanded, assembled, and then finished, with workers from each department leaving in turn. Finally the piece went to rub and pack, where it was prepared for shipping and then boxed. The last piece on the line was ready to be sent away. And so were the last workers. You finished your job. You were called away from your department an hour or so before closing time. You sat in the personnel room and signed some papers. The personnel officer shook your hand. And then it was over.[3]

And so it went for the workers in Jamestown and Batesville. They were out of work, and the prospects of landing similar jobs in these towns were remote. The sales reps would be slow to replace the income generated by the once "hot" line, and the suppliers would never be paid for their efforts to keep the place running. Dealers scrambled to replace the product in their assortment, and the management had to find jobs. The losers were obvious, but it was hard to see who the winners were. So it goes in the Furniture Wars.

Seven months later, fate made sure Jamestown Sterling would never return to the Furniture Wars. The empty plant caught fire one Saturday afternoon in early September and burned to the ground within a matter of hours. Smoke was visible 20 miles away, and workers cut power to the area because of high-voltage lines that ran close to the plant. The result was a blackout over a wide area and traffic jams at major intersections.

Jamestown Sterling did not go gentle into that good night. It's as if the plant raged against the bad managers and misguided owners whose weak leadership had shut it down. By burning so intensely and so completely, it was as if the very heart of the building was saying it would take no more abuse.

Yet the soul of Jamestown Sterling refused to die. John Scarsella, the company's top sales rep and one-time vice president of sales and marketing, joined a small Canadian company in late 1995 and, employing many of the same principles, transformed the company. Sales under his direction went from $6 million to $70 million (Canadian) in five years. "The Jamestown Sterling spirit lives on and is embodied in this company," said Scarsella, who had been instrumental in shaping the original operating philosophy of both ventures.

LESSONS LEARNED

Webb Turner crashed and burned. This man was only guilty of a few furniture sins. It is a shame his venture did not succeed. His respect for the industry and his willingness to dive into the fray were refreshing. His Wall Street savvy and his risk-taking nature made things a lot more interesting. His overreaching and his insistence on getting involved with operations and organizations led to his downfall, but you can't say he was dull.

Because Webb Turner had studied the industry before his invasion, he avoided many of the glaring mistakes made by his predecessors, but the properties he acquired were damaged goods. Most were beyond repair. Consequently, the lessons to be learned from his ventures are at a postgraduate level:

CONFEDERACY OF NICHES: Time spent looking for an opening in the market pays big dividends. The relative success of Jamestown Sterling resulted from attacking an open niche. The "gap" uncovered by Jamestown Sterling led to a quick breakout and considerable success on the battlefield against difficult odds. A strong sales force that is closely linked to the company can be a tremendous asset in exploiting the opening. They will go out of their way to support the company and represent its products. They can prop up a weak or wounded company and can generate big results for a strong company, but they will drift away if not cared for and motivated.

ALIGNMENT: Note how Jamestown Sterling management realigned its product line, sales force, and dealer base concurrently. It did not try to sell the new products to the old dealer network through the old sales force. Contrast this with Williams' attempt to sell a youth furniture line without a sales force experienced in those products. The attempt to market waterbeds at Williams was another case of misalignment, like firing small caliber shells through cannons.

PEOPLE: There is a shortage of capable managers in the industry. The really good "furniture guys" frequently are not broad-gauged enough to handle tough management situations, yet the outside "professional managers" typically fail. It is wise to hold on to managers who encompass both. Owners should let the managers manage and not interfere. The only justifiable interference by an owner is to terminate the manager. If he does not like the way the manager is running the company or not happy with the results, then he should replace him. He should not "help" him by getting too involved with operations. The Mr. Inside/Mr. Outside organization model works, but not the co-presidency model. Turner's problems at United Globe and the demise of Jamestown Sterling can be traced directly to the "team presidency" confusion.

DIEHARD CULTURES: In contrast with the botched marriage of Lea and American Drew, Turner was able to join two disparate cultures. This is rare, because the cultures fiercely resist change. The key is to select the dominant culture ahead of time. Union of Batesville and Jamestown Sterling had nothing in common, but the merger worked by making it clear at the start that the Jamestown culture was the designated choice. The put-together of the State culture with Jamestown culture failed because neither party saw the merit of the decision.

The Turner venture demonstrated clearly that synergy does not occur spontaneously in the furniture business. It may not occur at all. Yet synergy is exactly what our next invader thought could be found in the Briar Patch. As Webb Turner was withdrawing from the battlefield, a large plumbing products producer from Michigan was arriving in force. Never before, and probably never again, will the industry see anything like the Masco Invasion.

•

THE MASCO FIASCO: KING RICHARD'S CRUSADE

Strange but true, one of the hottest industries for merger activity recently has been neither high finance nor high technology, but the ancient and venerable business of furniture making. It's an industry in which about 600 companies share about $20 billion worth of business, roughly divided between office and home furniture. It is a business in which the size of the largest company can still be expressed in millions of dollars, not billions. . . .

Why is this happening? Partly it's the comedy of errors called corporate strategy, but also the industry is responding to changes in the way furniture is sold in America, to some increase in foreign competition and to a growing market among the so called baby boomers who, like Ken and Barbie grown up, are shopping for home furnishings. . . .

Who wins in this game? Well, most of all the shareholders of family owned furniture companies in North Carolina and

Virginia who are being paid a fancy price by the newcomers.
But there will be some losers, too, as there were before when big
companies bought into the furniture business.

What happened? The usual thing: Big companies buy out
family owners of profitable small companies in another indus-
try; say they intend to leave local management alone, except to
"help" with things such as finance. Then, soon after the honey-
moon, the big company is milking profits from the smaller to
meet earnings targets of its own, demeaning local management
and sapping local initiative. Small wonder the business goes
downhill. . . .

Makes you wonder if the acquisition-happy companies
wouldn't be better off paying premiums to their own sharehold-
ers and letting them invest in furniture if they want.[1]

James Flanigan

T HE JUNE 24, 1986, NEWS WAS STUNNING. Henredon,
the most revered, feared, and copied company in the business, was being sold – to a plumbing fixture company! A Northern
company! Henredon, the Empress of the Furniture Industry, the
one company everybody looked up to, everybody emulated, the
one countless suitors had tried to buy. Henredon – just to be associated with this classy company enhanced your reputation.

Its history was legendary. Even the name had a mystique about
it. Founded in 1945, in Morganton, North Carolina, by four furniture veterans who had broken away from Heritage Furniture,
the brand combined bits of three of their names – <u>Hen</u>ry Wilson,

Ralph Edwards, Donnell VanOppen, and Sterling Collett – to create a new word. Henredon found immediate acceptance of its vision to offer "Grand Rapids Quality at North Carolina Prices." By mirroring the styles and quality of the finest Michigan cabinetmakers while using cheap Southern labor, the company gradually became the dominant line in the high-end segment it served. Known for styling, quality, comfort, and prestige, the company represented the Southern furniture industry at its best. To think that a Northern company had acquired this gem was shocking. But that was only part of the story. The new buyer was in the plumbing business! They made faucets and towel racks, for heaven's sake. Who did they think they were? What were they trying to do? Why would they want to be in the furniture business in the first place? Why in the world would they pay so much money to buy Henredon? What did they know that the Insiders did not?

FULLY PRICED DAMAGED GOODS?

The $298 million purchase price was staggering – 27 times peak earnings, more than 2 times sales – for a company that, in spite of its storied past, had been showing signs of breaking down for several years. The 1986 sales of $127 million were down 11 percent from the year before, and profits were down 31 percent. Like a veteran pitcher who has lost his fastball and has yet to master the curve, Henredon was having some problems. Their wonderfully talented director of design, Ken Volz, who came to the company from Kittinger, had died three years before, and this ended the company's string of sensational new collections. Henredon had trouble shipping its best-selling group because of offshore parts supply difficulties, and they were having serious quality problems with another recent introduction. But the more troublesome issue was an entanglement with a high-tech, flat-line manufacturing process using polyester finishes. This costly venture took Henredon away from its historic niche and threatened to drag down the entire organization. Worse still, no solution was in sight. As the malaise spread, the plants were having morale problems and the front office was rife with politics. Their dealers were fed up with the company's longstanding habit of shipping incomplete orders, just like Pennsylvania House, and no longer felt privileged to carry the line. They loved the brand image and the status it conveyed on those associated with it, but they resented how they were treated by management.

A strong case could be made that Henredon had peaked five years earlier. In 1981, the company hit a phenomenal level of 13 percent after tax return on sales and a 21 percent return on equity. These results were largely fueled by a huge volume of high-margin sales coming from its popular Scene One collection. After that, sales grew as management introduced cheaper products, but profits gradually eroded. Knowing that the numbers lag behind the management decisions that produce those numbers, it could be argued that the real decline of the company began when then-President John Collett died in a house fire in 1979. Nevertheless, even in decline, it was still Henredon, and it was impressive even with a "tired arm."

MASCO, MASTERS OF THE MUNDANE

The buyer, Masco Corp., was also a highly regarded company with an enviable track record. Before invading the furniture industry in June 1986, the company recorded its 30th consecutive year of earnings growth. Sales in 1986 were expected to top $1.3 billion, and after-tax profits were close to 15 percent. Dubbed the "masters of the mundane," top management was proud of its ability to be a low-cost producer and an effective marketer of relatively unexciting products such as shower heads, bathtubs, door handles, and garbage disposals. Masco's emphasis on consumer products was a fairly recent development. In its early days, it was content to go after the original equipment market for automotive parts, making a variety of metal products such as screws, fasteners, stampings, tail pipes, and gearshift levers. Never was it involved with any fashion or style oriented products, unless you thought new faucets were stylish. Masco did.

Responding to Wall Street criticism regarding the company's confusing mixture of original equipment market products and consumer goods, Chairman Richard A. Manoogian split the company in 1984. Masco Tech encompassed industrial products, and Masco Corp. housed consumer products. With this spin-off successfully behind him, he was now diversifying beyond the core building products business into home furnishings. "This is a stepping stone for us into furniture, and we are pleased to start out with the best," Manoogian said, adding that Henredon management would remain in place after the acquisition.

Manoogian's meal ticket was the single-handle faucet, which was protected by multiple patents that gave it a virtual monopoly. It was a huge profit generator for Masco's Delta Faucet group. This division represented Masco at its best – employing solid marketing tactics and advanced manufacturing techniques to carve out impressive market share numbers and even more impressive factory margins. Its approach to the marketplace made Masco the preferred supplier for "big box" retailers such as Home Depot, and its aggressive management of the plants was the envy of the industry. If its skill set could somehow be transported, this could be exactly what the furniture industry needed. The big question was why Masco paid so much for a troubled company. Were its top brass perhaps not as smart as they appeared to be, or did they have a master plan that would only be revealed in time?

Masco's stated goal was to become "The Procter & Gamble of Consumer Durable Goods." No longer was General Motors the standard of excellence, as it was during Colin Carpi's quest a generation earlier. They wanted to leverage their innovative product skills, their manufacturing expertise, and what they called "Power Marketing" among the furniture natives. The phrase had an intriguing sound to it. Yet no one in Masco was ever able to define it with any clarity. The 1989 annual report put it this way: "Power Marketing results from our placing comprehensive and innovative focus on all elements of the marketing function to achieve desired results." Was the copywriter serious? How does one have "*comprehensive* focus?" And how do you "focus on *all* elements?" And note the way this is worded: Power Marketing "results from" that focus; it does not get results. The furniture marketing people, as backward as they were, scoffed at this corporate doubletalk.

Insiders asked the question they had asked when other Outsiders arrived: "What is different that makes them think they will not fail with furniture just as so many other previously successful invaders had done?" "These guys are not stupid," remarked one industry observer. "They must have a plan, but what can they possibly do to avoid the misfortunes that plagued their predecessors? It's going to be interesting to see how it plays out."

LIFE IN THE BRIAR PATCH, CIRCA 1986

The residential furniture industry had changed little in the 20 years since Carpi's Lewisburg invasion. The competition was still fierce, and the structure was still fragmented with some 2,500 manufacturers shipping $14 billion in merchandise. The top 400 accounted for 80 percent of the total, but the Top 10 held just 23 percent of the market. Only 19 companies topped $100 million in sales. After-tax profits were in the 4 percent range, and the working capital required was very high.[2] This is about as close to a real world example of the economists' model of Perfect Competition as you can find, but it was producing less-than-perfect results. Since Carpi's failed attempt to lead the consolidation movement, the furniture industry had grown but remained stubbornly fragmented. And consumer purchases of furniture products had been declining as a percentage of discretionary income, indicating that the industry was doing a poor job convincing consumers of the merits of its products.

The shopping experience was still frustrating, and consumers ignored conventional retailers who failed to excite them. As a consequence, the number of stores carrying furniture fell 27 percent since 1978, to 16,000 in 1986. The mix was changing also, as chains and specialty stores displaced the old-line furniture stores. Manufacturers' galleries, such as the one pioneered by Pennsylvania House, were increasing in importance as consumers responded to their focused assortment of goods. Perhaps Masco could reformat this concept – or, better yet, open the Masco stores that many had suspected.

On the manufacturing side, little had changed during the past 15 years in methods, machinery, and management. Repeated attempts to import techniques from other fields invariably failed, simply because wood does not behave like metal. Nevertheless, Masco had done some remarkable things with its Delta Faucet division, and one of its more recent acquisitions was Merrillat, a rapid delivery kitchen cabinet producer. Perhaps Masco could transfer some of those techniques to furniture. Industry insiders watched with growing fascination.

Do We Really Need Another Plumber?

Masco's longtime plumbing rival, Wisconsin based Kohler Co., grabbed center stage in the furniture industry in September 1986 by buying Henredon's longtime rival, Baker Furniture. Baker's sales were estimated at $100 million, including its chain of designer showrooms, Baker Knapp and Tubbs. Unconfirmed reports said the purchase price was comparable to Henredon's 27 times earnings, but Baker's profits were not as high as Henredon's. Widespread rumors claimed the two plumbing product rivals had bid against each other for the two properties, which drove up the purchase prices. According to legend, Kohler had an agreement to buy Henredon before Masco showed up, but Manoogian made a "take out" offer that the Henredon board could not refuse. The legend says CEO Herb Kohler was on the Bloomingdale's New York furniture floor not long afterward and, still smarting at this affront by his adversary, he asked a Bloomingdale's person what brand would be the first choice if Henredon were not available. The answer was Baker, and Kohler decided to pursue it even though he was not particularly familiar with that brand.

HEY, HERB, WATCH THIS

Kohler's move made it impossible for Masco to tie up the high-end furniture segment. Putting Henredon and Baker under the same battle flag might have made a formidable combination, but Kohler prevented this from occurring. Now, the two rivals were destined to continue engaging in hand-to-hand combat during the '90s to see who would claim the top position in the luxury segment. In late September 1986, Masco made headlines again with its $256 million purchase of Drexel Heritage. The deal further shocked the industry. Drexel Heritage had experienced a successful 10-year run led by Howard Haworth, its peerless CEO, but he had retired in 1985. The company was put in the hands of the charismatic but untested Fred Copeland. Within three months, the three best-known upper-end brands had been sold to a pair of Outsiders with no experience in furniture. The moves triggered a great deal of questions. What did these plumbers see in the Briar Patch that led them to bid against each other and run the valuations so high? Obviously, professional jealousy had more than a little bit to do with it. Kohler had for many years been engaged in a fierce rivalry with Masco to see who would be King of the Bathroom. Kohler had the edge when it came to toilets, sinks and bathtubs, but Masco owned the lead in faucets. The privately held Kohler had estimated annual sales of $1 billion compared to Masco's $1.3 billion, and neither could stand to see the other take the lead in escaping from the bathroom. They ended up costing each other a lot of money.

POWER MARKETING + JUST IN TIME = MASCO HOME

The plumbers' appetite for furniture companies closely followed Webb Turner's highly publicized crash-and-burn act. You would think the previous failures would give them pause, but such was not the case. In the fall of 1987, after buying Drexel Heritage, Masco confidently stated that it expected to develop a $500 million business in the upper-end but denied that it had a master plan to revolutionize the industry. It just wanted to diversify into a related field and extend the range of the "Masco Home." Its approach was simple – modernize the manufacturing operations by introducing "Just-in-Time" methods to drive out waste, and apply some "Power Marketing" tactics to the selling side of the business. Masco's strategy was so simple, but it never bothered to develop plans to make it happen. Masco just told the furniture people how great Delta was and invited them to copy the Delta methods.

The idea sounded good to the casual observer, but both of the newly acquired divisions had serious problems that Masco would soon need to address. A parallel is the rise and fall of the ancient oriental dynasties, which often decayed from within long before outside observers took notice. Often they created wonderful art and culture at the beginning of their decline. So too, furniture cultures can appear to be flourishing when they are actually headed downward. A strong case could be made that both Henredon and Drexel Heritage had seen better days. For example, Henredon's ill-fated venture into producing furniture with a deep gloss polyester finish would prove to be one of the costliest mistakes in the history of the industry. By 1986, the polyester mistake had already hit the bottom line hard, and more agony was on the way. Yet in June 1986, Masco CEO Manoogian told the *Detroit Free Press* the process was "a big plus, because nobody in this country is doing it or able to do it, and now that they're getting it perfected, they'll have a big jump on everybody else." A big jump it certainly was – but without a parachute.

Drexel Heritage had a different set of problems. With Fred Copeland as the hand-picked successor to Howard Haworth, the company was going through the delicate transition period that often follows the departure of a strong CEO who drove the company to excel beyond its comfort zone. Haworth led the company effectively during the late '70s and '80s, when it was owned by Dominick and Dominick, a private investment group. Before that, the 83-year-old company was owned by U. S. Plywood – Champion Papers acquired it in 1968, shortly after Carpi made his moves. The "plywood paper" years were chaotic, but the company flourished in the hands of the private group that left the capable Haworth alone. As a result, the brand name became powerful; the product line was strengthened by the introduction of several legendary successes; and the company became a leader in both the gallery concept and the free-standing store format. However, the company's past looked brighter than its future. When Haworth retired, management had not addressed the issue of aging production facilities, and critics felt it was losing its clout in the marketplace. Yet Masco was obviously pleased with its new purchase as it reaffirmed its "conviction that Drexel is a logical and important complement to Henredon as a firmly established brand name at the upper end and its intention to keep the Copeland-led team in place."[3]

Wall Street did not respond favorably. Many analysts were highly skeptical of the furniture industry, and few could blame them. Some expressed concerns, especially regarding the apparent lack of proper due diligence, wondering whether Masco had completed its homework. John Stanley of Wertheim and Co. said "the deal carries extra risks for Masco because it is straying outside the areas where it has production and distribution experience. It's woodworking as opposed to metal bending." James Leonard, director of research at First of Michigan Corp., added, "These furniture companies are not as recession resistant as most of Masco's other products."

However, Masco was regarded so highly that most analysts were willing to give the company time to develop a plan. In defense of its controversial move, Masco officials countered that they had other home products that sold well even in downturns. If ever an Outsider existed who looked exactly like what the furniture business needed, Masco just might be the one. Unlike previous Outsider invasions, this one just might turn out to be good for the industry. Initially, the invaders were welcomed as potential saviors of a struggling industry. Most everyone agreed some fresh thinking was needed.

THE GOLD DUST TWINS

What Masco needed to make a success of its bold new venture was a world-class executive with a combination of broad-gauge

managerial skills and a keen understanding of the unique aspects
of the furniture business – a leader who could be Masco's all-
seeing navigator through the Briar Patch. Its pick would have the
most important position in the industry. This individual would be
under enormous pressure to make the massive investment in the
industry pay off.

At the time Masco had to choose, Michael Porter was teaching
students at Harvard that most conglomerates, like General Mills
and Masco, failed to add stockholder value. He stressed that consolidation of a fragmented industry could not be accomplished
unless you could change the underlying reasons for the fragmentation. The Business School later published two case studies on
the Masco furniture strategy.[4] But Masco boss Manoogian went
to Yale, not Harvard, and he believed "acquisitions can be an efficient means of entering attractive consumer-market segments
or obtaining particular product or marketing or technical capabilities. These often can be more expeditiously and economically
accomplished through acquisitions rather than by pursuing the
same goals through internal product development or by starting
a new business."[5]

The person Masco needed to lead its furniture division did not
exist. Masco bosses sensed that outside talent imported from another industry was not the way to go, but they found the ranks of
talent inside the industry to be exceedingly thin. What they got
was a package deal of two clever furniture warriors: Drexel Heritage president Fred Copeland and creative leader Darrell Ferguson. Copeland was appointed group vice president of the newly
formed Masco Home Furnishings Group in March 1987, and
Ferguson was appointed executive vice president of marketing.

Although neither individual could be described as being a broad-gauge business executive, both knew the furniture business. The two were close friends who complemented each other well. The intense, driven Copeland could sell anything and had an eye for talent. The easygoing, friendly Ferguson could design anything and had an eye for what would sell. Their rise to this level was rapid and filled with propitious timing. Their greatest asset by far was an abundance of charm, which went a long way to offset any lack of business skills. Besides, they had a wonderful way of never taking things too seriously, as if they knew it was all just a big game and the way to win was to have more fun than the other guy.

Copeland, a University of Georgia graduate, had been a mattress salesman and then a sales representative for Henredon before becoming the company's assistant sales manager in 1976 at age 31. In early 1977, he was made sales VP of the Marimont Division, a failed attempt at making low-cost sofas. In April 1979, he set up his own company in partnership with another Henredon sales representative, Edward Manderson. But he did this while still in the employ of Henredon without telling President Bill Smith. When Smith found out in the middle of the April Market, he fired Copeland and his accomplice. The Frederick Edward venture eventually got off the ground, but Manderson died unexpectedly. Manderson was replaced by Drexel Heritage creative director Darrell Ferguson, who was generally credited with building that company's product line into one of the best in the industry. A graduate of the University of North Carolina at Chapel Hill, where he majored in business administration, Ferguson also was trained as a furniture designer by the Kendall School of Design. He worked for Drexel Heritage as a product designer and distinguished himself by paying attention to what consumers and dealers wanted. Most designers stay close to their drafting tables and disdain the tawdry world of sales. Not Darrell – he loved the marketplace, could spot trends quickly, and then create designs to meet emerging consumer needs.

Even so, the struggling Frederick Edward Co. was just barely breaking even when Drexel Heritage President Howard Haworth decided to step down and needed a successor. Copeland was unproven, but Haworth figured with proper support, he would grow into the job. So, he bought out Frederick Edward primarily to get the two owners on board.

In 1985, Copeland was named president of Drexel Heritage, and Ferguson returned to his position as vice president, director of design. Before Copeland could demonstrate whether he was up to the challenge of running Drexel Heritage, Masco arrived with its checkbook. Less than 18 months before, they were casually running a tiny upholstery company that was not making any money. Now the Dynamic Duo was running Drexel Heritage and Henredon.

Keep on Shopping

Meanwhile, the Masco acquisition team continued its shopping spree and scooped up three small players. In January 1987, it acquired HickoryCraft, which held a strong niche in mid-priced upholstery led by J. Don Smith. It also picked up LaBarge Mirror, a modest-sized importer of brass accents led by Jim LaBarge, and Marbro Lamp, a small lighting producer led by Jim Caver. It looked a lot like the Carpi vision on a much grander scale. Did someone say, "Masco Home"? How else to explain the acquisition of these small family businesses? Each was totally dependent on the drive of its owner/entrepreneurs. What would motivate them now that they had sold out? Each company was only marginally profitable after providing the owner with a nice lifestyle. How would they ever get earnings up to Masco's goal of 15 percent to 20 percent return on sales? Masco, under pressure from trade publications, implied that the grand plan would soon be revealed. When asked how HickoryCraft would fit in, Treasurer John Nichols quickly countered: "In time, you'll understand how it will complement our total picture." For good measure, they reminded people that in all the acquisitions they had made, "We haven't lost a single management team."[6]

Industry observers looked on in amazement. "They must have a plan," was the most common response, and many felt certain that the only way Masco could justify overpaying for these properties was to support a vertical consolidation strategy involving retail stores. But no plan was ever revealed. These plumbers were not that subtle. They simply figured they were good at making and selling home products like faucets and such, they knew how to make acquisitions, and they had a lot of cash to invest. Their research pointed out that there were not many places where they could find a home for all the cash they had to invest, and the furniture business looked so easy to them. How hard could it be to make bedrooms and dining rooms? Besides, if they just kept buying companies, they could surely have a sustainable competitive advantage. By now, Kohler had stopped trying to keep up with Masco, perhaps because of the problems with Baker. They picked up a few small companies who were suppliers to the Baker designer showrooms, but they prudently chose not to match Masco's "shop-till-you-drop" frenzy.

In April 1987, Masco made a few changes. The Frederick Edward upholstery division was put together with HickoryCraft to form a new upholstery division to be headed by J. Don Smith. Making Smith a group executive meant he would be one step removed from his own operation, causing some customers to wonder if HickoryCraft would suffer as a result. Frederick Edward had been languishing at Drexel Heritage, despite having the potentially lucrative Ralph Lauren license, and it was hoped putting it under Smith would rejuvenate it.

In August 1987, Masco bought three more furniture companies – Lexington Furniture Industries for $225 million, Maitland-Smith Hong Kong for $10 million, and Marge Carson Inc. for an undisclosed amount. Masco, like Webb Turner, thought nothing of buying a company just to get talented individuals. What they failed to understand was that those individuals might not use their talents as productively in a corporate environment as they did in their own companies. But for now, everybody was happy. Bob and Carole Carson, the talented husband/wife team who had made their small West Coast upholstery company esteemed by their peers if not very profitable, got a bunch of Masco money. So too did Paul Maitland-Smith, the creative and prolific Englishman who pioneered highly stylized products sourced in the Far East. Fred and Darrell brought some respected competitors on board and now could pick their brains at will. And Masco executives were having a lot more fun than they ever did selling faucets to Home Depot.

Then there was Lexington, the furniture man's furniture company, the toughest kid on the block, the one warrior you did not want to challenge. Lexington was a true low-cost producer with a sense for the marketplace that could knock you out with a well-executed and sharply priced group usually copied blatantly from a higher end competitor. It was led by J. Smith Young, a tough ex-Navy officer who shelled the Germans while on a destroyer during the landings at Normandy on D-Day. In good times or bad, the former Dixie Furniture could be counted on to do well. Recently, the company had begun to extend its range with the introduction of some original designs, thanks to the marketing and merchandising skills of Jeff Young, Smith's son. Lexington was, arguably, the best company in the middle of the market and putting it together with Henredon and Drexel Heritage was downright intimidating. Lexington sales were above $200 million.

The Maitland-Smith acquisition completed an earlier transaction in which Henredon had acquired half of the company with an option to pick up the balance. Henredon, in effect, had served as the midwife for Maitland-Smith, striking a deal with founder Paul Maitland-Smith and giving his fabulous designs a prominent showroom, a sales force with access to the best retailers in the country, a North American delivery system, and a visibility it would never have had on its own. Maitland-Smith, in return, gave Henredon some great values and a style excitement it had lost since the demise of Ken Volz. Because the product was made in the Philippines with low-cost skilled labor, it was very well priced. This allowed Henredon to make a nice profit margin on top of the Maitland-Smith margin. Sales worldwide were only $15 million, but they were growing rapidly. The problem was the venture was hard to manage because of its remote location and could not make the goods fast enough.

Now What

Masco's invasion of the furniture industry had now gone well beyond the original targets. In 1986, Masco said it aimed to hit $500 million in sales within five years and would focus on the upper end.[7] Now it had extended into the mid-market and openly talked about going for $1 billion within five years.[8] It had certainly acquired the leading companies and had accumulated some of the best talent in the business. If it could create an environment in which the entrepreneurs would remain motivated and the talent would be channeled into the larger divisions, these expensive acquisitions might pay off. If, on the other hand, the talented entrepreneurs became frustrated and constrained by corporate impediments, Masco would find itself with a garage full of fine cars it would not know how to drive. Top managers seemed to understand this and pointed with pride to their history of acquisitions. "Once a company is acquired, Masco pursues a 'hands-off' management approach that preserves company culture and rewards individual initiative. The managers of the new Masco division continue to function as entrepreneurs who set their own goals and strategies."[9] Perhaps more importantly, they bragged about their small corporate staff in Taylor, Michigan, and insisted that they had no plans to centralize any functions beyond the obvious areas like legal, finance, and benefits administration.

As Colin Carpi, Jim Mills, Webb Turner, and a host of other would-be "furniture conquerors" discovered, buying furniture companies is easy but running them is altogether different. The combination of Masco's vaunted expertise and the Gold Dust Twins' furniture savvy might not have been enough to tame the beast collected by Masco's voracious acquisition team. In retrospect, it appears that Masco gave little thought to what to do with its patchwork quilt of clashing elements. Under the best of circumstances, it would have been incredibly difficult to manage, much less to meet Masco's expectations. By their own admission, they had just assumed the retail channel would welcome their arrival. Instead, dealers resented and resisted the plumbers at every turn. The highly touted "Power Marketing" system failed to impress anyone, and the fashion side of the business baffled the technically oriented men from Michigan. Instead of unleashing a well-conceived strategy, perhaps involving a chain of retail stores with a white glove home delivery system and some powerful national advertising, Masco reverted to the engineering side of the business, where they were more comfortable. They hoped they could "modernize" what they considered to be antiquated manufacturing methods. But even in this area, the initiatives were tentative. They acted as if a transformation would happen by osmosis. Simply expose the furniture guys to a Delta Faucet plant and they would see the light. A steady stream of "experts" were sent from Michigan to North Carolina to convert the "unwashed," but those experts invariably were confused by the complexity of the furniture-making process and failed to make any improvements. Had the furniture types been more receptive to new methods and less protective of the old ways, it might have been a different story.

Copeland and Ferguson were left to handle the day-to-day duties, which were considerable. In July 1987, Masco made Copeland president of the Home Furnishings Group and Ferguson a senior vice president. Organizationally, they faced a challenge coming out of the gates. Henredon's long-time president, Bill Smith, had retired shortly after the arrival of Masco. Working for an Outsider did not appeal to him, and he sensed Ferguson's star was on the rise. Considering the fact that Smith had fired Copeland eight years earlier, he made the easy decision to leave before being asked. Filling this slot proved to be difficult. Henredon people had strong, almost arrogant beliefs in their own superiority, making it very hard for a newcomer to take control. Yet no capable "number two" inside person existed. Masco naturally wanted a "world-class" CEO to fill this position, but Copeland instinctively knew that an outsider would have a hard time being accepted. A lot was at stake. Henredon needed a turnaround, but Masco could not bear to admit that it paid that much for a dysfunctional company.

Copeland and the Masco headhunter, Dave Kinsella, searched the industry for talent. The pickings were slim. This portent should have had a sobering effect on Masco, but they were still in the "Lotus eating" phase and ignored the signal. Steve Pond, the insightful founder/publisher of the trade journal *Furniture Today*, was asked what he thought of Masco's furniture invasion and his prophetic reply was, "I just don't see how they are going to be able to find enough managers to run these companies the way they want them to be run." At Drexel Heritage, earlier in the year, the choice for president had been W. Paul Monroe, a veteran insider who had been the company's chief financial officer for years. Henredon tried hard to select a president from within but was not comfortable with the likely candidates. So it went outside the company, but not the industry, and recruited the author from Jamestown Sterling.

With the armies assembled and generals selected, very little had been done to formulate a strategic battle plan. All the warriors knew was that they were expected to win, and that meant a 20 percent pretax return on sales, higher than anyone had seen in many years. Copeland's style was to pick the best people he could find and then turn them loose. Masco's style, in the beginning, was not much different. They bragged about the small size of their corporate staff was and insisted "our businesses are run by people who know their industries and the people in the industries. We let our companies make their own judgments and we support that."[10]

THE MARKETS SHOW DISPLEASURE

By late 1987, things had already started to go wrong. Soon after Masco paid peak multiples on peak earnings to acquire the first group of cyclically driven furniture companies, the stock market collapsed. On a single day during the October Market that year, the Dow Jones Industrial Average dropped 616 points – more than 20 percent – signaling the end of Reagan era of "conspicuous consumption" patterns for upper-end consumers. This, in turn, rattled the upper-end dealers who de-emphasized the luxury segment by adjusting their merchandise assortment downward. Many never recovered. The shrinkage in the dealer base hit Henredon and Drexel hard. The original Masco acquisition strategy had been to concentrate on the high-end. Now, the high-end fell out of favor with investors as retailers and consumers pulled back. It would eventually cost Masco close to a $1 billion to get out of the Briar Patch.

To make matters worse, Fred Copeland's streak of good fortune ran out. In December, he and Darrell Ferguson flew to Cebu, Philippines, where Paul Maitland-Smith, the eponymous head of Maitland-Smith Ltd, presided over a tropical community like a British colonial governor. Copeland and Ferguson needed time to get away, relax, and think about what to do next. The responsibilities they had been handed by Masco were far beyond anything they had ever seen. The thought of it was exciting; the reality of all this responsibility was sobering. While in the Philippines, Fred Copeland's wife of 20 years was found shot to death in the master bedroom of their home in Morganton, North Carolina. She had committed suicide.

Susan Copeland's tragic death shocked the Morganton community, where she was well liked and had many friends. Speculation was rampant as to what might drive a mother of two young children to end her life, just as her husband had landed the top job in the furniture industry, but a definitive answer was never found. Just as Laura Carpi's death seemed senseless, so too did Susan's. Fred was grief-stricken but received a great deal of sympathy and support from his many friends.

In the meantime, Masco Home Furnishings finished 1987 as the largest upper-end manufacturer in the country and the second-largest furniture company overall. It reported sales of $799 million and $122 million in operating profits. The 15 percent operating profits were respectable by furniture standards, but Masco made it clear to divisional management that they were far below what was expected. Nothing short of 20 percent was worth noting, and even that level was only barely acceptable, especially when compared to the Delta Faucet division and its patented, single handle faucet that made 35 percent operating margins. Chief Operating Officer Wayne B. Lyon made it clear in a group meeting that Masco liked interesting companies, and only profitable companies could be called interesting. The furniture managers wondered how they could produce those kinds of numbers when the rest of the industry had trouble reaching double-digit margins.

Briar Patch Invasion

At this point, Masco management had so deeply invaded the Briar Patch that they could not think of turning back. The heady feeling associated with buying companies so easily was quite intoxicating. And then there was the sheer joy of being able to buy all these beautiful products at wholesale. One of the first strategic moves Masco made was to make sure that all the furniture lines were included in the Masco Employee Purchase Plan, which let employees buy Masco products from other divisions at factory cost.

Having set that up, they went back to the acquisition game and picked off a fabric distributor, Robert Allen, paying $125 million for a business whose primary asset was the talent residing in the husband/wife team who founded it. As long as Alan and Carol Wyatt remained motivated to work round the clock, this investment would pay off. Otherwise, it was a high-risk move, because neither Masco nor any of its furniture companies knew anything about the fabric business. For good measure, Masco later bought another fabric company, Sunbury Textiles, a small weaver with sales of less than $20 million. Although these companies were suppliers to the industry, they had little in common with the furniture companies, and rather than fitting into the group's complexity, they added to it.

By this time, Wall Street analysts were openly questioning Masco's diversification move, and investors reacted accordingly. The stock, after hitting a high of $39, fell to $26 by midyear 1988. While Masco historically had traded at a price-to-earnings ratio of 25 percent to 35 percent higher than the Standard and Poor average, it was now selling at a 15 percent discount.

Operating results continued to fall short of Masco standards, but they were still well above average by historic furniture standards. This was because the original entrepreneurs were still in charge, and the companies themselves had positive momentum when they were acquired. After all, Masco had selected the best and the brightest people and brands the industry had to offer. These companies were leaders in their respective categories. Also, the economy was still strong, although the first telltale signs of a slowdown were already in evidence. The stock market crash of 1987 began to impact the furniture business slowly as the inevitable down cycle began. Furniture was always one of the first categories to feel it as consumers tightened their belts. Faucets were different, as were the other products Masco made, and management had a difficult time accepting the cyclicality of furniture. Denying it was much easier. Instead of paring back and getting ready to ride out the expected downturn, they added overhead at the corporate and division levels. Like many other outside invaders, Masco never seemed to understand that the margins in furniture couldn't support the expenses associated with many desirable projects.

There's a New Kid in Town

Throughout the year after his wife's death, Fred Copeland's personal problems continued, and his cavalier management style began to wear a little thin with the Faucet Barons. Copeland worked intensely, but not for long hours. He was effective in one-on-one situations but rarely bothered to read his mail or return phone calls. He became bored easily and liked to change the scenery, restlessly moving on to more interesting pastures. It was inevitable that he would become disenchanted with the more serious demeanor of Masco. The Plumbers wanted someone more attuned to their thinking, someone who was less independent and more inclined to make changes in the furniture operations. They found Ron Jones, who on August 11 was appointed to the newly created post of President–Furniture Group, reporting to Copeland. Masco must have felt pleased to find a professional executive like Jones who was not a "furniture person." He had an MBA from Southern Methodist University and a divinity degree, which may well have been needed. Plus, to their way of thinking, he had furniture experience, having served as the president and COO of HON Industries, a producer of low priced filing cabinets and desks. In contrast, the furniture insiders dismissed experience with office furniture, because the production methods and the marketing channels were so different. Only rarely have managers successfully moved from the office furniture field to the residential furniture industry.

More Overhead Gets Layered on Top

Recognizing that the transition from Copeland to Jones may be problematic, Masco tried to soften the impact with an odd office arrangement. With Jones' appointment came news that Ferguson and Copeland would set up offices in Atlanta while Jones would set up offices in High Point. The divisional CEOs, instinctively distrustful of all bosses, now had three corporate offices to contend with – one in Taylor, Michigan, one in High Point, and one in Atlanta. As the old saying goes, "If my boss calls, get his name."

Masco had a very lean headquarters staff in Michigan when it moved into the furniture business, and the original Home Furnishings Group office consisted of only six people – Ferguson and Copeland, their two secretaries, an assistant to help Ferguson stay organized, plus Group Controller Jim Melton. They were housed in a small rented office over a bank in Morganton, North Carolina. At the time the office opened, Copeland told a *Furniture Today* reporter, "We will stay right here. We need to be on the scene on a day-to-day basis so we'll keep these offices here in the heart of the furniture manufacturing industry."[11] The operating divisions themselves had learned long ago to operate with a minimal staff. The money they spent on overhead was usually aimed at either making or selling the products. The margins could not support additional costs.

Yet, like a relentless plague, overhead spending increased at all four levels. Ferguson and Copeland built a stunningly expensive office in Atlanta. Jones set up his base in a newly purchased building in High Point. And Masco added a huge new wing to its Michigan main headquarters. More people were added at all locations, and those people needed staffs to support them, so still more people were added. Then, the various main headquarters people and their staffs needed projects to work on, so they visited the divisions looking for problems that might fit their pre-conceived solutions. Not to be outdone, the group people also visited the divisions. While there, they invariably found something to criticize and wrote reports designed to demonstrate their value. To respond to the critical reports and to deal with the home office people, the group headquarters hired more people and staff. These people needed staffs to help them, so still more people were added. Then the divisions had to add people to correct the problems spotted by the group and headquarters people. Division reports were written in response to the headquarters reports; before long, a great deal of time and money was being spent on activities that had nothing to do with adding value to the products.

In a move that said a lot about the contrasting directions of both companies, the building purchased by Masco to house the Home Furnishings Group had been a large, freestanding market showroom owned by LADD. In the transaction, LADD's Dick Allen was converting a superfluous asset to cash, while Masco was creating a larger, more elaborate home for its rapidly growing overhead staff.

Sales in 1988 climbed to $1.358 billion, and operating profits were $186 million. Not bad at all considering the distractions at the top, but margins slipped slightly from 15 percent to 13.6 percent. Masco management continued to express their displeasure with the numbers and made it clear that they would see to it that next year things would turn around. Little did they realize that future results would make these numbers look marvelous.

MASCO GOES GLOBAL

The economy refused to cooperate in 1989, especially for high-end, big-ticket goods. Consumers began to turn away from conspicuous consumption as the "good enough" syndrome took hold. Instead of generating "Masco type" margins, the furniture companies headed in the wrong direction. Masco management, to its credit, did not flinch. It bravely continued to advance, so much so, that it made still another substantial acquisition. In March, Masco bought Universal Furniture Ltd., a Hong Kong based producer of popularly priced wood furniture. With sales of $500 million, Universal became the industry's fourth largest company. The purchase price was $480 million, a hefty sum for a company whose margins were far below Masco's minimum expectation. In fact, the purchase actually resulted in a dilution of Masco's earnings in the amount of 7 cents per share in 1988. However, the added volume put Masco's home furnishings sales at $1.5 billion, propelling them to the top and setting a new industry record.

Industry veterans questioned why Masco wanted to take on this complicated entity before it figured out what to do with its earlier purchases. Cynical observers predicted that the high-end oriented group running Masco was going to find out in a hurry that the world of Universal was very different from the world to which they had become accustomed. What the industry sages failed to realize was that several Wall Street analysts had been ripping Masco for placing too much emphasis on the upper end. So, rather than focusing on the upper segment within the industry, they decided to spread the risk by doing what they knew how to do – pay top dollar for the leader of the low end. The official rationale lamely talked about "permitting us to offer our customers a true good-better-best selection."

Universal was the brain child of Laurance Zung and Larry Moh, who pioneered the model of a furniture company that combined high-powered North American marketing savvy with low-cost Far Eastern labor to become the preeminent low-cost producer of well-designed collections and suites. They revolutionized the industry with their brilliant concept of making pre-finished parts in Taiwan, where labor costs were minuscule, shipping them disassembled to save freight costs, and quickly assembling furniture at strategically located plants across America. The company struck fear in the hearts of its competitors because of its amazing values, but that was not the only advantage it held. Universal placed a high value on recruiting talented marketing and sales types who made sure the products and promotions were at the leading edge. The acquisition gave Masco a presence in the Far East, which many felt was the wave of the future. Once again, the challenge was how to make the talent productive so that the opportunity would pay off. Universal was not like anything Masco had seen before. Unlike the other Masco divisions, Universal operated in the mass market, distributing its goods through stores like Levitz, Sears, Rhodes, and Heilig-Myers. This retail channel was a world apart from Henredon and Drexel Heritage. And Universal's production facilities were now spread across 10 countries, but Taiwan remained the center of its manufacturing power in spite of an alarming rise in wages there. It was hard to rationalize the purchase of this multinational, complex organization, but as long as the Hong Kong-based founders, Zung and Moh, stuck around, and the High Point based marketing and sales wizards stayed focused, maybe it would be okay. Otherwise, it wouldn't take much to flip this tank into a ditch. Either way, things just became a whole lot more complicated for top management.

THE GOLD DUST TWINS JUST FADE AWAY

At this point, Masco had too many furniture entities to manage effectively – and too many managers managing them. Jones and Copeland respectfully kept their distance from each other, but each clearly considered himself to be the commander in chief. Then, of course, there was Masco President Wayne Lyon, who made it clear that he was the true commander in chief. The division commanders struggled with their own battles not knowing what was happening at headquarters. In September 1989, Lyon issued a corporate proclamation intended to clear everything up, but it was so carefully proofread and sanitized that it only confused matters even more. "Major multi-million dollar coordinated sales opportunities are developing requiring enhanced inter-divisional cooperation," it started. "To optimize these initiatives and provide operating leadership that will guide our future growth, I am pleased to announce the following executive promotions and appointments." The memo said "Ron Jones, formerly President – Furniture Group had been made President – Home Furnishings Products" and "Fred Copeland, formerly Group President home furnishings group, will assume additional corporate responsibilities in the newly created position of Chairman – Home Furnishings Products."

The rank and file tried to decipher what it meant. Who was the boss? A chairman outranked a president, or did he? "Furnishings" seemed to be bigger than "Furniture," or was it? And, why was part of Copeland's former title set in lower case? Was this possibly the beginning of his disappearance, not unlike the way Stalin would erase the photos and records of party officials who had fallen from favor? Who could tell?

The clearest signals came from the grapevine, which reported that Ferguson had bought a house in Charleston. Sure enough, a small notice in *Furniture Today* said Masco would set up a design center there that Ferguson would head. The cost would top $1 million by the time it was completed, but it was nicer than the Atlanta office that now stood empty. In day-to-day activities, Copeland was nowhere to be seen, while Jones was very much in evidence. That is not to say Copeland's presence was not felt. His stature as a living legend continued, and his propensity for audacious behavior was unchecked. It was obvious to the troops that the scepter was being passed from General Copeland to General Jones.

WAR COSTS ESCALATE

On January 3, 1990, Masco reported that, for the first time in 33 years, its earnings actually declined over the prior year. The sensational track record, started by Alex Manoogian in 1956 and continued by his son, Richard, was a casualty of the Furniture Wars. "We're embarrassed," said Treasurer John Nichols. "It's our first down year in more than three decades."[12] The lavish Annual Report referred to it as "a humbling experience." Earnings per share were expected to be $1.50 vs. $2.03 the year before. The Furnishings Group ended the year at the top of the industry with sales of $1.460 billion, including Universal, but profits fell 23 percent to $142 million. Even though the operating margin of 9.75 percent was an embarrassment to Masco, it still looked awfully good to the furniture Insiders.[13]

Privately, the mood of Masco's top brass was tough. The public humiliation was too much to bear, and the woeful performance of the furniture group was intolerable. Even the next tier of managers, people in the plumbing products divisions who had nothing to do with furniture, were hostile toward the furniture group because their Masco stock holdings had declined in value. All at headquarters in Taylor, Michigan, agreed: The furniture mess simply had to be fixed, or else. The problem was no one knew what to do next. They still did not seem to grasp the realities of the industry they had paid too much to enter, and they had yet to develop a coherent strategy. But, they had a new general and fervently hoped that Ron Jones could make their huge investment pay off. The furniture industry had a lot at stake as well. If Masco failed, it would deter other outside investors and be a major setback for the industry in serious need of outside help and capital. If it succeeded, it might wipe out some weaker competitors. All eyes were trained on the Man from HON.

LESSONS LEARNED

Masco and Kohler launched major invasions of the Furniture Zone in the mid to late '80s. Their well-financed armies met no resistance in the early battles, and many of the industry's prized territories were captured. That is to say, they were bought off. Like those who proceeded them, these invaders then discovered that capturing ground was much easier than occupying it. Life in the Briar Patch was reasonably pleasant if the occupation forces accepted its limitations, but they ran into trouble as soon as they tried to remake its culture, to transform it, or to dominate it. The industry's Border Patrol is weak, but its Resistance Movement is implacable.

The Plumbers were not good students of history. They chose to ignore the lessons learned by earlier invaders. In spite of this, here are lessons from the Plumbers' early days in the Briar Patch.

NEED TO DO HOMEWORK: Masco made a dramatic entry with the purchase of the "crown jewel" Henredon and followed with an equally dramatic capture of Drexel Heritage, but it did nothing to follow through except continuing to buy companies. If there were a plan or a strategy, they never revealed it, and a golden opportunity was missed because they lacked strategic discipline. Better intelligence would have helped. Robert E. Lee's forces were handicapped at Gettysburg because General Jeb Stuart and his cavalry were off looking for a boot factory and failed to provide Lee with a complete picture of the enemy forces. Masco studied the manufacturing side of the furniture business and saw opportunity, but it neglected to study the distribution side – which by far is the more challenging of the two. More diligence might have revealed more than the raw numbers. Success in the furniture business can slip away quickly. Misreading the subtle signals can be costly, and current statements will not tell you what will happen. Smart decisions and great designs made in the 1970s fueled Henredon successes in the '80s, just as costly decisions and weak designs made in the '80s hurt Henredon in the '90s. The same could be said of Drexel Heritage.

MICHAEL PORTER SHOULD HAVE BEEN HEARD: Porter was remarkably prescient when he showed how diversification strategies don't work. "The track record of corporate strategies has been dismal. . . . The corporate strategies of most companies have dissipated instead of created shareholder value."[14] He also specifically warned against entering highly fragmented industries. "In the economists' perfectly competitive world, jockeying for position is unbridled and entry to the industry very easy. This kind of industry structure, of course, offers the worst prospect for long-run profitability."[15]

BE WARY OF EASY SOLUTIONS: Masco management tended to act as if the furniture practitioners were not all that bright. Much was made of Delta's vaunted Power Marketing tactic that Masco assumed it would take the industry by storm. When the furniture people saw the plan, it turned out to be less sophisticated than some programs already in existence. Take a look at what Pennsylvania House did in the 1970s and you will see a level of marketing effectiveness higher than Delta Faucet's in the '80s. Furniture marketing is more art than science, and importing tactics from other industries is like panning for fool's gold.

BEWARE OF SMALL COMPANIES: More caution should have been exercised evaluating the small companies – before the acquisitions. They are just as hard to manage as big ones and, invariably, they must have motivated entrepreneurs to lead them. The small operating units in furniture can easily drain management time, making it impossible to focus on the big units. "They weren't really tuck-ins, which would have made sense, they were glop-ons. All of these just soaked up management time," said Budd Bugatch, an industry expert with Raymond James & Associates and a former furniture retailer.[16]

CORPORATE STAFF DRAINS DIVISION STRENGTH: As the old military adage puts it: "Lead, follow, or get out of the way." Masco loaded the corporate office with high-priced staff people who only managed to frustrate the divisional people. These corporate people, for the most part, could not justify the added costs they brought to the table. The result was confusion in the ranks and erosion of the margins.

Had Masco been able to create an environment in which entrepreneurial people could thrive, the results likely would have been different. The furniture business is entrepreneurially driven, and if your best managers are frustrated by corporate restrictions and not allowed to "do their thing," your competitors will take your market share and your entrepreneurs away. Masco claimed to be a big believer in this philosophy and paid a premium to attract the industry's best entrepreneurs, but it did not give them adequate running room.[17]

KEEPING UP
WITH THE JONESES

"Some of those who have invested in Masco's shares over the years have wondered why management chose to enter what has up to now been a rather prosaic industry with mediocre returns and growth rates. We believe that the appropriate answer reflects both what the company has always been and what the furniture industry could become." Richard Manoogian, chairman and chief executive officer of Masco, was recently quoted as saying, "We think our strategy is simple. It amazes us that nobody else seems to practice it."

Smith Barney Research Report, June 19, 1990

IN THE TWO YEARS AFTER the stock market crash of 1987, upper-end furniture companies resembled a squadron of B-24 bombers returning from a bombing run in Germany. Hit by enemy fire, some crashed and burned while others kept on flying. High-end furniture manufacturers and especially retailers found themselves in similar straits. The unique "top-down" aspect of the 1989–1992 recessions hit the white collar, well-to-do consumer particularly hard, and purveyors of top-of-the-line goods suffered along with their customers.

Order rates for high-end goods declined as consumers pulled back or traded down. Manufacturers promoted like mad, driving down margins but not stimulating business. Retailers cut inventory levels and advertising expenditures, which only worsened the picture. When the economy recovered, it was led by non-durables and services, but the furniture industry did not come back with the rest of the economy. The painfully familiar pattern of the furniture cycle had struck again – leading the downturn, lagging the upturn. By early 1990, Masco stock was trading at $23.50, 43 percent below 1987 levels. The heat was on to make the diversification move into the Furniture Zone pay off – but how?

JONES & JONES

In 1988 Ron Jones, an amiable, hardworking Missourian, had been handed the keys to Masco Home Furnishings, an agglomeration of companies that some said was impossible to manage. He was told to lead this amorphous pile of assets to unprecedented levels of profitability. The situation reminded one of a *New Yorker* cartoon in which the boss, speaking with another executive whom he has just hired, says, "Look, Jones, your job is simple. All you have to do is make sense out of these broken-down companies I paid too much for, so I'll look like a genius." Masco President Wayne Lyon, who prided himself on being a Jimmy Cagney-like tough guy, always demanding results "or else," was now seriously concerned by the way business was going in the furniture group. Not only had the group failed to produce the "Masco-type margins" he insisted on, they were now headed downward. This was not what the Masco Board had in mind when it agreed to fund this invasion.

Now that the flamboyant furniture guy, Fred Copeland, was being removed, Lyon had an individual more to his liking. In his own courteous way, Jones was also a bit of a maverick, but he had neither Copeland's verve nor his reckless tendencies. During his initial introduction to the furniture group, he surprised the image-conscious audience by appearing in a warm-up suit. Lyon pointedly explained that Jones had recently lost a great deal of weight and had no suits that fit. In spite of this, he impressed people with his quiet self-assurance. Tall and broad shouldered, his imposing physical presence was balanced by a quick smile and a friendly, soft-spoken manner.

Although Jones had spent five years at HON industries, a producer of low-cost desks and file cabinets for offices, nothing in his background could have prepared him for what he was about to experience. The office contract furniture field bears no resemblance to the residential furniture game, so it offered Jones little transferable experience. Earlier in his career, he had experience making beer barrels, but it was a stretch to see how this would help him with the fashion aspects of the furniture business. Finally, he had experience and training as a minister, but he would need more than sanctifying grace to deal with all the entrepreneurial egos in his new parish. His journey into the Furniture Zone would be challenging, especially when he attempted to make the difficult passage between the treacherous rocks at Masco headquarters in

Taylor, Michigan, and the whirlpool of the low-margin industry. Jones was in for a wild ride with the demanding Wayne Lyon on one side and cantankerous furniture warlords on the other.

He needed help in navigating these waters, and he correctly sensed that the furniture veterans might view him as a usurper and might not give him their undying loyalty. There was no animosity toward him, and the divisional heads certainly wanted him to succeed. It's just that they were not used to having a boss of any kind, and dealing with one who had not shared the Furniture Zone experience with them was difficult. The battle-scarred commanders of the Masco furniture armies knew that the intensity level was rising, and they were understandably nervous about their new leader. The economy was souring, Lyon was pressuring, and the competition was poised to exploit Masco's confusion. These were not good times to have anything less than a commander-in-chief with a great deal of furniture experience, and Jones did not have it. But he was very likable and trustworthy, so the division CEOs tried hard to please him. Although he tended to become caught up in the details, he demonstrated a great deal of self-confidence and kept his troops on the attack even when his battle plans were failing. The thought of retreating and regrouping was not in his playbook.

As the early battle lines were being drawn, Jones announced he had retained someone to help the divisions become more sophisticated in marketing and public relations. The divisions were not overly impressed. Marketing was not their long suit, and publicity was thought to be a waste of time. The person just happened to be a woman, which by itself was hard for some of the good-old furniture boys to swallow. She had no residential furniture experience, which was a problem for others. But what really upset the crew was the openly acknowledged fact that she and Ron Jones were dating and planned to get married. They did so in January 1989, creating the highest profile husband/wife team in the furniture business. Husband and wife teams were not unusual in the furniture business, and everyone at Masco tried to make the best of the situation, but the comfort level was not there for many people. Linda worked hard and brought numerous ideas to the table, but many of them were not on target, given her lack of residential furniture experience. Because of her relationship with Ron and because he enthusiastically endorsed her ideas, no one challenged her.

LET'S REWRITE THE RULES

As a Semi-Outsider, Jones tried hard to understand the residential furniture business and explain it to Lyon, but the more Jones explained it, the less Lyon liked it. Without Copeland around to defend the furniture point of view, it became fashionable at Masco's upper level to criticize the furniture methods and to dispute the advice of the experienced furniture people. Curiously, these were the same experts Masco paid so much to have in the first place. Rather than taking the time to comprehend the industry practices and fully engage the wealth of talent on board, Masco's top brass decided to rewrite the rules. They spared no expense in the process. By this time, Masco had accumulated close to 40 different furniture brand names, from Polo Ralph Lauren and Henredon at the top, to Universal and Benchcraft at the bottom. Yet it was decided that the industry needed another brand – one that would be started from scratch. This meant that the Jones/Lyon group could control every element and break away from the annoying objections of the furniture people, without wasting any more time learning the foolish tricks of the trade that didn't work anyway. Instead of learning the intricacies of the Furniture Game, they would just ignore them. When the new brand became a big hit, as it surely would, they could then demonstrate how the furniture people should go about their jobs the right way. Best of all, they had Linda Jones to apply her talents to the task.

•

LINEAGE LAUNCHED

Jones and Jones could hardly wait to get started. And who could blame them? After months of being patronized by the recalcitrant good-old boys, patiently dealing with constraints set by Masco, and encountering resistance from retailers, they were free to design a company exactly as they felt it should be designed. Their intentions were good. By doing market research, they hoped to have a better understanding of consumers. From their perspective, their vision of a retailer- and consumer-focused furniture company designed to address the Baby Boomer market seemed like the perfect answer to Masco's dilemma. Others thought it was insane.

In November 1989, they selected Tom Tilley, a respected Thomasville product man, to head the new division. Jones used a *cherchez le creneau* type matrix to rationalize the move. Using the matrix like Colin Carpi used his grid, Jones pointed out that Masco had plenty of coverage with widely distributed, moderately priced lines (such as Universal and Lexington) and plenty of coverage with limited-distribution, higher priced lines (such as Henredon and Drexel Heritage), but nothing in the category of moderately priced lines with limited distribution. The origin of this observation came from the countless times dealers told Jones that they loved what Lexington and Universal offered but wished they could have it exclusively. This age-old retail complaint fell on deaf ears at the division level. When Wes Collins of Universal or Smith Young of Lexington were asked why they did not grant more exclusives by limiting their dealer base, they would just smile and say, "Because we don't have to. As long as the product is good enough, the dealers will tolerate broad distribution. That means we sell more, have longer production runs, and keep our costs down. That's just the way it is in the furniture business." Jones felt he could change this. Where he came from, suppliers took customer complaints seriously. Overlooked in this analysis was the fact that Masco already had Drexel Heritage, a furniture company with moderately priced products and narrow distribution. The problem was that the Drexel product line was not very strong. It would have been simpler and more effective to fix this line, but Jones and Lyon chose a more dramatic route.

The troubles started quickly. Those closest to the project – which was named "Lineage" – insisted on mispronouncing the brand, giving it two syllables, "LIN-idge," rather than the proper three syllables, "LIN-ee-idge." Masco charged ahead anyway. On April 16, 1990, Tom Tilley announced, "The goal of Lineage Home Furnishings is to create an entirely new furniture company, one that is consumer-driven, retailer-responsive and innovative in every way.

With the power of Masco Home Furnishings Group behind it, Lineage is positioned and committed to serve key retailers with a comprehensive assortment of casegoods, upholstery, accessories, fabrics, and retail support programs."[1] The annoying undercurrent, of course, was the implication that all other furniture companies are *not* responsive to their retailers or driven by consumers. Ron Jones expressed it differently with the correct "Mascotalk" haze, saying, "The new company will reflect the strategic opportunities offered through the cooperative strengths of the group of Masco companies now assembled."[2]

The furniture veterans urged Jones to go slowly in order to avoid the huge risk associated with this campaign. According to them, there were other battles that needed attention. The Drexel Heritage store program had big problems, and Universal needed help with logistics to manage the ever-increasing flow of goods from Asia. Many believed it would have made more sense to leverage one of the smaller brands, such as Maitland-Smith or Frederick Edward. They felt there was something about Lineage that did not ring true. Committing so many resources to it might expose the core divisions to competitive attacks, in their view. Jones and Lyon were not swayed by these arguments, because they had heard them all before. Like the legendary cavalry officer who mounted his horse and rode off in all directions, Jones and Lyon ignored the entreaties of the seasoned veterans. Besides, the real audience here was the Wall Street analysts who had been nagging Masco since the day it entered the Briar Patch. They had an annoying habit of asking Manoogian what his plan was, and he, in turn, would ask his staff to spell out the strategy. The pressure to come up with a plan was huge, and Lineage looked like the best bone to throw to the analysts.

PRUDENCE VS. PROFLIGACY

Profligacy often fills the void when prudence is absent, and Masco had money to spend. All the expenses that the core divisions had learned to live without – such as ad agencies, public relations, top-notch photography, elaborate catalogs, and fancy offices – were part of Lineage long before it sold the first piece of furniture. Even before the products were designed, the decision was made to build a new showroom and distribution center in Greensboro. Drexel and Henredon both needed new showrooms, but they were told to put their needs on hold for the time being. Lineage was more important. Drexel Heritage and Henredon could have used an extra creative person or two to help improve their product lines, but they were told to get by with what they had. Meanwhile, new Lineage president Tom Tilley hired five vice presidents.

Having paid close to $500 million dollars for Henredon and Drexel Heritage, Masco invested another $125 million or so to create a new in-house competitor. The effect on Henredon and Drexel was demoralizing, especially when answering incredulous questions from the retailers. Lyon and Jones were convinced that the creation of this new company, free from the insidious influence of the furniture Insiders, would prove that they were right about how things should be. Nothing could stand in their way, certainly not the counsel of the in-house rivals. Confident in their own brilliance, they disconnected from reality and ignored the dangers inherent to this situation.

With Lineage, the Outsiders tried to rewrite the rules to coincide with their views. It was somewhat like government officials casting aside military leaders in order to conduct a war on their own. Defying conventional furniture thinking, the Jones and Jones team introduced many innovations. In fact, all of these elements had been done before, or at least tried, but never had all of them been attempted at the same time and with so much money behind the effort. The Insiders were barely able to conceal their envy as they learned what Lineage was doing:

✝ A Retail Advisory Panel was set up to meet dealer needs. Virtually every major decision was made with close involvement by 10 of the best retailers in the industry.

✝ Focus groups made sure the voice of the consumer was heard.

✝ Instead of using a veteran, commissioned sales force, they paid salaries to young men and women who were largely new to the business.

✝ The catalogs were much more elaborate and costlier than normal. Only the best talent was used, no matter what the cost. The basic catalog cost $375,000 just to develop, and it was obsolete within a year.

✝ Copious amounts of sales collateral material were developed.

✝ Dealers received generous incentives up front, including 120 to 160 days dating, 10 percent to 15 percent discounts on the opening order, 25 percent guaranteed markdown money, and funds to cover build-out expenses.

✝ Lineage merchandisers had free access to the showrooms and the confidential rates-of-sale for other Masco divisions, including Henredon, Ralph Lauren, Drexel Heritage, Lexington, Maitland-Smith, Marge Carson, and Universal.

✝ The creative product assignment was put in the capable hands of Darrell Ferguson, who was now settled into his lavish Charleston design center.

✝ To top it all off, Lineage was given a mothballed Henredon plant to be retooled as a "Plant of the Future" facility. It would employ the most up-to-date operations, referred to as "Just in Time" manufacturing.

LINEAGE TAKES OFF

Lineage launched with much fanfare in April 1990. Despite all the effort and money that went into it, initial reviews of its line of products were just fair. The presentation of the product in the showroom was superb, thanks to a huge budget and last-minute help from Henredon and Drexel Heritage, who were told to strip accessories from their showrooms to help Lineage. Some of the designs were quite good, thanks to Ferguson's talent and the freedom to knock off Henredon and Drexel Heritage with impunity, but there was a noticeable lack of freshness. The prices came in higher than expected, falling more in the Drexel Heritage range. This should have been no surprise to anyone. After all, Drexel Heritage made most of the products, and Ferguson designed them. Yet dealer reaction was less than expected. Something seemed out of line, and instinctively, the retailers sensed it. There were too many elements that had a utopian feeling about them, and these dealers were too cynical to believe everything would go according to plan. The retailers *feared* something would go wrong. The manufacturing veterans knew something would go wrong.

Many things did. The initial launch to the trade was like a major air strike, with lots of noise and fireworks, but the ground troops still had to go in and capture the enemy position. Management had not paid enough attention to this aspect, so the ground campaign immediately faltered. The interplant logistics were unmanageable and inventories climbed. The "Plant of the Future" with its "Just in Time" approach turned out to be just too costly. The costs came in above targets because the plants could not handle the small lot sizes they required. The retail prices were high because the promised dealer margins were so generous. In spite of management's best efforts, quality problems surfaced because scant attention had been paid to this area. The lack of a brand name underwhelmed consumers, and the designs did not have the right appeal. Except for one Ralph Lauren-inspired group, the collections were rather ordinary. The narrow dealer base meant the retailer could "sit on" the line and not bother to promote it against competitors. There was no competitor across town to keep the pressure on. The service-oriented sales force was not good at selling.

LINEAGE CRASH LANDS

Lineage was probably way ahead of its time, and the hidebound furniture industry wasn't ready for it. Had the prices been lower due to off-shore sourcing, perhaps it might have been received better. Given time and the right adjustments, it could have had a big impact on the industry. It was intended to bring out the best in the industry. Instead, it exposed the weakness of the industry. It was predicated on several naïve assumptions and faith in benevolent illusions, and it did not work out the way it had been planned. Most retailers did not embrace it. The goal was to have 150 Lineage Pavilions open by 1992.[3] At the end of 1991, only 19 were open with plans to add about 50 more in 1992. These numbers came nowhere near adding up to the announced goal of 150 that was projected in the beginning. And, worse still, the product did not produce at retail. The dogs would not eat the dog food.

The press releases claimed victory anyway. In a December 30, 1991, interview with *Furniture Today*, Lineage President Tilley did a masterful job positioning the venture as a success despite of the reality of the situation. What follows are the key Tilley quotes intended to reassure dealers that everything was fine and that they should sign up for the wonderful Lineage program. In contrast are a few comments representing what Tilley *might* have said, had he been perfectly candid:

WHAT HE SAID	WHAT HE MIGHT HAVE SAID
"We are firmly committed to maintaining the integrity of our service and quality."	*What integrity? Both service and quality levels have been terrible because we are dealing with too many plants and we have no control over them.*
"To achieve that, we must be careful not to open up locations faster than we can service them. We are still in the process of fine-tuning all the logistics of production and delivery, and we want to make sure everything is right."	*We can't service the dealers we have now, much less the ones we have not yet opened. "Fine-tuning?" Hell, we are out of stock in the best sellers, overloaded with the rest of the line, and the plants won't return our calls.*
"We have a very good list of potential partners. We want to meet this demand as quickly as possible, but we want to make sure we don't sacrifice any of the cornerstones of service that our company is built on."	*That list is the one we drew up of dealers we would like to open. "Cornerstones?" Don't I wish we had a few? This company was built on sand and has no cornerstones because it is not linked to any factory. It's just a marketing creation.*

WHAT HE SAID	WHAT HE MIGHT HAVE SAID
"We don't want to bump out other Masco products."	*At the outset, we of course wanted to avoid replacing other Masco lines, but now, we'll take anything we can get. The Drexel Heritage dealers seem very interested.*
"We've had good retail activity so far. Upholstery and occasional are off to a fast start, and a lot of our unique items are doing well."	*Traffic has been fair. Sales are disappointing, but we did sell a few sofas and we actually sold one of those crazy birdcages that we can't get delivery on.*
"In case goods, we have a number of solid patterns that are selling well, although that seems to depend more on the strength of a particular market."	*Not much is selling, but what has sold has been on a regional basis, which means the groups are limited and will be hard to support.*
"Overall, we feel very positive about the consumer response to our line. But we would welcome an upturn in the economy."	*Overall, we feel terrible. Sales are rotten. No one's buying anything right now, least of all an unproven brand no one ever heard of.*

Tilley was in an untenable position. Others had prepared his battle plan, and he was ordered to execute it. Now he was getting blasted from all sides, and no help was on the way. In the meantime, the other Masco furniture divisions struggled to defend their positions in the midst of crossfire and competitive counterattacks. Competitors saw this move as a mistake and were quick to exploit it. As one wag put it, "Masco took aim at Thomasville and scored a direct hit on Drexel." Retailers seemed to be rooting against Masco for having the arrogance to attempt the Lineage initiative. The guilt-by-association phenomenon spilled to other Masco furniture companies, and each had to do a lot of explaining to their dealers who took delight in comparing Lineage to New Coke and the Edsel. Even the "Just in Time, Plant of the Future" facility came in for scorn when it struggled mightily to make furniture. One expert called it "the Potemkin Village of 'Just in Time' manufacturing."[4]

Lineage would turn out to be an unmitigated disaster. Not on a scale with the Edsel or New Coke, but by furniture standards in the Pantheon of strategic blunders. No one at the top would admit it at this point, but the furniture warriors knew the battle was lost as soon as it began.

In retrospect, the concept was right out of Thomas More's *Utopia*. While it looked wonderful to the non-furniture group, like Jones, Lyons, and Jones, it looked insane to the Insiders. Lineage foreshadowed the offshore pattern of today – with marketing detached from production. It contained elements that the industry has since adopted, and it was reminiscent of Colin Carpi's vision. However, it was a big mistake to think that the plants of three separate companies could make small quantities of product with specs that were radically different from their own. It was a mistake to think a full-blown company could emerge overnight. And it was a mistake to think the retailers would implement the concept properly.

It might have been a different story had Masco emulated Ethan Allen or La-Z-Boy and gone the whole way by opening Lineage stores and controlling the access to consumers while avoiding the "plant of the future" pitfalls. Instead, they created a beautiful failure. Because so much was at stake, no one dared to admit this fact, but the expensively constructed Lineage Army had no firepower. Like the French Army in World War II, the Lineage troops had marvelous uniforms and many generals, but when the shooting started, they were quickly overrun. The strategy was flawed and the execution was weak. The competition quickly destroyed it.

OUTSIDERS PREVAIL, PRESIDE OVER WASTELAND

Contained within this humiliating defeat is the essence of the Insider vs. Outsider struggle. Outsider thinking permeated the creation of Lineage. During 1990, the balance of power between the insiders and the outsiders at Masco had shifted decidedly to the outside. Outsiders Lyon and Jones were finally running the business their way, and the furniture point of view was rapidly falling out of favor. Sales for the year were flat at $1.475 billion, and operating profits fell to $96 million, down 32 percent and a mere 6.5 percent of sales. Of course, the Insiders were blamed. Masco's stock price dropped below $15 a share at the end of the year, a shocking number for the Manoogian family and anyone else who had become accustomed to an ever-increasing stock price.

DISCOVER THE WORLD OF MASCO,
ALL EXPENSES PAID

Jones and Jones correctly observed that the furniture business largely depends upon relationships between retailers and manufacturers. When people like and trust each other, they are inclined to do business together. These relationships are based on complex connections and events, and they take years to develop. At their core, they defy logic and corporate attempts to organize them do not work. This frustrates outsiders because they know they cannot participate in these enigmatic business drivers. But the Joneses were certain something could be done to take charge of these relationships and change them from being division-based to being Masco-based.

In 1991, the company debuted its "Discover the World of Masco" sales incentive contest that awarded trips to dealers who met certain sales volume requirements. Rather than a conventional launch, Masco did it with extravagance. Sensing correctly that there would be some resistance to the program by the old-guard furniture types, Ron and Linda launched a full-blown launch to counter resistance. All sales and marketing people, including some 600 reps, were flown to Maritz Incentive headquarters in St. Louis to get pumped up about it. The expense was big, and the reaction from the participants was the opposite of what was intended. Many were offended by the crass appeal to materialism and greed that permeated the presentations. The big launch failed to convert the players; it actually turned off many of them.

The reaction from the dealers, at first, ranged from indifference to outright hostility. These programs had been used before, and the general conclusion was they were not cost effective. But Masco plowed ahead, acting as if it were the first company to think of this promotion. Power Marketing had failed. Perhaps they could redeem themselves through a few relationship-building trips overseas. Applying their typical "more-is-better" élan, they made the trips more and more elaborate and lowered the requirements so nearly any dealer could win. The trips were indeed wonderful. No expense was spared, and dealers admittedly had a great time. Relationships between people who naturally liked each other were enhanced, but these relationships remained largely between the retailers and the divisions, not corporate as originally hoped. Ironically, many dealers did get to know the corporate people better on these trips, but they did not particularly like what they observed.

It was not for any lack of spending. Masco poured money into the trips as they became grander and grander each year. Spain, Switzerland, Bermuda, Turkey, The Greek Islands, and Argentina were among the destinations for the major trips. Cozumel, the Dominican Republic, Puerto Rico, and Nassau were chosen for "minor" trips. The divisional management had to go along to "work on those relationships" and basically remove themselves from their busy schedules for two more weeks each year, weeks they could ill afford to spend. Wayne Lyon would kick off each trip by reminding everyone they had better work hard on forging relationships, "or else."

The net result of this program was that a lot of people had some wonderful experiences, and many friendships started. Sales increases probably resulted, but they were not measurable. For sure, the Jones duo was given an enormous boost. These two people from the office furniture business quickly became the most prominent couple in the Furniture Zone. The cost to the furniture group was $4 to $5 million a year for five consecutive years. The furniture types were incredulous, but neither the Joneses nor Masco seemed to mind. The attitude was consistent with the belief that somehow you could spend your way to higher profits.

For good measure, they tossed in a few more expensive programs, but they were only marginally effective. Among these were numerous "Dealer Support Loans" which provided money to retailers in return for display space; the Masco Art display which provided serious art to dealers who rarely had interest in it; and the CARE program as a way to contribute to the United Nations charity. In the end it disrupted divisional product development plans and contributed very little to the philanthropic entity it was intended to serve. These and other ill-conceived plans consumed money without generating much in return.

Faced with an extremely tough economy in 1991, sales declined slightly and operating profits dropped another 60 percent to hit the embarrassing level of $38 million, just 2.6 percent of sales. The stock price closed the year at $23.50, up from the previous year but well below Masco's stock price before it began buying furniture companies.

PERSEVERANCE AND CAPITAL EXPENDITURES

The Jones and Jones team was not deterred by the obvious failure of their initial schemes. Wayne Lyon remained supportive, at least outwardly, as they continued on the path of spending money and moving further and further away from the more conventional furniture approach. By this time, Ron and Linda had become so accustomed to the furniture veterans telling them their ideas would not work, that they had stopped listening.

In addition to costly marketing programs that missed the mark, Masco spent money on offices and showrooms in the High Point area. After remodeling the main office on Thomasville Highway, purchased from LADD, they gave the go-ahead to a $7 million new showroom for Lexington. Then Lineage got a beautiful new $8 million complex , and Drexel Heritage blew them both away with a $9 million showroom on Oak Hollow Lake. Not to be ignored, the money-losing Masco Contract Division was given the go-ahead to do a million-dollar makeover of the Frederick Edward showroom, and Maitland-Smith built a new showroom as well. In the meantime, Henredon, the most prestigious division, made do with its factory showroom in a run-down industrial area.

What must they have been thinking? The organization was now becoming dysfunctional as the furniture insiders conceded control to the outsiders at the top. The experienced people simply stopped trying to express their concerns, because they knew that the leadership no longer cared what they thought. Defections began as the more independent individuals bailed out. As early as 1991, Allen and Carol Wyatt, the founders and prime movers of the Robert Allen Co., left after many disputes and went off to Florida to spend their Masco money. This left Ron Jones in a jam with no one in the organization knowing how to run a decorative showroom chain. He replaced the Wyatts with the Carsons, the talented creative team behind Marge Carson. He bought the Kaplan & Fox showroom in Boston and put its respected president, David Kaplan Sr., in charge of the whole chain. At this point, both Robert Allen and Marge Carson were losing money, and the former owners had trouble being effective in the corporate environment.

Masco also struggled with what to do with Ferguson and Copeland. With their "long goodbye" now in its second year, it was announced in January 1992 that the Dynamic Duo and Masco had formed a joint venture to operate Marge Carson. In another carefully crafted press release, Wayne Lyon outdid himself explaining the whole thing in "Mascotalk." "This joint venture provides us with an exciting opportunity to bring a seasoned leadership focus to the merchandising promotion and expanded product development efforts of Marge Carson, Inc. This specialty company has consistently been identified as a California fashion trendsetter and we are confident that role will expand significantly."[5]

This move triggered a chain reaction, sending Marge Carson chief Birger Rasmussen to a new position heading up Hickorycraft and Frederick Edward, while putting J. Don Smith upstairs to become an "executive consultant" with Masco. In a few short years, all three of these specialty niche players had been converted from modestly successful entrepreneurial companies to money-losing corporate divisions. Masco had paid a handsome amount for all three with the expectation they would flourish under the Masco umbrella. Instead they languished. Similar trouble was brewing far away in the Philippines, as Paul Maitland-Smith was becoming openly critical of how his company was being handled. Earlier, Jones had made Vince Burns president of Maitland-Smith U.S.A. Burns had no experience in anything remotely connected with the world of Maitland-Smith, and his tenure was understandably brief. In March 1992, Jones selected Larry Milan to replace Burns. Milan was a corporate accounting person who was familiar with the numbers, but he had no experience or skill in the marketing side of the business. Meanwhile, trouble was brewing with the Drexel Heritage organization. President John Pastrone, former chief of Pennsylvania House, informed Jones that he wanted out. Privately, he told friends that he had no confidence in Masco's ability to understand the furniture business. Having commanded troops under three "corporate" owners – General Mills, Hoover, and Maytag – Pastrone could see the warning signs clearly and he decided to leave before the trouble began. To save face, Masco convinced him to remain until a successor could be groomed. Once again, finding a suitable candidate was tough. They made Pastrone a group vice president and named Dan Grow as his successor.[6] Grow had been a sales manager at Thomasville and had no general management experience. Ill-equipped to contend with the serious challenges facing the company, he became the fifth Drexel Heritage president in seven years.[7]

Masco Home Furnishing's sales rose slightly in 1992, to $1.564 billion, but profit margins languished at 3.9 percent. After six years of Masco guidance, the gap between actual margins and the Masco expectations was bigger than ever. The share price was $27, down from the peak of $40 in the Spring 1987, and some Wall Street analysts were finally beginning to note that Masco's earnings target for furniture was unrealistic. Those analysts predicted that Masco would spin off or divest its furniture group.

Once More into the Breech

With profits disappearing and market share declining, it would seem logical at this point for someone to step forward to say,

"Wait a minute. Things are not working as we had expected. Why don't we pause to review what we are doing and candidly assess the results? Obviously, some changes should be made." Either no one did, or if they did, they were ignored. Yet Masco plunged ahead with more programs as if nothing were amiss. In addition to Lineage, it spent more money on startup ventures like Smith and Gaines, a leather company; The Roberts Co., a recliner company; Devan Designs, a self-assembly company; and Marion Frame, an upholstery frame producer. Each effort was costly and took management time away from the divisions. Each effort failed.

To add to the list of failed ventures, a new division was formed in 1992 to centralize the sales and customer service functions relating to "contract" sales, the industry term for sales to hotels, restaurants, and governments. This business is tricky and can have a major impact on a conventional furniture plant. The divisions themselves had previously managed this function locally, and in some cases, it had been a valuable part of the division's sales mix. Handled poorly, it was a money loser that disrupted the regular production schedule. Masco turned it into a corporate group function, where it became a perennial money loser. Every year the Contract Division president would make optimistic forecasts and then proceed to miss the numbers and lose more money. It was finally abandoned in 2001.

The cost of these and other ill-conceived adventures was substantial, probably in the $150 million vicinity. And, of course, the real costs were the countless opportunities lost. In military terms it was like pulling the best troops from your best divisions in order to set up Special Forces who were sent on suicide missions. In effect, you weaken your core strengths and gain nothing. Your enemies can attack your home territory, and you will have a difficult time defending it. Had that money been directed at the badly needed improvement of the core divisions, Masco could have had far more profitable results, and the inherent strength of the acquired divisions would have been sustained. As it was, the core divisions kept deteriorating and losing ground to the competition.

Group sales in 1993 actually grew to $1.698 billion, but operating profits declined to 3.5 percent of sales – far below the 20 percent demanded by Masco in previous years. Wall Street analysts covering Masco stock were putting pressure on Manoogian to make sense out if the furniture holdings. Yet thanks to the results at other Masco divisions, such as Delta Faucet, the stock closed out the year at $37, well above the prior year.

More Warlords Go AWOL

The Insiders were deeply dismayed by these ill-advised ventures and became increasingly tired of trying to put a good face on them when talking with retailers. The whole thing seemed so naive, so insane, and so pointless that many of them abandoned their hope that Masco would eventually come to its senses. One by one, the experienced furniture people began making plans to desert the Masco Army. They knew Jones and Lyon no longer wanted to hear their objections to the direction Masco was taking, and they knew their opinions had lost credibility within the hierarchy. Many remained out of loyalty to the people in their divisions, but this could not go on forever.

A significant number of defections occurred during these years, starting with people who bailed out before the advent of Lineage. Although many of were termed retirements, the individuals still had contributions to make and their departures meant a loss to the company. In addition to the defections noted earlier, the following Insiders left the Masco ranks:

LEXINGTON: Mr. Inside, Bruce Hinkle, retired along with Jeff Young's brother soon after the company was bought. Then Lexington lost most of its top management when the incomparable Smith Young retired, followed by operations wizard Willis Hedrick.

UNIVERSAL: Co-founders Laurence Zung and Larry Moh left not long after the acquisition. Moh later built a magnificent plant in mainland China that soon became a direct competitor to Masco. Universal's North American president, Ron Hahn, resigned to pursue an entrepreneurial opportunity competing with a rival import company. Wes Collins, brought back to turn Universal around, retired for the second time. Collins' successor, Don Mitchell, resigned in a dispute with Wayne Lyon and became the number two executive at LADD and competed effectively with his alma mater. Mitchell's successor, George Revington, was dismissed and now heads another competitor.

DREXEL HERITAGE: President Paul Monroe resigned in frustration over "too many meetings." His replacement, John Pastrone, also resigned as soon as he realized how Masco planned to manage the divisions.

MAITLAND-SMITH: The founder, Paul Maitland-Smith, re-signed and, after a non-compete year, founded Theodore and Alexander. The new company is much like the original and competes successfully with his former division.

FREDERICK EDWARD: President Rick Hopkins resigned to work for Sherrill, a competitor. Hopkins' successor, Birger Rasmussen, lasted a short while before moving through a number of positions at corporate and division levels. He eventually left to work for Vanguard, an entrepreneurial competitor.

LABARGE: President and former owner Jim LaBarge resigned to buy Marge Carson from Masco. He remains a competitor today. LaBarge's successor was a magazine advertising salesman who was removed within a year. The LaBarge Co. eventually was folded into Maitland-Smith.

CORPORATE: Fred Copeland and Darrell Ferguson, after a failed attempt to acquire Marge Carson, founded a new company, Ferguson Copeland, which competes with Henredon and Drexel Heritage.

HICKORYCRAFT: Founder J. Don Smith, after being placed in a number of corporate posts, resigned in frustration and is now fully retired. His former company no longer exists.

MARGE CARSON: Founders Bob and Carole Carson were put in meaningless corporate positions and left to go "freelance."

MARBRO: President Jim Caver died unexpectedly. His company was folded into LaBarge and later into Maitland-Smith, where it languished.

Each case was different – and several defections had nothing to do with Masco – but the huge number of departures surely signaled that the mindset of the typical furniture entrepreneur was not compatible with the Masco mindset. And this was the company that had boasted over and over again in all its acquisitions that it "had never lost a management team." The cumulative effect of this brain drain weakened the already-broken Masco properties so severely that some did not recover.

LEXINGTON RULES

Masco put the best possible spin on the pathetic furniture performance in its 1993 annual report, boldly promising that they would experience 11 percent annual sales growth from '93 to '97. Henredon, Drexel Heritage, and Universal had shown improvements, but Lexington was clearly the star performer. Thanks to a hot product line and an aggressive distribution policy, incoming orders kept climbing. By offering the line to any and all dealers, Lexington sold a lot of goods but annoyed its big customers by refusing to yield to the retail pressure to keep the line from their competitors. When asked about "distribution" plans during markets, President Smith Young would sometimes thunder, "Distribution? We don't make 'distribution.' We make furniture! Don't ask me for 'distribution.' I don't have any." On another occasion, he claimed the Lexington distribution policy was, "If you can breathe and pay your bills, we want you as a dealer."

Consistent with the traditional practices in the industry, Lexington's marketing effort consisted of catalogs and fabric swatches. It had no national advertising, no market research, and no marketing strategy. All Lexington did was make great-looking, affordable products at the lowest possible price and then harangue their sales force to peddle them to any and all comers. Lexington was the prototypical furniture company, a true reflection of its strong leadership. But it was most certainly not the typical Masco division.

Young's counterpart in operations was a feisty furniture veteran named Willis Hedrick, who ran the plants with an iron hand and kept score with a small notepad. There were no production control systems, no engineered standards, no formal controls, no bills of material, no quality systems, yet Hedrick knew where every part, every board, and every labor hour was every day in every plant. Masco sent in countless operations experts to observe the Lexington money machine, and they all came to the same conclusion – the place could not continue to be run this way. It defied logic and was alien to anything they had ever seen. Something had to be done to fix it – and Masco engineers were itching to do it – but Willis Hedrick would not let them near his plants. Incidentally, this "mess" doubled its sales from 1988 to 1994, managing to make close to 10 percent operating income each year. In '92 and '93, Lexington made half of the entire Home Furnishings Group's earnings. Just think what it could do if the dinosaurs retired and let the corporate wizards do things right.

Unable to penetrate the Willis Hedrick protected plants, the

Jones duo managed to infiltrate the marketing area and made some needed improvements. In merchandising, Lexington felt tremendous pressure to come up with another licensed collection to match its hugely successful Timberlake Collection. Timberlake had broad consumer appeal and was well suited to Lexington's plants and sales force. The *alignment* was perfect, but like all groups, it followed a typical sales life-cycle pattern and could not keep growing forever. When Universal launched an even bigger hit with the Alexander Julian Collection, the race was on to develop more licenses. Lexington management had a relationship of sorts with Arnold and Winnie Palmer, and this led to the creation of the Palmer Home Collection. The market samples looked fabulous and the dealer reaction was overwhelming, as many people commented that it looked a lot like Henredon for a lot less money. Henredon management was miffed to see their designs copied by a sister company, but they knew a protest would be viewed as insubordination. They, too, were amazed at the low costs. Harold Kirby, the Henredon operations chief, saw the market introduction of the Palmer group and commented prophetically that the Lexington plants would have a tough time executing the designs. "That is not the kind of product those boys know how to slap together," was how he put it. "They will be sorry they took this on."

DREXEL GETS "HELPED"

The corporate office operations experts had better luck making changes at Drexel Heritage, whose president was much more accommodating than Lexington's Willis Hedrick. When not working on Lineage, the corporate experts made many "improvements" in the operations and marketing efforts at Drexel Heritage. These changes proved to be costly, and when combined with tough economic conditions they drove earnings down, almost to a loss. When the economy recovered by 1994, margins were equal to half of what they were before the "improvements" were made. Between 1990 and 1994, operating earnings at Drexel Heritage declined 43 percent.

Meanwhile, at Henredon, the president was more inclined to keep the corporate "helpers" at bay. During the same period, Henredon's earnings increased by 35 percent despite being held back by the general malaise in the upper-end segment.

The insane logic of Joseph Heller's *Catch-22* was applicable here. The divisions lived under a constant threat of getting "corporate help" if they slipped up. Yet when the "corporate help" was applied, the division's results got worse and division management got blamed.

No End of Ideas or Shopping Opportunities

Jones kept plowing ahead, like a fullback who has been stripped of the ball but still refuses to let tacklers bring him down. As a sideshow, the Joneses became caught up in another new product startup called "Simply Together" involving cheap-looking, ready-to-assemble sofas. The furniture veterans tried to point out that the RTA sofa cost more to make than a comparable conventional sofa and quietly wondered why anyone would pay a premium for a sofa they had to assemble themselves when they could buy a whole one for less? Not wishing to offend the Joneses, who enthusiastically endorsed the idea, the veterans tried to distance themselves from it as much as possible.

This was around the time that Linda Jones introduced a company-wide fundraising effort for CARE. Each division was told it must introduce a collection of products that related to a Third World country on the CARE list. Sales from the collections would then generate a donation to CARE. It would have been simpler and far cheaper if the Joneses had just written a check, but the divisions instead spent a lot of money building samples of unneeded products like the Cameroon Collection from Henredon. Merchandisers, designers, and sample makers spent valuable time away from needed products to pursue this boondoggle. When the products were launched at the April Market, the corporate wizards were giddy with excitement and no expense was spared. However, the dealers responded with icy indifference, and not one collection was successful.

The Joneses kept giving it their best shot, but they were still unable to get the earnings anywhere near the level Masco expected. Not only had Masco failed to generate margins above industry standards, they had not even matched industry averages. All the initiatives, all the programs, and all the startups had failed to generate any noticeable internal growth. So, like a one-trick pony in need of a drink, Masco reverted to what it knew best by going to the acquisition trough to buy some more sales and earnings. In June 1994, Masco announced that it had bought Berkline, a fast-growing producer of motion furniture and recliners. The addition of Berkline's sales of $165 million put the Home Furnishings Group close to $2 billion in sales and solidified the company's position as the largest in the industry. "If you can't beat 'em, buy 'em," seemed to be the mindset. But investors weren't buying it. By the end of 1994, the Masco stock had drifted down to $22 a share, its lowest point since 1990. Sales for the Home Furnishings Group, including Berkline, were up 14 percent to $1.945 billion, but profits were only $89 million, 4.6 percent of sales.

1995: The Case of the Disappearing Companies

All the attention that was given to Lineage was not able to make it successful. It was a costly dud. Most of Masco's small furniture companies were left to fend for themselves during the brief "Lineage Era." This neglect might have been benign in nature had the original owners of these companies still been on the scene. But they had left long ago, and these companies fared poorly without them. Occasionally, Masco turned its attention to these smaller companies, but as with the larger divisions, the corporate "helpers" lacked the wisdom and knowledge to truly help. As a result, these companies never thrived in the "supportive" Masco atmosphere. The body count included five viable companies in 1987, each worthy of a Masco takeover but turned into *los desaparecidos*, the disappeared ones, by 1995.

Marge Carson was an example of one of the smaller Masco furniture companies that suffered under Masco ownership. This was the hot little brand Copeland and Ferguson lusted for back in 1988, the company that "practically invented the California Contemporary look," according to Wayne Lyon. Before it was acquired, it provided a nice living for the owners but made no profits beyond that. It lost money after it was brought in under the Masco Umbrella. Former owners, Bob and Carole Carson, were eased out in 1992 and replaced by Birger Rasmussen. The losses continued. In 1992, the company was handed to Copeland in a joint venture, but

Copeland quickly handed it back to corporate in 1993. Ferguson was made president in August 1993, and in 1995 it was sold to Jim LaBarge. The company had five presidents in five years, each with a distinctly different opinion of what the company should be.

The Frederick Edward Co. had a similarly traumatic experience, going through three CEOs in four years before it disappeared into Drexel Heritage and died from neglect. Marbro Lamps disappeared into LaBarge, which in turn, was folded into Maitland-Smith, rarely to be seen again. Finally, the once-hot upholstery line, Hickorycraft, went through three CEOs in three years and was then folded into Lexington, where the name was erased quickly.

•

MASCO TURNS OFF THE FAUCET

But those five companies were not the only things Masco managed to make disappear. After an all-out nine year effort to invade, capture, and dominate the furniture industry, Masco's $1.7 billion investment was earning about 5 percent before taxes, a pitiful reward for the once proud Masters of the Mundane. No industry consolidation had occurred. No major victories could be claimed, and none were in sight. Masco's top management could no longer put a bright face on the Furniture Group results, and speculation regarding a probable spin-off was rampant. In the thorny thicket of the Briar Patch, its weapons did not work, its officers were ineffective, and its troops wanted to go AWOL. What's more, even when it won battles it could not occupy the area it captured.

To no one's surprise, Masco finally faced up to the obvious in the second quarter of 1995. After countless assurances that they were in it for the long haul, the company abruptly said it would "evaluate the possible divestiture of home furnishings."[8] The question now was how Manoogian could extricate himself from the mess without losing the pants to his uniform. Would anybody want to buy the whole venture? If so, how much would they pay?

All that remained was to negotiate a cease-fire and to arrange for an orderly withdrawal from the Briar Patch. It was embarrassing for Masco management to admit that the whole crusade had been a mistake and hard to explain why their stewardship was such a failure, but Wall Street generally applauded Masco for raising the white flag. The concern, of course, was the cost to withdraw. The possibility of finding a buyer willing to pay anything close to the $1.7 billion book value was remote, and the appraised valuation would be anybody's guess until accountants put a true value on the Home Furnishings Group. The company placed this value in excess of $1 billion, and securities analysts estimated it to be between $800 million and $1.2 billion. Masco's stock price at this point was around $30 a share, well below its peak of $41 in 1987, nine months after it began buying home furnishings companies. The cost of this buying spree was staggering. As reported in *Furniture Today*, Gregory Nejmeh of Lehman Brothers "concluded that on a net basis, Masco has lost money on furniture each year since 1990. Last year, the loss was 2 cents per share, while building products earned $1.70 per share. . . . If Masco had never gotten into furniture – never issued shares to buy furniture companies – its building products alone would have earned $3.10 per share in 1994."[9]

Despite all the resources committed to the campaign, Masco finally had to admit it could not conquer the furniture industry.

"A prospective divestiture of our home furnishings business would enable us to better focus on our traditional home improvement and building products business, which have historically demonstrated outstanding operating performance," said Chairman Richard Manoogian. According to published reports at the time, the Home Furnishings Group comprised 42 percent of Masco sales but only 14 percent of the profits.[10]

Lessons Learned

The Masco army invaded the Briar Patch in a manner that recalled Sherman's march through Georgia, except Sherman was victorious. Masco, supported by its air force of corporate planes, captured the high ground and had more firepower than the opposition. However, it had a cavalier disregard for the realities of the industry and fell into a number of strategic traps. Only because of its overwhelming numeric superiority could it keep going despite the staggering setbacks. Strategically, Masco sought dominance but disregarded the evidence showing that was not possible. Masco over-centralized in several key areas, adding overhead costs that hindered the divisions' ability to compete with lower-cost rivals.

Masco's biggest fault was its lack of a plan, which meant it tended to lose focus and distract the divisions from maintaining their focus. Headquarters never seemed to realize that it takes a major effort to run a division, and the constant shuffling of people – along with countless meetings at corporate headquarters – eventually take a toll.

Future furniture leaders can benefit by studying Masco's expensive campaign – the largest, best funded, and most spectacular invasion ever attempted. It is hard to imagine it could ever happen again, but then, people felt the same way when Colin Carpi imploded decades earlier. Here are the main lessons:

PUT THE RIGHT PEOPLE ON THE BUS: Use caution when hiring non-furniture executives to run furniture companies. The pool of highly capable furniture executives is small, but making an outsider the commander-in-chief of the largest agglomeration of furniture producers ever assembled was like putting an admiral in charge of land forces. The redoubtable Howard Haworth would have been a wiser choice. It is probably wise to avoid hiring your spouse, no matter how talented, unless you own the company. Hold onto the good furniture warriors. Group head Ron Jones had to steer between Wayne Lyon and a host of furniture warlords. He was so intent on avoiding the Lyon vortex that he lost much of his crew.

SALES FORCE IMPORTANCE: They make a lot of money, but the good ones are worth every penny. Two-legged assets need maintenance just as machines do. You must provide the right environment to hold onto the entrepreneur owners. Entrepreneurs choose to be entrepreneurs for a reason. Paying them a lot of money for their creations and expecting them to become good corporate citizens is a foolish exercise.

LEAD, FOLLOW, OR GET OUT OF THE WAY: Corporate staffs drain division strength. Masco loaded the corporate office with high-priced staff people who only managed to frustrate the divisional people. These corporate people, for the most part, could not justify the added costs they brought to the table. The result was confusion in the ranks and erosion of the margins.

CONTROL COSTS: Operational expenses must be controlled constantly. The competitive intensity of the furniture business drives down prices close to factory costs, leaving no room for expensive programs and functions. You cannot spend yourself to profitability. Don't mess with success. Study it and learn from it. Lexington, under Smith Young and Willis Hedrick, was a monster hit. Their "country boy" demeanor was part of the act. There was a reason for the way those plants were set up and a reason why they sold to everybody. The result was a great furniture company that struck fear in the hearts of competitors. Masco should have studied how they did it and shared the formula with the other divisions.

RULES ARE RULES: There is a big difference between rewriting the rules and breaking them. Good rules derive from realities, and realities are immutable. Unless you wrote them in the first place, you cannot rewrite them. Lineage broke the rules and paid dearly for it. Also, it is unwise to neglect your main divisions when creating a new one. While Lineage was being assembled from scratch, the mature divisions were neglected and lost market share that took years to recapture.

In sharp contrast with the Masco surrender, their primary furniture rival, Interco, announced plans in November 1995 to acquire Thomasville Furniture Industries. This would put their sales at $1.6 billion. The headline in the November 27 issue of *Furniture Today* proclaimed "Masco, Thomasville sales set." Just as Masco was bailing out, Interco was surging forward. One corporate behemoth was betting the ranch on furniture; the other was walking away from the table. Once again the Outsiders had failed, but this time, the Insiders had fought so hard to protect their beloved Briar Patch, they were now in dire straits. Should someone come along and mount a concerted assault, there might not be any defenders left to protect the fort.

WAYNE'S WORLD

*A point of view can be a dangerous luxury
when substituted for insight and understanding.*

Marshall McLuhan

PLENTY OF POTENTIAL BUYERS were interested in Masco's furniture holdings, but none agreed with the value that Masco chief Richard Manoogian placed on the assets. With a personal net worth estimated at $570 million,[1] Manoogian was unusually skillful in asset deployment. Part of his genius lay more in balance sheet management than in operations. The balance sheet mattered most to him, and the profit-and-loss statement mattered because it reflected the accumulation or consumption of cash. When it came to companies and his art collection, Manoogian had a reputation for knowing when to buy, when to hold, and when to sell. It was definitely time to sell the furniture group. As a collection, the individual pieces were oddly matched, and some had not been well cared for. The stated "book value" on Masco's balance sheet was $1.7 billion, but the investment in furniture was worth far less. Manoogian was eager to get out of the Briar Patch so he could focus on the product areas he knew would produce more impressive margins. He was willing to sell below book value, but did not want to take a bath.

FURNITURE SALE, COMPANIES AT 40 PERCENT OFF

Savvy consumers know that fine furniture products are sold every day at "40% off," and potential buyers expected a similar discount for the Masco Home Furnishings Group. No matter how hard Masco tried to put an attractive veneer on the package, potential buyers insisted that the properties were not worth the book value. After four months of investment banking activity, Masco announced in November 1995 an agreement to sell the furniture holdings to a Morgan Stanley-backed group for $1.075 billion in cash, plus the assumption of another $25 million of debt. This meant Masco would have to take a $600 million write-down. But Manoogian's company would receive nearly $1 billion in cash and, better still, be rid of the furniture companies. No one knew much about the new owners, who appeared out of nowhere to beat out the other suitors. The furniture Insiders fretted about who might run the new company, and they noted that designated President Vince Langone had no furniture experience. He had been president of the Formica Corp., which supplied plastic laminates to producers of cheap dinettes, but otherwise he knew nothing about the furniture industry. He did, however, possess an abundance of that self-confident, almost arrogant, manner that non-furniture people use to intimidate Insiders. The impression he made was that of a person who suspected he was in over his head but thought he was the only one who noticed. The Insiders envisioned Masco-like ownership without the compassion or the deep pockets. As it turns out, the Insiders never discovered whether this was true. The more the potential new owners looked, the less they liked what they saw and the less comfortable Masco became. The deal was called off abruptly in January 1996.

JONES LEAVES, LYON STAYS

Another mad scramble was put in motion, and the value of the assets was again questioned. To no one's surprise, Ron Jones resigned in March 1996 to become president and CEO of Sealy, the mattress company, leaving Wayne Lyon to manage the furniture group directly.[2]

Another deal was put together, this time led by Citicorp Venture Capital, and a new agreement was reached to sell the companies again for $1.1 billion. But this package included $300 million of "seller notes." In simple terms, this meant the buyers gave Masco $800 million of cash, but Masco paid itself an additional $300 million in the form of Payment in Kind promissory notes. This is like selling your house to someone who won't meet your asking price, so you give the buyer a second mortgage. The plan called for Lyon to apply his leadership and strategic skills to increase earnings, pay down debt, and take the new company public. If successful, everyone would win. Masco would get back its $300 million plus 13 percent interest; management would get stock in the new company; and Lyon would salvage his reputation while making a bundle. With a collective sigh, the deal was signed and a new company was born in August 1996. The new name, Life*Style*

Furnishings International, reflected a grandiose vision. It encompassed entire lifestyles, involving more than mere furniture, and it was global in scope. It even had two fonts. Behind the logo, it looked a lot like the old Masco Home Furnishings group with one ominous exception. This time, there was a lot of debt on the balance sheet and interest payments that needed to be paid.

During his first interview with the trade press, Lyon gave no hint of big changes. "Life*Style*'s executive structure remains unchanged from the Masco Home Furnishings days" reported *Furniture Today*. "Operating company presidents report to him, and the headquarters staff of about 20 handles financial, human resources and administrative duties. Life*Style* has a nine-month agreement with Masco to provide certain corporate services. Lyon said the home office staff would grow as it weans itself from Masco, though it won't get too big. 'We'll stay lean,' he said."

The choice of Wayne B. Lyon to run the new venture was curious to some. As president and chief operating officer of Masco, he had played a role in the decision to get Masco into furniture to begin with, the same man charged with the responsibility of making it pay off, and the same man who hired and closely directed Ron Jones. Masco assembled a $1 billion furniture company under his leadership, but at a $2 billion cost. After overseeing this investment turn into a $1.1 billion divestiture, he then was given the responsibility of recouping part of the loss by running the spinoff company. Because of the nature of the deal, even though Masco "sold" the furniture holdings, the only way it would be paid in full is if the spinoff succeeded. Presumably Manoogian felt that since Lyon had led the way into the quagmire, he was qualified to find his way out. The challenge was to manage the company well enough for it to go public so the heavy debt load could be reduced. He had the right companies in the stable. This time, the objectives were more reasonable. A 10 percent operating margin and prudent management of working capital ought to do it, and now Lyon had the benefit of his own on-the-job training in the furniture business. His 10-year stint surely qualified him for an advanced degree in Furniture, if not a Ph.D. The many million dollars of "tuition" that Masco paid surely must have taught him how to get around in the Briar Patch, at the very least. He would get it right this time – or else.

The plan looked fine on paper, but the problem was how to make it happen. As a young chemical engineer, Lyon was involved with a number of product development projects usually made of plastic. His accomplishments included working on the design and development of plastic garbage cans and cottage cheese containers. At Masco, he had oversight responsibility for many divisions, but the Masco philosophy was strictly hands off, so he rarely got into the day-to-day operating realities. He was a "big-picture guy," more of a Merger-and-Acquisitions type than a true operating type, and this background would shape his management style.

Hunting from the Lodge

Determined to produce better results than he had seen working through Ron Jones, Lyon asserted himself early and imposed his vision of the perfect furniture company on Life*Style* Furnishings International, known by many by its initials, LFI. He was a proponent of lean manufacturing techniques, especially if it meant speedy deliveries, and he believed in Delta Faucet-type Power

Marketing. His big picture world-view led him to believe that the industry was headed for a crisis of gargantuan proportions. The Chinese invasion into the furniture industry would destroy American producers who did not radically change their ways, and there was little time to get ready for the all-out attack. He was right, but he still had to contend with obstinate furniture veterans who did not see it the way he did. Efforts to resolve these differences just hardened the battle lines. To circumvent them, he decided to create an extensive headquarters staff and to centralize everything he could get his arms around. He was not comfortable with the divisions making their own decisions. In fact, he was not comfortable with the divisions at all, and the feelings of distrust were mutual.

During the Jones era, headquarters leaned toward marketing solutions and left operational programs up to the divisions. Lyon shifted the emphasis to operations, an area with which he was more comfortable. He was determined to change how furniture was made, and he remained convinced the conventional techniques were outmoded. He often expressed admiration for GE chief Jack Welch, who bragged, "I always reminded myself headquarters doesn't make anything or sell anything. Banging around the field was my best shot at getting some idea about what was really going on."[3] Lyon's management style was more like the hunter who is such a good shot that he believes he can bag a deer from the lodge porch without sallying forth into the woods. Lyon rarely visited customers at their stores and spent little time at the division sites, relying instead on reports given to him by the ever-expanding staff of non-furniture operations people he hired.

Lyon also held on to the trappings of corporate life. Some felt he was subconsciously trying to create another Masco, or "Masco

Lite," as some called it. Discarding the spacious offices used by Ron Jones, Lyon directed a contractor to transform the former Lineage complex into a palatial corporate office. It was too big at 60,000 square feet, but not for the staff Lyon had in mind. Masco provided a corporate jet despite adequate commercial airline service nearby. A powerful mainframe computer was installed even though there was little to run on it, and many other "goodies" were built into the new offices, including a caterer hired to run the company dining room. When the divisions complained about the extravagant example set by the Potemkin-like headquarters, they were reminded in a patronizing tone that there was a need to impress future investors and customers. The consuming need to go public, and the compelling need to build an impressive "corporate structure," were the hallmarks of Wayne's World.

In noteworthy contrast, LFI's chief rival, Interco, took a different route. In 1994, it spun off its shoe company holdings to focus solely on furniture. Then, in November 1995, the same month that Masco announced it had reached an agreement to dump its furniture holdings, Interco bought Thomasville for $339 million. The addition of Thomasville's sales put Interco at the $1.6 billion level, tops in the industry. *Furniture Today* said, "The Thomasville deal continues a stunning turnaround for Interco, coming just three years after the company emerged from Chapter 11 bankruptcy protection."[4] Interco had been one of the suitors that considered buying the furniture group from Masco earlier, but it passed because their top people felt it was too complicated to manage.

Interco changed its name to Furniture Brands International in October 1996, explaining that its focus was on the furniture business to the exclusion of all others. The same month, as

Masco's Home Furnishing Group was being reborn as LFI, Furniture Brands CEO Richard Loynd announced that he was going to step aside and named as his successor Mickey Holliman, a furniture person to the core. In a remarkably candid assessment, Loynd said, "Mickey knows furniture backward and forward. I don't particularly understand the furniture business. I'm the kind of guy who understands how to run businesses and make money. The company needed a guy like me when it had financial problems, and it needs a guy like Mickey now."⁵ Loynd turned out to be right. Holliman had demonstrated at Lane he not only understood the furniture business, he also knew how to make money.

A Strategic Divisional Assessment, 1996

The Lyon management style would be tested many times in Wayne's World. The Masco years had not been good for the strength of the divisions, and each one had its own unique set of challenges. How any one person could make all the needed repairs is hard to imagine. Lyon approached the daunting task with an abundance of confidence but little imagination. Here is what he faced:

UNIVERSAL FURNITURE had been the most challenging division to run, and Masco management never seemed certain what to do with this powerhouse. Nevertheless, it appeared to be thriving in late 1995, at least in its North American division. It is true that Far Eastern operations began a slow decline after the late 1980s departure of brilliant founder/CEO Larry Moh. But in North America, the appointment of industry veteran Wes Collins to a second term as president led to a resurgence in marketing and sales. And the company continued to move forward when Collins anointed Don Mitchell to succeed him. With the introduction of the hugely successful Alexander Julian Collection in 1994, Universal traded up markedly and showed it could compete at the next level. It gave up some market share in the lower end of their product range in the process, but management felt this could be recovered. As the biggest low-cost producer, Universal had concerns. The company's Taiwan-based production facilities were beset with rising labor costs and could no longer maintain their low-cost advantage. The success of the Alexander Julian line masked the real problem for a while, but their historic low-cost niche was under a severe threat as other companies migrated production from Taiwan to the People's Republic of China. It was time to move to Mainland China, where the real action was beginning to take place.

Universal sales had peaked at close to $600 million in 1993, and earnings that year were almost $40 million. In launching the Alexander Julian product, the company served notice that it could successfully attack the price points normally belonging to Lexington. All Universal had to do was retain its low-cost capabilities by gradually shifting production from Taiwan to lower-cost sites on the mainland, where it already had a foothold. Larry Moh had the foresight to build three flooring plants in the People's Republic, and converting them to furniture production seemed plausible. If needed, new facilities could also be built. Universal was in a position to become the dominant force in the middle of the market, competing with Lexington, Broyhill, Bassett, and even Thomasville. The problem was that after founding genius Larry Moh left, no one had replaced him and the American executives neglected the crucial overseas operations.

LEXINGTON had performed well during the Jones years, introducing one successful collection after another and watching sales and profits soar. The sales growth was fueled by the decision to provide much of the production from Drexel plants. One of the few synergies Masco found was the practice of feeding a hot line like Lexington with production from a cold line like Drexel Heritage. Headquarters developed a formula so each plant showed a normal profit, and the supplier kept his plants running while the recipient received help to meet customer demand. This "Marxist Capitalism" took from each according to his available capacity and gave to each according to his backlog need. The program worked well on the surface, but it covered up some deep-seated problems at Drexel that management needed to address. Its proprietary product line had weakened; its position in the field was losing strength; and morale in the plants was deteriorating. Lexington, however, flourished beyond anyone's dreams. It added upholstery to its lineup in 1994, when the struggling Hickorycraft Division, unable to survive without J. Don Smith, was given over to Lexington. Sales nearly doubled from 1989 to 1995, and operating profits remained above 10 percent.

In October 1995, Lexington went over the top by introducing the Palmer Home Collection, a stunning new group developed by Jeff Young that had the added attraction of being licensed by Arnold Palmer. Prospects were bright at Lexington as it sent a clear signal that it could compete with product in the Drexel price range. The product lines were hot, and divisional profits topped 10 percent. There were, however, some land mines beneath the pretty surface at Lexington. The transition from the tough-as-nails duo of Smith Young and Willis Hedrick to the unproven leadership of Jeff Young was not going to be smooth. The preliminary cost estimates on the Palmer Home Collection turned out to be understated, requiring three price increases before it ever shipped. Harold Kirby's prediction was on the mark, and the group proved to be too complicated for the Lexington plants to produce. The decision to stress licensed collections such as Timberlake and Palmer could easily lead to a competitive attack on Lexington's core businesses of youth bedrooms and mid-priced suites. Stanley Furniture did just that, and within two years Lexington lost what had been an important part of its core business. Also, the import challenge had not been taken seriously. Making things even more challenging was the self-imposed "cultural isolation" practiced by Lexington's management. The owners sold the company and cashed Masco's checks, but they acted as if the sale had never taken place.

DREXEL HERITAGE had not prospered under the Masco banner, contracting as Lexington grew. The company had been a true success story under the leadership of Howard Haworth in the late 1970s and early '80s, but conditions gradually deteriorated after his departure in 1986. Just as John Wooden's successors at UCLA failed to stick, so too did a series of replacement CEOs at Drexel Heritage. Haworth was brought back to be a group president in 1990, but in the midst of correcting things, he clashed with Wayne Lyon and gracefully departed again, leaving Drexel in the hands of a former Thomasville sales manager. Unable to keep sales and profits from spiraling downward, management desperately tried to please headquarters and became a pilot for many ill-conceived corporate efforts. The result was a steady decline in Drexel Heritage branded sales and a company propped up by the addition of contracted work for Lexington and Lineage. The paper profits from this business put a small Band-Aid on some serious self-inflicted wounds. During the early '90s, Drexel's product development efforts were off the mark, its store program declined, and its brand lost much of its cachet. Morale suffered accordingly. Major reconstructive surgery was needed, and with the demise of Lineage, which was folded into Drexel for proper burial in August 1995, it was time to get on with fixing the core problems. In spite of its significant challenges, Drexel still had a great brand name and a prominent position in the industry. Given proper leadership, it could have been restored to fighting strength.

HENREDON, like Lexington, stood apart from the pack. Though it had been badly wounded by the upper-end recession in the early '90s, it managed to hold on to its dominant market share. Further, as the category gradually recovered, Henredon's sales and earnings became more respectable. Masco was instinctively reluctant to tamper with this division. And unlike the executives at Drexel Heritage, Henredon management aggressively kept the corporate staff at bay. This meant the division largely avoided the debilitating impact of Masco guidance, even if its management was continually second-guessed and rendered the object of much sniper fire. Management felt constrained by the awareness that Corporate would seize the reins the minute anyone stumbled, but it nonetheless carried on successfully.

In 1996 Henredon took the Polo Ralph Lauren license from Frederick Edward, overcoming the strong objections of Jones and his staff. Although the line had failed to produce results at Frederick Edward, it fit well with Henredon and, handled properly, would be a real plus. In addition, Henredon's brand image kept growing stronger, its product line was again producing winners, and the quality problems and systems deficiencies were getting resolved. The future of the "jewel in the crown" looked reasonably sunny at the time LFI was formed – as long as the parent resisted the temptation to tamper with it. Since it had little to gain from its association with the other divisions, attempts to draw it closer to the corporate bosom made no sense. Going forward, it would not be easy to preserve the special, elite mystique of this brand.

BERKLINE BENCHCRAFT had strong organizations in place, and Berkline held a well-defended market position in "motion" upholstery, a category that was growing faster than the industry. Benchcraft once was reasonably well positioned in the fast-paced promotional upholstery market. By 1996, they had lost their edge, and both companies were subject to powerful competitive forces in their niches. They needed to maintain sharp focus or they would get wiped out quickly. The last thing they needed was distraction. The best thing would be for LFI to leave them alone. These divisions had experienced less interference from corporate and for the most part, managed to avoid friendly fire.

ROBERT ALLEN / AMETEX / SUNBURY had been misunderstood by Masco right from the start. This basically was a company of old-line fabric mills, but Masco always stressed its jobber/ distributor division called Robert Allen. In neglecting the less-glamorous part of the business, Masco had turned off the veterans running the mills. One by one, they took early retirement instead of sticking around to watch the plumbers take a monkey wrench to the intricately woven tapestry of the fabric business. The departures of the top people at Robert Allen and its divisions knocked these companies on their heels, and the upward momentum they had when acquired was soon dissipated. Masco seemed puzzled by this business and surprised that it was so different from furniture. The home textile industry had its own Briar Patch and a geography that was different from the furniture version. In 1994, Masco recruited Ron Kass to run the division and scrambled to shore up a depleted management staff. Fortunately, he was no stranger to the business, having been the head of Knoll International's European operation when it was owned by Marshall Cogan, the former director of General Interiors.

MAITLAND-SMITH had so much upward velocity when Masco bought it that it took on a life of its own. This offshore furniture warrior doubled sales and tripled profits in the early '90s as the company combined a low-cost labor base in the Philippines with a pronounced styling edge. However, the fuel for this growth was provided by the eponymous Paul Maitland-Smith, and his 1996 departure left the company's future success less than assured. Somehow, the new owners at LFI had to survive the "Post-Paul" era and maintain the impetus without the founding genius around to dazzle customers with his creative product development legerdemain. What LFI needed to do was fix the infamous delivery reliability problems that Paul had neglected to address and to sustain the creative energy that he had provided in abundance.

The other companies, in the aggregate, managed to lose a good deal of money in the early 1990s. Only Sunbury Textiles showed a consistent profit, but it was small. The rest of the group failed year after year to make a profit no matter how hard headquarters tried to "help" them. Nothing made a difference – not money, management changes, nor expert advice. What LFI needed to do was to dispose of these misfits or fold them into the larger entities.

WAYNE WAGES WAR

The armies placed under Wayne Lyon's direct command in 1996 needed refitting, retraining, and reenergizing to bring them back to fighting strength. The distractions during the Masco era had depleted their energy, and the competition had taken advantage of their weakened condition. Dealers remained skeptical. Many were wary of the new company. What the divisions needed, from their perspective, was strong leadership and more autonomy. Under Ron Jones, divisional management had been forced to take on too many projects that made little sense. The last thing they needed was more top-down initiatives. They needed to focus on better product lines and finding good people to replace people who had been driven off. What they quickly got, however, was a large central headquarters staff determined to show the divisions how to get the job done. Lyon surveyed the same battlefield that the division commanders saw and came to completely different conclusions. The divisional executives came from varying backgrounds, but each had developed a feel for the intricacies of the Briar Patch. They were accustomed to hand-to-hand combat and had little respect for the corporate world. Lyon, on the other hand, came from the corporate world populated with boardrooms, bankers, big deals, and big budgets. The furniture warriors flew coach. Lyon flew on a corporate jet. They loved the business. He loathed it.

Lyon embarked with gusto on his quest to be victorious on the furniture battlefield, to prove to Manoogian that he was worthy of the trust placed in him, and to recoup some of the money that had been lost during his previous watch. His opening moves were watched closely, because everyone was eager to know what leadership he would provide. In an October 1997 interview with the *Greensboro News and Record*, Lyon replayed the old tunes from the Masco era and avoided striking any new chords. The story ran under the sardonic headline, "Life*Style*: New Name, Same Plan."[6] In a meeting with divisional executives, he stressed speed of delivery as his favorite mantra, as he called it. The furniture veterans cringed, because they knew meeting the objective would be costly and produce a small payoff. This was the familiar Delta Faucet refrain, exactly the type of theme that would appeal to a person who is only superficially tuned into the business, like Colin Carpi's "Have it your way" mantra. In the press, he defended the basic principles behind Lineage and ruminated on the idea of selling furniture like clothing, allowing consumers to express themselves. Again, echoes of Colin Carpi could be heard with clothing substituted for cosmetics.

This would have been a great time for a candid reassessment, a time to acknowledge mistakes and to set new strategies. Obviously, a continuation of the failed strategies of the past was not going to yield results any different from previous years of lackluster earnings. Unfortunately, no such new strategies were developed.

Lyon's Lieutenants

Charging forward, Wayne Lyon knew he would need a team of

officers to carry out his commands He assembled a handful of people he felt were right for the challenge – just one of which was a furniture man. His choices included Don Barefoot, an Emerson veteran as top operations person, a Unilever executive as head of human resources, Masco people as chief financial officer and chief legal officer, and Berkline Benchcraft President Alan Cole as chief marketing officer. Cole was the only furniture person in the group. This was consistent with Lyon's lack of respect for furniture people. It would have been out of character for him to choose Insiders, because his mission was to shape up the industry and transform the company into a Delta Faucet-type money-maker. For this he needed a higher-level executive than the furniture industry could supply. LFI reeled under the burden of this cumbersome, meddling bureaucracy. You don't recruit infidels to convert infidels.

These executives hired their own staff to carry out the orders they issued while carrying out Lyon's orders, and the corporate staff grew along with the corporate directives to the divisions. The headquarters staff had grown under Jones from fewer than 10 people to 24 with an annual payroll of $5 million. Now the number grew to 137. They were well paid and hardworking, yet few knew anything about making or selling furniture. But the corporate employees needed to fill those hours and earn those paychecks, so they carried on the former Masco way of "helping" the divisions. The divisions in turn staggered under the load of one corporate initiative after another.

And it was largely redundant, trying to perform functions the divisions were already doing. For example, in the Human Resource area, LFI combined the divisions' patchwork pension plans into one plan that nobody liked. They then set up a new 401(k) plan that later proved unmanageable and depressed morale. Finally, they put in a new medical insurance program that raised the division expenses by 30 percent the first year and led to a sharp increase in the employee contributions the second year. All three of these major corporate moves had to be abandoned within two years.

ORACULAR PRONOUNCEMENTS

The information technology chief made a name for himself by quickly implementing a Wayne Lyon initiative to buy $18 million worth of enterprise software from Oracle. This system – whereby nearly all activities of the enterprise were linked – was very much in vogue at this time, and Lyon believed that this was just what the divisions needed. Unfortunately, he reached this conclusion without taking the time to make sure the divisions were ready for something this sophisticated.[7] In addition, Lyon and Barefoot committed the company to an undetermined amount each year for consulting services to make the software work. The whole venture turned out to be a blunder as the divisions struggled to force the ill-suited software programs into manufacturing processes that were just too complex for them. Five years and $54 million later, the project was scrapped. During that time, little was done to correct the more fundamental systems needs at many of the divisions. Installing Oracle in companies like Lexington was like putting a turbocharged engine in a Model T Ford. Yet Lyon, who was not particularly knowledgeable regarding information technology, kept insisting the divisions must move faster to install the questionable software, perhaps because it sounded good to the bankers on Wall Street.

It was clear that Lyon was focused on one overriding goal: going public. Beyond that, he did not have the appetite to get involved with hand-to-hand combat, yet he continued to make decisions as if he knew what the battlefield conditions were. For certain, he did not involve the furniture veterans in his decision-making process. In his view, they were out of touch and incapable of understanding his grand vision. "Kittens do not devour Lyons" could well have been his motto; or, "Lyons can outrun Furniture People." The dramatic gestures, like the grandiose purchase of enterprise software, played well with analysts and therefore took on an exalted importance. The more mundane elements that were crying out for attention – like consumer marketing, quality, and cost containment – were neglected.

In spite of this, LFI got off to a decent start, reporting reasonably good first quarter results in May 1997. Sales were flat at $490 million, but operating earnings were up 15 percent, to $39 million. The outlook looked favorable on the surface, but the house of cards within the ranks was teetering.

THE BAREFOOT GENERAL ATTACKS

The Oracle software debacle was mild compared to the attempts to "modernize" time-honored and change-resistant manufacturing methods. This assault was led by a messianic Outsider named Donald L. Barefoot, Lyon's handpicked choice in July 1997 to be the top corporate "Operations Guy." He was ideally suited to play the role of Garth in Wayne Lyon's world – smart, tough, well educated, and technically proficient in the latest operations methods. He was also arrogant, opinionated, devoid of furniture experience

and convinced the industry was full of backward people just waiting to be shown the way, if not the door. He was the furniture
person's worst nightmare and before long would prove to be a
powerful force for change in multiple locations. A graduate of the
General Motors Institute, he went on to earn an MBA at MIT and
was wonderfully up to speed on countless technical matters. At
Emerson he turned around a division making convertible tops for
General Motors. This was a company with an abundance of engineering talent and a lack of marketing and branding, the antithesis
of the furniture business. His management style was abrasive. As
one division CEO put it, "He's the only person I know who can
walk into a room and annoy everyone, including the wallpaper,
before he sits down." For Barefoot, listening meant waiting for you
to stop speaking so he could tell you what to do.

Armed with extensive knowledge of the latest operations planning and management fashions, he became deeply engaged with
Lexington, Universal, and Drexel Heritage. He overwhelmed them
with initiatives, projects, and techniques. Henredon managed to
keep him at bay, but even there he had an impact as management
spent a good deal of time convincing him they were already doing
what he espoused.

Barefoot was consumed with what he called "Operational Excellence" some days and "Lean Manufacturing" other days. Regardless what he called it, he was determined to destroy resistance
put up by old-line furniture manufacturing people who thought
he was deranged. It was not so much that his ideas were wrong,
as it was that his ideas were risky and costly. He never acknowledged that his projects would cost money. When Insiders tried to
tell him this, they were accused of being troublemakers and – in

some cases – dismissed. When confronted with the consequences of his projects, he would change the subject. Barefoot had little patience with the Insiders, many of whom were equally stubborn in refusing to follow orders. This put them in an impossible situation because their bosses, the division CEOs, would be dismissed if they failed to hit their numbers. At some point they would be forced to choose their poison and, sadly, more than a few were sacrificed.

Right when the entire company should have been narrowly focused on meeting budget targets, Barefoot's message was that divisions must transform how they did things – no matter the cost. Lyon wanted to go public while shipping faster; Barefoot wanted to make everyone more operations oriented while transforming the industry; Alan Cole wanted the divisions to become more marketing oriented. This put division commanders in a difficult spot, especially when Lyon proclaimed that he was setting up an Office of the Presidency in which all three would share in all decisions and a directive from one was like a directive from all. "If my boss calls, get his name," the division CEOs howled once again.

RESULTS

By the end of its first year, Wayne's World was not exactly breaking records for sales and profitability. Sales fell slightly to $1.960 billion and operating profits were only $100 million, 5 percent of sales. As corporate expenses accelerated, the situation at the largest two divisions deteriorated. Conditions were especially bad at Universal, and a reserve of nearly $50 million was set up to cover some long-overdue restructuring costs. At Lexington, production problems began to surface in plants that had traditionally made enviable profits. In 1997, Lyon had used a special consulting firm to modernize the operations, and longtime operations chief Willis Hedrick had been pushed out of the way. Since Universal and Lexington comprised nearly half of the total Life*Style* sales, problems here impacted the whole corporation. Lyon crafted a wordy press release that tried to put the right spin on the mediocre numbers, but those close to the company knew otherwise. "1997, the first full year of Life*Style* Furnishings International's existence, has been at once positive and transitional for the company," was the way he clarified the otherwise murky picture. Privately, he expressed frustration with the divisions for being so slow to respond to his directives. If only the divisions would get with the program and listen to Barefoot, the opportunities were wonderful.

Chance to Get Whole

In June 1998, despite the continued margin decline, Life*Style* Furnishings International was tantalizingly close to launching the coveted Initial Public Offering of stock – the modern-day business equivalent of winning the lottery. The paperwork was completed and the Wall Street Wizards were ready to hit the road with Wayne Lyon to sell the offering to the institutional investors. Proceeds were expected to be $400 million, enough to pay off $334 million of debt and $12 million of accumulated interest. This move would strengthen the company's balance sheet and sharply reduce interest expenses going forward.

There was only one problem. The company was not performing well. Sales in the first quarter of 1998 were level at $498 million, but net income dropped 36 percent to $4.8 million after some restructuring charges. This was below the paltry $7.5 million the prior year.

Lyon needed his unexpurgated corporate dictionary to explain these numbers. Here is how he put it:

> *We are pleased to start the year with positive momentum in order volume with customer orders showing double-digit increases over the comparable period of 1997. First quarter shipments, however, were impacted as the initial implementation of manufacturing and technology initiatives at several business units combined to limit product availability. Similarly, operating profits were impacted by: – Additional costs related to the previously announced restructuring efforts designed to improve quality, reduce order-to-ship times and enhance product values at our Universal Furniture business unit; – New product production start-up inefficiencies resulting from LFI's successful October 1997 market introductions; – A complex computer system conversion at the Robert Allen Group; and – Continued reduction of inventory level company-wide. While these initiatives temporarily disrupted operating efficiency, we are confident that the resultant long term improvement in our customer satisfaction levels will justify the short term costs.*[8]

The corporate response was to put pressure on the divisions to perform better in the second quarter, but there was no relief granted regarding the special projects. The Briar Patch residents knew the culprit was the headlong thrust to transform the production process, and earnings would continue to fall until this reality was addressed. To the headquarters staff, the setbacks were only temporary. There had to be another explanation. Going forward, the constant vacillating between long-range projects and short-term earnings took its toll. When the second quarter results were tallied, sales were still flat at $479 million compared to the prior year. Net income dropped 17 percent, to $13.6 million.

What Went Wrong?

According to Lyon, "Second quarter shipments continued to be temporarily impacted as the initial implementation and rollout of planned manufacturing and technology initiatives at several business units combined to limit production availability. While these initiatives are temporarily disruptive, we are confident that the resultant benefit to our customers and our consumers will more than justify the short-term costs."[9] Without giving details, he went on to say that operating results were hit by "transition costs" related to the restructuring and re-engineering programs spearheaded by Barefoot's army in the pursuit of the overriding goal of shipping faster. Had he chosen to be candid, the explanation would have been quite different. What should have been said was, "Instead of stressing cost controls and concentrating on making the divisions stronger, we wasted money and time on expensive, unproven projects." But no such candid acknowledgment was ever uttered as he plowed forward. He was too tough to admit defeat.

While waiting for earnings to improve, the stock market turned soft and the window of opportunity for IPOs closed. By September, Lyon was forced to acknowledge that with these markets, it probably was not a wonderful time to start." The window would open again, that was certain, but it was not at all certain that LFI's earnings would be acceptable when the breeze blew in.

By the end of 1998, it was even more obvious that the operational strategy was not working. Things looked okay on the surface with sales for the year at $2 billion, up 2%, with profits of $137 million. But inside, things were not going well. Rather than stepping back to assess the real world, Barefoot just put his head down and knocked aside anyone who stood between him and his "Superior Business Model." He was especially hard on the furniture veterans who dared to question his moves, and the purging of the ranks continued. Lexington's Jeff Young resigned in August 1999 in protest of the destruction of what had been his family's company. Earlier that summer George Revington, a furniture person, had been dismissed as CEO of Universal and replaced by Harvey Dondero, who had been the CEO of Maitland-Smith. He, in turn, was replaced by Seamus Bateson, another non-furniture person. Later, Young's position would be filled by a person with a menswear background. Barefoot now could carry out his vision without fear of interference from those annoying furniture warriors who insisted on confronting him with facts.

BAREFOOT GOES TO WORK ON HENREDON

Barefoot's impact on the divisions was broad and corrosive. The depth of his negative influence can start to be imagined by looking at what he engineered at Henredon, the least-affected division. What follows is a partial list of what Barefoot and his troops had Henredon working on by the middle of 1999, in addition to projects that Henredon management had started. Bear in mind, this was happening when the company should have been cutting costs and streamlining operations.

1: *Assemble-to-Order-Focused Factories*

The massive Assemble-to-Order project called for product to be put together from a supply of parts, and it involved an expensive re-layout of the entire manufacturing space. Incidentally, Kittinger made furniture this way 50 years ago, but it was costly and required highly skilled cabinetmakers to do it. Henredon management felt strongly that if you were going to go to all this trouble, Make-to-Order – whereby you built furniture from raw materials forward – was the way to go. Barefoot, they insisted, had sold out and compromised on Assemble to Order. With Make-to-Order, the work cell could produce one-at-a-time products; with Assemble-to-Order, the work cell built products from pre-machined parts and subassemblies. Barefoot's plan for Henredon's Morganton facility alone would require the creation of an $8 million, 200,000 square foot storage area in the middle of the plant to house 110,000 linear feet of shelf space. This would presumably let the plant ship dining room product faster, yet the dealers said deliveries were already fast enough. When confronted with these facts, Barefoot just scowled and changed the subject.

2: *Project Delphi*

This was Henredon's company-wide effort to install and use the enterprise software Lyon and Best had bought from Oracle. Those who understood the furniture manufacturing process were convinced that it would not lend itself to the "cookie-cutter" logic of Oracle. The process was too complicated and had too many parts. Identical installations had failed with two of Henredon's rivals,

Baker Furniture and Century Furniture, and everyone knew it. Yet LFI pushed onward. While Henredon was preparing for LFI's "Project Leap" team to arrive with the costly package, the LFI roll-out team became helplessly ensnarled at Lexington and never made it to Morganton. Nevertheless, LFI assessed Henredon to cover some costs of the worthless software. Meanwhile, without letting LFI know, Henredon's IT team developed its own home-grown system that was superior to Oracle. It eventually would be adopted by several other furniture divisions and could easily have been used from the outset.

3: *Quality*

Barefoot had little interest in quality initiatives, but it was important to Henredon and its customers, so the division quietly worked on it without corporate support. With Barefoot's metalworking background at Emerson and General Motors, he was out of his element in the wood Briar Patch, and this frustrated him. Classic quality systems called for strict conformance to standards, but standards for wood are so variable that the textbook system does not work. This is especially true at the high-end of the market, where each piece of furniture is unique and no universal standard applies. What was needed was a quality system uniquely tailored to furniture, not one imported from a metalworking assembly plant. Berkline had developed one, but Barefoot dismissed it.

4: *New Product Development*

With Barefoot's urging and with Henredon's active support, the manufacturing and marketing teams were transforming the entire process of creating new products. This was a case of an advanced organization reaching even higher levels, and the results were impressive as Henredon removed waste from the way new products were introduced to the trade and to the plants. This was an area where corporate was helpful, yet the more successful Henredon became, the more the Henredon team sensed that Barefoot resented it.

5: *Marketing Strategy Revitalization*

A new marketing plan was drawn up in 1998, and management involvement was extensive. This initiative was a result of Alan Cole's urging, and it galvanized Henredon's marketing efforts to make them more centered on their highest achievers. The results were notable, and the backing from headquarters was worthwhile. Cole did not get caught up in the hyperactivity that others favored, but instead picked his openings and made the most of them.

6: *Upholstery Division Breakout*

Barefoot had sneered at the 10 percent margins in the upholstery division and challenged the management team to develop no less than a "Superior Business Model." This led to a massive restructuring of Henredon's upholstery division, including the closing of the flagship factory in downtown High Point and the loss of dozens of skilled workers. The project cost the company a great deal of money and after two years, there were very few tangible benefits to cite.

In addition to these major projects, Henredon was also involved with seven additional programs monitored by LFI. These included separate programs for safety, computer-aided design and engineering, set-up reduction, kaizens, lumber yield improvement, computerized traffic management, and environmental. Some were worthwhile and coincided with division needs. Many were boondoggles dreamed up by misinformed headquarters staff. All were given high-priority status by Corporate, and since different people were driving them, conflicts over the allocation of scarce resources were never resolved. The Corporate minions all had their own agendas, and the divisions were constantly being distracted from their primary purpose of making money by making furniture. Division management again felt trapped between the conflicting goals of producing "good numbers" to satisfy their CEOs' directives or making progress on the corporate projects to satisfy LFI. The CEOs had to make similar choices as they navigated between Scylla and Charybdis, pondering the means of their own destruction.

ANOTHER HUSBAND/WIFE TEAM

To help with his crusade, Barefoot had convinced Lyon to hire a husband/wife team, Ed and Julie Heard, who had parlayed their working knowledge of operations management techniques into a consulting and teaching career. Ed Heard had taught at Tennessee State as an academic, and as a consultant he dabbled with several companies. His wife, Julie, served as a confidant/assistant. Barefoot and Lyon were impressed with this duo and signed them up for a long-term stint as in-house gurus. With typical LFI pretension, their venture was named the "Life*Style* Center for Creative

Vitality," or LCCV to those in the know. The furniture people now had the Heards on board in addition to having Barefoot and his extensive staff to show them how to do their jobs. The result of this zealotry was a continued downward slope in earnings. No longer required to report earnings publicly, the actual numbers were not released, but there is no doubt they were "disappointing."

The House of Cards Wobbles

Meanwhile, as Don Barefoot was storming through the ranks, chief marketing officer Alan Cole was quietly making the case for a more rational approach to the business. Astutely sensing that Barefoot had Wayne Lyon's full support, Cole held back at first but during 2000 could no longer stand by and watch the demolition project. Cole was a furniture Insider who could think and act like an outsider when it made sense to do so. He had run a division successfully and knew the subtleties of the business. What's more, he had the support of the division people who saw him as their only chance at saving the company. His naturally polite, soft-spoken manner belied a strong will. Within Lyon's inner circle he had to overcome the stigma of being a furniture person, and this held him back at first. But he was slowly able to transform into more of a "corporate animal" and became accepted by Lyon's team. In the short-term, this caused him to lose a strong feel for the divisions, but in August 1999 he returned to full contact when he stepped into the acting CEO role to replace Jeff Young at Lexington. Cole had suspected the divisions were getting hammered by the various corporate projects, but he quickly saw that conditions were much worse than anyone at corporate could imagine. Something had to be done. In his quiet way, Cole kept trying to steer LFI away from the course set by Lyon and Barefoot.

LYON LETS GO

Finally, under tremendous pressure from Citicorp and Masco, Lyon agreed to a reorganization of the failed "Office of the Presidency." In February 2000, Alan Cole was promoted to president and CEO of LFI, and Barefoot was named chief operating officer. Lyon remained as chairman of the Board and still wielded great influence. This included Lyon's continued support of Barefoot, even in the face of overwhelming evidence that his methods were not working.

Barefoot must have been disappointed at being passed over for the top job. This perceived injustice only served to stiffen his resolve to push forward with his agenda. In a newspaper interview, he claimed that his lack of furniture experience was no handicap and suggested the furniture business was no different from any other. "Good fundamentals are good fundamentals," he said. "While I've been in other industries outside of furniture, the fact is, the subjects are the same."[10]

With Cole at the top, the division officers had at least a slim chance of surviving despite their depleted ranks. But as chief operating officer, Barefoot was the direct supervisor of the CEOs – not Cole – and the remaining furniture veterans wondered how long it would take for them to be designated for removal.

It's Simple, Stupid

Just when the divisional operating people thought things could not get any worse, they did. In October, the divisional staff people were brought in for a presentation by a consulting company called Simpler. Their designated presenter was a former chief executive officer of the HON Co., where Ron Jones had earned his spurs. He began the presentation by stating flatly that the furniture business was no different from any other business, and that every one in the room was stupid if they did not get their act together and make the conversion to "Lean Manufacturing." In a question-and-answer session that followed, someone pointed out to him that his own company suffered a sharp drop in earnings during the years when they made their conversion to "lean methods." When the guest speaker bristled, Barefoot and Lyon jumped in to keep the situation under control. Dissent was quickly shut down, and still another opportunity was missed to assess what was really happening. Among the questions that were on people's minds but were not asked that fateful day were the following:

✝ Why was Simpler Consulting needed on top of LCCV on top of the LFI staff?

✝ Why could LFI not do a better job of convincing the divisions that Lean Manufacturing was the way to go and that they must work together to make it happen?

✝ How was Simpler any different from the Universal Consulting Co. that did so much damage earlier?

✝ How much money had already been spent on Lean Manufacturing, and could LFI point to even one case where it actually worked?

✝ Did LFI really think it could succeed in the furniture business by firing the most knowledgeable people and replacing
them with inexperienced people?

✝ Why have so many previous "corporate initiatives" failed,
such as Oracle, LCCV LFI WorldWide, LFI Contract, Assemble-to-Order, Internet Marketing, Logistics, single-
source cushion buying, and centralized lumber buying?

✝ Why did Furniture Brands International have one third as
many people in their corporate office as LFI but with better
profits?

✝ Did anyone really believe that Universal and Lexington
were on track to return to profitability?

✝ What would happen if LFI were to shut all but the essential functions at corporate, eliminate LifeStyle Contract
and LifeStyle Worldwide, and let the divisions absorb these
functions?

✝ What if the direction of LFI's strategy was to manage the
company to generate cash flow first, margins second and
market share third, using the funds to pay down debt now
and to go public later?

✝ What if LFI were to eliminate the corporate constraints and measure the divisional CEOs on results?

A sense of impending doom pervaded headquarters and the divisions while the competition attacked what they saw as weakened forces. The divisions put up a brave defense, but market share was lost. Something had to be done to avoid a massive implosion. As it turned out, the Simpler presentation was Barefoot's last hurrah. Within a month he was dismissed from his command, along with several of his staff and a few other corporate executives. Alan Cole had finally taken control in November 2000 and was making the right moves. The question was whether or not they were too late to save the Life*Style* armies from defeat.

RESUSCITATION FOLLOWED BY DISINTEGRATION

After five years under the centralized command of Wayne's Watch, the divisions were no longer the leaders of the industry – and several were in disarray.

Cole tried gamely to keep the LFI forces on the field and to avoid a rout, but conditions were not in his favor. The economy turned bleak; four key retail customers went bankrupt; Chinese imports swamped the domestic industry; and the damage done over the last dozen years had robbed the divisions of their fighting strength. Cole knew his efforts, no matter how well conceived, would not be enough to turn the battle around, and as early as April 2001, he began to seek buyers for some properties. Caught in the cross fire of enemy attacks and "friendly fire" from headquarters, the

Life*Style* armies had little to bargain with as they sought a negotiated peace.

A STRATEGIC DIVISIONAL ASSESSMENT, 2001

Serving under the Life*Style* banner was not good for the health of the divisions. A situation report on each of the main flags circa 2001 revealed the following:

UNIVERSAL failed to make the sorely needed move to Mainland China, and now was trying to compete despite higher labor costs at its Taiwan plants. The company that had invented and perfected the offshore furniture concept was now getting pounded by copycat rivals who took the Universal concept to the Chinese Mainland. The company had lost its competitive edge in manufacturing, experienced constant turnover in its executive ranks, and failed to come up with a successor to the Alexander Julian Collection. They lost market share to mainland producers rather quickly and had to shut down some factories. Realizing the game was over, Cole sold the name and marketing organization to Samuel Kuo, the upstart Chinese manufacturer who owned LacquerCraft. The sale price was rumored to be less than $50 million. No one wanted the plants, and LFI still would have to contend with the liabilities associated with shutting them down. Masco had paid $500 million for Universal in 1989.

LEXINGTON withered under the smothering attention given to it by corporate during the previous five years. Instead of leaving this prodigious moneymaker alone, LFI could not resist the temptation to fix what was not broken. Three successive waves of "efficiency experts" were sent in to change the manufacturing process, and their cumulative effect crippled the operation. The entire marketing and distribution approach also was changed during this time, and the impact was to drive sales down sharply. Finally, the best people were driven off and replaced by inexperienced managers who failed to sustain the product development successes that made the line so strong in the Jones era. By 2001, the division was up for sale, but no one wanted to pay much for it.

DREXEL HERITAGE continued to stumble during Wayne's watch just as it had done under Jones. Little was done to correct the core problems, and the same CEO was left in place despite continuous profit shortfalls. The product development and merchandising efforts continued to be off the mark and sales declined accordingly. The top line kept falling, and profits dropped dangerously close to the red line. No one wanted to buy this once-dominant army, and LFI had to package it with other more desirable divisions to sell it.

HENREDON managed to avoid headquarters' help during Wayne's watch despite a constant barrage by Barefoot. The tough defensive battle Henredon had to wage to protect itself from corporate undoubtedly kept the company from reaching its true potential, but it remained successful in many ways. Sales and profits reached record levels in early 2001, and the brand name was more powerful than ever. There was no shortage of interested buyers. Recognizing the appeal of this property, Cole bundled it with Maitland-Smith and Drexel Heritage as a package deal.

BERKLINE AND BENCHCRAFT were also left alone by Corporate, and CEO Bill Wittenberg deflected attempts to infiltrate their operations. These divisions were in Tennessee and Mississippi, just far enough away to discourage visits by corporate executives. As a result, they performed well. What they needed was working capital to remain competitive in the fast-growing, but highly competitive motion furniture segment. The companies were certainly viable, but not dominant in a field ruled by La-Z-Boy and Action Lane.

ROBERT ALLEN was largely left alone as well and was capable of being spun off. Masco was focused on the distribution wing, which featured the rapid delivery of cut-order yardage of fabric to upholsterers. The bulk of the company was comprised of old-line fabric mills that never interested Masco or LFI. As such, there was no connection with the other divisions. Lyon would occasionally try to cajole and browbeat the upholstery divisions to buy more fabric from the company-owned mills, but everyone knew this only made sense if the fabrics were right for that particular company. This kind of vertical integration benefited no one. At the first Masco meeting with the Citicorp investors, one of the division CEOs asked Dave Thomas of Citicorp why they did not just spin the fabric group off and use the proceeds to pay down debt. His reply was, "Because the assets will be worth so much more when we go public." To his way of thinking, it mattered not that the business unit did not fit with the other companies. Now, after five more years of neglect, it was worth less.

MAITLAND-SMITH flourished during the LFI years, and money was poured into this amazing offshore company. This investment in facilities, combined with the skilled, cheap labor of the Philippines, helped it grow sales and earnings sharply despite the loss of founder Paul Maitland-Smith. However, the lack of his brilliant creative direction gradually took its toll, and his prior company felt the heat when he launched his new venture, Theodore Alexander. Despite LFI's handling of Maitland-Smith, it was a desirable property especially in view of its Far Eastern base.

RUMORS

The dissolution of Wayne's World continued to gain speed as 2001 came to close. In November, as rumors of the sale of various divisions swirled around the industry, stockholder Masco announced that it was taking a $460 million write-down of its furniture stake. Manoogian refused to say whether the divisions were for sale, but it was obvious they were. In December, the sale of Henredon, Drexel Heritage and Maitland-Smith to Furniture Brands International was announced. "Life*Style* breaking up" shouted the *Furniture Today* headline of its lead story on December 10. "The moves will bring to an end the concept launched by Masco, Life-*Style*'s former owner, which once hoped to achieve synergy and high performance by assembling a stable of manufacturers."[11] The price: $176.5 million in cash and $110.6 million in Furniture Brand International shares.

It was not a pretty sight to see the once-proud armies struggle to cover their retreat as they tried to avoid a rout. The mighty Universal had been recaptured by the Chinese. Life*Style*'s chief rival had captured Henredon, Drexel Heritage and Maitland-Smith.

Berkline and Benchcraft were about to surrender, and the other divisions were negotiating a cease-fire that would lead to surrender.

The demolition of the Lexington "aircraft carrier" was particularly sad. After Barefoot and Lyon succeeded in removing the top tier of furniture officers and replacing them with people with little furniture experience, the company's fortunes soured. In 1996, sales had reached $440 million, operating profits were above 10 percent, and the company was the envy of its rivals. But LFI insisted on transforming it into a "superior business model" of making and marketing furniture. Five years later, it had sales of $290 million and a $13 million operating loss.

FBI Captures the Most Wanted Brands

As Alan Cole struggled with the remains of the Life*Style* army, the leader of Furniture Brands International, Mickey Holliman, could hardly believe how well the battle had turned out. For a price of $176.5 million in cash plus shares of FBI stock worth $110.6 million, he had captured the high end of Life*Style* and strengthened his hold atop the industry. He now owned Henredon and Drexel Heritage as well as Thomasville, Broyhill, and Lane, without question the strongest line up of brands ever imagined in the furniture industry. Not even Colin Carpi could have envisioned this collection.

In September 2001, when rumors of the impending sale first broke, Furniture Brands stock was trading at $22. As the agreement was announced in December, the value had climbed to $30, and it was trading above $35 by mid-January 2002.

The irony of the transaction is that Interco and Masco originally converged in how they operated; they then diverged markedly under different leaders, upon entering the furniture business. The St. Louis-based Interco originally was engaged in footwear, apparel, and retailing; Michigan-based Masco made industrial parts, plumbing products and fasteners. As they both divested the less-promising categories they elected to diversify into furniture. From there they took radically different paths. The contrast between Mickey Holliman and Wayne Lyon and their respective operating philosophies was startling. Lyon never reached a clear understanding of the industry and never grew to love it. Likewise, he never learned to respect or to trust the furniture Insiders. Holliman was an unalloyed Insider, "born and raised in the Briar Patch," and he loved it with all his heart. While Lyon tried to make the industry fit his predetermined point of view, Holliman used common sense to put together the right people in the right slots so that they could create the right products. The rest would take care of itself, he believed, and it did. While LifeStyle stumbled toward defeat, Furniture Brands prepared for its victory march.

THE EMPIRE CONTINUES TO DISSOLVE

One by one, LFI's divisions were discarded during late 2001 and early 2002. The Robert Allen Fabric Group, including the Beacon Hill showrooms, was sold to an investment group led by Ron Cordover, the New York businessman who had sold Berkline to Masco. The art of selling high to the Outsiders and later buying back low from them was not lost on the astute Mr. Cordover. Incumbent CEO Ron Kass resigned. In March 2002, a deal was announced to sell Lexington to a management-led investment group. Former London Fog executive Bob Stec remained as CEO. And the Berkline Benchcraft sale to another management-led investment group was finalized in April, along with the sale of Sunbury Textiles to another management group. With the exception of Lexington, these companies were sold to industry Insiders who knew the industry well. The purchase prices were not revealed, but they were well below what Masco had paid for them.

At one time, this conglutinate collection of companies had 30,000 employees and sales of $2 billion. In April 2002, LFI was reduced to a lease on the now-empty headquarters, some carryover obligations for a few pensions, and 4 million shares of Furniture Brands stock. At the time of the divestiture of Henredon, Drexel Heritage and Maitland-Smith, these shares were worth $110 million at market price. Now they were worth $160 million. Richard Manoogian had finally discovered how to make money in the furniture industry – by shutting down his own operation and acquiring stock in his rival's. As Michael Porter predicted years earlier, if a stockholder wants to own stock in a company in another industry, he can buy the stock directly. He does not need to buy it indirectly through an acquiring company's ownership.

LifeStyle Furniture Disappears

Alan Cole resigned in May 2002, and LFI disappeared quietly. Various "post mortems" were offered as the Masco/LFI occupation ended. It was a bad acquisition strategy in the first place, some experts said. The group of companies had no synergy and were impossible to manage, they reasoned. Victims of a changing industry, said others. Cole was quoted in *Furniture Today* on February 11, as saying, "With where the industry is going, if you are going to be a large company, you can't sacrifice responsiveness and strategic unity for the sake of being big. While we were large, we didn't have that one strategy that worked for all our divisions." "The fast eat the slow," was a favorite expression of Mickey Holliman's. "So, it's not the peculiarities of furniture that have doomed virtually every major consolidation effort in the business. It's the execution of those efforts, or lack of execution – the inability of the corporate entities to pull the trigger and reduce some of the excess overhead to sawdust – that has spelled disaster for most of the failed furniture conglomerates," intoned Warren Shoulberg of InFurniture.[12] David Perry of *Furniture Today* concluded that the Life*Style* business model was flawed and "had little new to offer the industry."[13] Jerry Epperson offered a mild defense of Masco, if not Life*Style* management, and pointed out that "as an industry, we need to learn from other industries about how they are succeeding and how they could help us. We need to embrace these solutions, not resist them. Maybe we can learn one day."

The obituaries missed the most insidious cause of death: Globalization. LFI's leadership made countless mistakes, but the wave of imports, especially from China, were the real killers. Others would find out soon enough.

LESSONS LEARNED

The downfall of Life*Style* Furnishings International came for the same reasons spelled out in previous chapters with previous companies. This was a big-budget sequel to the S&H experience. The consequences were more severe, but the refrain was familiar. Colin Carpi could have told LFI that the acquired companies did not fit well together and that the thrill of launching an IPO transcended the tedium of running the companies. The Furniture Realities were denied; the Seven Deadly Sins were committed; and the Strategic Traps ensnared the invaders. For Carpi, S&H, Turner, Masco, LFI and scores of other firms, the trip to the Briar Patch proved to be costly. Lyon could have avoided making the same mistakes, but stifling debate and surrounding himself with non-furniture people created an anti-furniture mindset that led to the collapse of the entire group. Like a noted Briar Patch resident quipped, "Some folks didn't have the sense they should have been born with." By studying the history of Life*Style* Furnishings and Masco and then contrasting that with the operating style of Furniture Brands, the keys that lead to success in the furniture business can be found.

There is no substitute for having capable people who know how to create, to make and to sell furniture. Next, the product must be right, or nothing else matters. Those capable people must develop products that sell in to the retailers, sell through to the consumer, and can be made at a profit. And, finally, you must have a passion for the business. Even though it can and will break your heart, you must love it to survive in it.

MAN IN MOTION

A ND SO THE LONG OUTSIDER CRUSADE was over. The invaders had been repelled for now and banished from the Furniture Zone. They were not so much defeated as they were outnumbered and outlasted. The skilled ones went back to work for companies that were more appreciative of their skills, to work with people who spoke their language and shared their desire for continuous improvement. The Insider forces retook control of what was left of the furniture industry and purged the last vestiges of the Outsider Invasion. Nevertheless, there were no victory celebrations, because there was no time to celebrate.

The affected companies had been seriously weakened by the conflict, as surely as America was drained by the War Between the States. Furniture facilities had been neglected, and brand building was abandoned. Instead of adopting the valid ideas and methods espoused by the Outsiders, the furniture people rejected everything and deprived the industry of some greatly needed innovations. Like a patient refusing to take the medications prescribed by a doctor because the doctor has an offensive bedside manner, the furniture veterans were still walking around with a host of untreated ailments.

The retail channel also suffered as independent dealers understandably stopped aligning themselves with any one manufacturer. The turmoil in manufacturing and the changes in ownership had fractured many of the relationships between factories and retailers. At a time when buyer/supplier partnerships were needed, uncertainty took over and the key players drifted apart. Historically, independent furniture retailers allied themselves with certain factories and grew comfortable with the owners and managers. This unspoken bond helped the factory remain in touch with the field and helped the retailer receive extra support from key suppliers. These fragile loyalties were often driven by the personalities of the owners. Paul Broyhill used a company plane to make visits to dealers so often that he was said to have more than "800 close personal friends." Unfortunately, the new breed of manufacturing executives brought on board by the outsiders didn't last long enough to build solid relationships, and the emerging retail chains were too focused on driving down costs to bother cultivating friendships with vendors. The result was a weakening of the supply chain that linked producers with retailers. Never very efficient, it nevertheless was based on mutual trust. Now that was gone.

The Outsiders lost the war, but the Insiders may have lost even more. They lost the thirst for innovation that the invaders brought with them. In many cases the Outsiders simply wanted to make improvements, and they were not afraid to pour money into the industry. Watching them leave the battlefield was depressing, especially in view of the threat on the horizon – imports from China. Like coalition forces that need each other, but can't seem to get along, the Insiders, Outsiders, and Retailers split up just when they should have been pulling together.

MAN IN MOTION

Into this postwar wasteland rode Wilbert G. "Mickey" Holliman, the chairman, president and CEO of Furniture Brands International, the largest and arguably best furniture army in the world. Holliman rode not on horseback but in a sleek Raytheon Hawker, one of the fastest corporate jets on the market. He loved the plane, not because it symbolized success but because it allowed him to stay close to his operating divisions and his customers. Even though his schedule was packed with store visits, meetings with his division executives, key suppliers, investors, and countless others, he could effortlessly shift gears as he sized up each situation, dealt with the issues, and headed home. Home to Holliman was Tupelo, Mississippi, where he was so comfortable that he turned down the top job when he was first offered to him. The headquarters were in St. Louis, but Holliman had no desire to leave Tupelo. The board relented and told him he could live wherever he wanted. He stayed in Tupelo.

Born in Columbus, Mississippi, Holliman was raised in Shuqualak, a town of 500 people not far from Scooba, a town of 600 people. After graduating from nearby Mississippi State with a degree in industrial engineering, Holliman went to work for the Futorian Corp, a promotional upholstery producer. Its head was Morrie Futorian, a showman with great instincts for merchandising and the ability to predict what would sell. After coming to Chicago from the Ukraine, Futorian and his father set up a small "garage" type upholstery shop, which he soon outgrew because of his remarkable selling ability.

Futorian greatly influenced Mickey Holliman, helping him to

understand the "promotional" game that he could play with the best of them. To say a line was "promotional" implied that dealers used it to promote the store, which invariably meant high value or "a lot of look for the money." Put another way, it meant cheap. It may look like the high-end sofa that inspired its design, especially in the newspaper ad, but it was not built that way. The promotional furniture universe was a fast-track, take-no-prisoners game. Success depended on your reputation for being able to deliver the goods. It required a sixth sense to know which designs to knock off and when to do it. Futorian's merchandising genius would have been wasted had he not been able to find a few manufacturing geniuses who knew how to cut costs and to deliver the goods.

NORTH CAROLINA COMES TO MISSISSIPPI

Futorian learned early that the low-cost card trumped everything else. Consumers and retailers never quite understood how the sofa was built and they had precious few brand names to rely on, but they did comprehend the difference between a $299 price point and a $399 price point. Noticing the rising labor rates for skilled upholsterers, even in North Carolina, he was clever enough and gutsy enough to build a factory in a region with lower labor costs. Long before NAFTA, Futorian was sensitive to the benefits of transplanting factories to gain access to cheap labor, even in the United States. When Futorian discovered an economic development initiative in Mississippi that provided him with the money to build an upholstery plant, he took advantage of the opportunity. Starting with a plant in New Albany, later built a frame plant in Eupora and a recliner plant in Okolona. He had the temerity to venture outside the customary bounds of North Carolina and Virginia, and he incurred the disdainful scorn of the established producers in the North Carolina-Virginia Briar Patch. "There is no way he can make it work without skilled upholsterers," was the establishment's reaction. The trickiest part of making sofas and chairs is the task performed by "outside" upholsterers, who apply the fabric to the piece and complete the job by tacking it neatly in place. The skill takes years to develop, and good "outside upholsterers" can make $30,000 a year. "Those boys in Mississippi are not going to make it," scoffed the skeptics. Futorian and others surprised the establishment, revealing that the upholstering skills of the trained "outsiders" may have been overrated.

Observers who had witnessed the transfer of old-line upholstery operations from Grand Rapids, Michigan, to North Carolina in the 1960s were not surprised to see history repeat itself. On several occasions, the furniture industry had demonstrated that it could be transported quite readily. Mute testimony to this fact can be seen in the empty factories still standing in New England, Pennsylvania, Upstate New York, Indiana, and Michigan.

Morrie, Mickey & Bo

Futorian's real genius was in re-engineering production lines to lower labor costs. In effect, he introduced Henry Ford-type, mass production techniques to the upholstery lines in eastern Mississippi. This gave him a cost advantage over competitors who clung to the old ways of production. He needed bright young engineers to do this, and one of the brightest was Mickey Holliman. The wizened old Ukrainian and the young Mississippian developed a close relationship as the company grew. The assembly line method let them price Futorian sofas lower than the "bench made" sofas from other regions. Nobody told Morrie you were not supposed to do that. His New Albany plant became the largest upholstery plant in the world, ultimately reaching 1.2 million square feet and employing 2,000 workers. Beyond that, he spawned numerous spin offs and start-ups by former employees. It has been estimated that 50 to 60 furniture factories in Mississippi can trace their roots to Futorian.

Mickey Holliman learned all he could from Futorian and cherished the relationship. Nevertheless, he had bigger dreams. What if, he wondered, I could start my own company? Unlike wood, which requires a lot of capital, an upholstery company can be started with very little money – which is exactly what Mickey had. With luck and resourcefulness, he figured the startup company could find an empty building, get a few sewing machines, buy materials on credit and – if they made the goods and shipped them fast enough – collect before they were out too far. In 1970, a restless Mickey Holliman partnered with Alvin E. "Bo" Bland, the vice president of manufacturing at the Futorian Corp., to do just that. They got Morrie Futorian's reluctant blessing and started their own upholstery company in a 20,000-square-foot leased warehouse in Tupelo. They called it the Action Co.

Their new company shrewdly tapped into the fastest-growing segment of the furniture business, the reclining chair, and they never looked back. This versatile design, with its clunky silhouette and ungainly "gear shift," was usually tailored in a garish fabric made of a stain-proof, wear-proof, seemingly bullet-proof fiber such as nylon or Herculon. Something about this magic combination caused the recliner to catch on with blue-collar America in a very big way. The aloof home shelter magazines were aghast; interior designers refused to allow them in the room; and upper-end producers ignored them, but Archie Bunker had to have his "La-Z-Boy." Action went beyond "clunky" with style and, above all, comfort. The problem with most furniture is that it just sits there. But this furniture did something. It moved. It reclined. It had a concealed ottoman that dropped out of sight when not needed. It let the user recline in comfort. And it sold like no other product category.

The category kept expanding. One day, somebody said, "Hey, if we can make chairs that recline, why not make sofas that recline?" Mickey Holliman and the Action team did just that, and a new segment was created. Dubbed "motion furniture" by industry insiders, it was a huge success with consumers. Sectionals followed, and the motion category soon was bigger than life. Producers who could deliver the goods could make decent margins, and mass market retailers could make even higher margins on these hot sellers that needed no prep work or after-market servicing. Retailers just ran their ads on television or in the paper. The floor salesman invited the shopper to sit in it and wrote up the order. The desk person arranged for extended financing and directed the customer to the dock, where a few burley guys loaded the recliner onto your pickup or SUV. What fun.

Usually startups like Action involve a production person and a sales type. One makes the goods and the other sells the goods. Mickey and Bo only had experience in making the goods. But Mickey Holliman never had to worry about expressing himself and being persuasive. His intensity got your attention; his honesty won your trust; and his way with words won you over. He approached people and problems the same way, candidly and directly. He was a naturally gifted speaker who was as comfortable chatting with a Northeast Mississippi hourly worker as he was negotiating with a New York banker. But his real talent was listening. He always paid close attention to what others were saying – always listening, observing, evaluating, questioning, learning, thinking. And then applied what he learned with the tenacity of a Mississippi State Bulldog.

VIRGINIA COMES TO MISSISSIPPI

Action, not surprisingly, grew so fast it ran out of working capital and had to seek shelter in order to keep growing. In the meantime, the conventional furniture manufacturers stood by and wondered why they were left out of this crazy game. The most conventional of conventional companies, Altavista, Virginia-based Lane, jumped in and in 1972 negotiated a deal to buy Action for an unspecified number of Lane shares.

Lane wisely insisted that Holliman and Bland stay on. From the very beginning, however, the cultures of Lane and Action clashed. Lane was formal, courtly, deliberative, and proud of its lineage, not unlike Virginia war hero Robert E. Lee. Action was casual, brash, impulsive, and determined to prove itself, not unlike Mississippi war hero Nathan Bedford Forrest. Forrest's key to victory was "to get there firstest with the mostest." Mickey Holliman expressed it differently but did not dispute that bit of advice.

The Lane Co., founded in 1912, made a fortune producing and selling "Hope Chests" lined with cedar. For decades these storage cabinets were popular with young women, and Lane built and maintained the major share of this profitable niche. They also produced collections of case goods and upholstery, but those product lines were less than memorable and not particularly profitable. As the popularity of the Hope Chests waned in the 1980s, management failed to correct its operational weaknesses and earnings declined steadily. Action, on the other hand, grew rapidly. At the time of acquisition, sales were only $4.6 million, but 20 percent increases year after year were not unusual. They passed the $130 million mark by 1985, and profits from Mississippi soon outstripped those of Virginia. The Mississippians got the working capital they needed. The Virginians got the earnings they needed.

To the outside, everything was copasetic. "This merger has been good for Action and Lane," Holliman said in a 1985 *Forbes* interview. Added Bernard B. Lane, family patriarch and board chairman: "Lane's strength comes from the fact that we're like a bundle of sticks bound together. Everybody knows that he or she has a shot at running his own show."[1] But privately, the tension between the two entities was increasing. Lane earnings kept declining and the stock price languished. This meant Holliman and Bland were not benefiting financially from the profits they were generating for Lane, and it began to be an irritant.

In 1970 Holliman and Bland approached Lane management and said they wanted to leave to pursue another start-up. Lane management objected, and instead of letting them go did the honorable and smart thing. They hired an independent consultant to put a value on the company and used the results to restructure the deal, giving Bland and Holliman more equity.

It paid off. In 1984, Lane earned $4.47 a share and returned 17 percent on shareholder equity with no debt. There were, however, a few clouds. In 1983 the company had invested heavily in a polyester coating operation from Italy that would prove to be a disaster for Lane the same way it had for Henredon. Also, the company acknowledged it was having trouble with its Venture division "where it tries to compete with imports."[2] Fortunately, there were few imports at that time.

MISSOURI COMES TO VIRGINIA

Lane stock was trading at $39 a share in 1987 when a St. Louis based conglomerate called Interco made an offer of $64, more than $500 million in total. The earnings of Holliman's Action division certainly helped to command such a premium. Lane's response to Interco's aggressive bidding tactics was cool. "B. B." Lane voted against the merger and resigned to devote his full attention to seeking a better offer.

This was not the first time outsiders had cast their eye on Lane. Notorious investor Victor Posner made a pass at buying it in 1980 and pocketed $550,000 in greenmail. This time, some of Interco's institutional investors balked at what they thought was a bad deal. "Lane is a great company," said Donald C. Geogerian, a Dreyfus vice president. "But it is too much money."[3] How Interco placed such a high value on Lane is not clear, but home office gossip attributed it to the previous experience of then-Chairman Harvey Saligman. Saligman supposedly lost the bidding for another company in the mid-1980s and he swore he would "never underpay for a company again." This time, the deal went through, and Lane became part of Interco in April 1987.

The Virginia gentry at Lane's Altavista headquarters were not happy despite the generous terms, and many of them never accepted what they called "the hostile takeover" by the Yankee outsiders from Missouri. In turn, Interco management eventually grew to resent the "Altavista attitude" and the lack of earnings. Nevertheless, the acquisition of Lane, when added to the previously acquired Ethan Allen and Broyhill, made Interco the largest furniture company in the world.

Interco once was called the International Shoe Co., the largest footwear manufacturer in the world with more than 80 factories in Missouri alone. The company diversified into apparel and retailing when the shoe business moved offshore in search of lower labor costs. In 1966, the company changed its name to reflect the move away from shoes. By 1988, Interco reported sales of $3.3 billion from its 23 operating divisions ranging from apparel manufacturing to retail merchandising. The company had made a remarkable transition from its origins as a shoe company, but as we saw with Masco, acquiring companies is one thing. Running them is another.

A CARDINAL COMES TO ST. LOUIS

Interco's stable of big-name furniture companies led some observers to conclude that the furniture industry finally was ready for consolidation. If it could integrate Broyhill's manufacturing skills with the retailing wizardry of Ethan Allen, the results could be impressive. But this was not the style of Interco, which preferred more of a conglomerate approach and treated divisions like holdings in a portfolio. "The Interco style was always hands-off – running a group of companies that reported to the corporate headquarters at the bottom line only. Concepts of integrating divisions were not put on the table until we disposed of all but the furniture companies and the pressure from offshore forced our hand. Eliminating redundancies was not part of the Interco agenda in the late 1980s."[4]

Even so, Interco had to defend itself from a hostile takeover attempt even before it could try out its new lineup. The Cardinal Acquisition Corp. in July 1988 literally faxed in a $2.4 billion tender offer for all the outstanding stock in Interco. This $64-a-share offer was well above the recent trading range of the stock at $35 to $40. The lead investors in this hostile takeover bid were Mitchell and Stephen Rales, who were backed by junk bond genius Michael Milken of Drexel, Burnham, Lambert. They also claimed to want to use the Toyota Production System to improve underperforming American manufacturing companies. Interco management, however, believed their intention was not to run the company but to make money by liquidating it and selling off the parts.

The board hired the investment banking firm of Wasserstein Perella to make the Rales go away. They employed an array of counter offensive techniques, including "poison pills" and "golden parachutes," while dismissing the bid as being below the real value of the assets. A titanic financial battle ensued. The Rales upped their offer to $74 a share. The board rejected it. Wasserstein Perella said the valuation should be $76 a share, or $2.9 billion. The bankers did not know the furniture business.

To keep the Rales at bay and to keep their jobs, the Interco board put together a restructuring package with Wasserstein Perella's help. It included borrowing nearly $2 billion from a consortium of banks, paying a $38-per-share cash dividend to stockholders, and distributing junk bonds to its shareholders. The package had a total value estimated by Wasserstein Perella to be in excess of the Rales offer. Interco sacrificed a great deal to get the Rales brothers off its back.

In November 1988, the Rales brothers let their offer expire and returned to D.C. Their visit to St. Louis was not a complete waste, however, because they pocketed $75 million of gains on the shares they owned. Interco's armed forces, aided by Wasserstein Perella's mercenaries, had defeated the "barbarians at the gates." The headquarters were secure. Now, all they had to do was live with the post-war consequences. Stockholders were weary; management was wary. That year, Interco's total earnings were $227 million, well below the $350 million needed to service the debt.

It might never be clear as to which deal was better – the Rales brothers' offer versus the Interco restructuring package. Lynn Chipperfield, chief counsel at Interco during the time of the competing offers, still expresses uncertainty nearly 20 years later:

> *I am not sure you can say for certain whether the Interco shareholders "won" or "lost" in the battle with the Rales brothers. The shareholders had been made an all-cash offer by the Rales, which would seem in retrospect to have been a good deal. But there was serious question whether the Rales ever had the money to pay the offer price, and a Delaware judge implied that they did not. Interco's Board, on the other hand, offered a mixture of cash and junk bonds and "stub value of the equity" that was valued by our financial advisors as greater than the Rales offer. This was advice the Board of Directors could not ignore. The cash was real, and the*

equity gave the shareholders the opportunity to participate in the future growth of the company, albeit in a highly leveraged environment. Even in hindsight and with seventeen years of second-guessing behind us, the relative value to the shareholders of the two proposals remains a jump ball.

The moral of the whole experience is that hostile takeovers can make money for the bankers and lawyers, but they do not make the target companies stronger.

POST WAR TRAVAILS

While Wasserstein Perella collected their fees and went back to Chicago, Interco had to start making good on its claim that the company was better off without the Rales. As Chipperfield recalled,

The mood at the corporate offices after the Rales offer was pulled ran the gamut from jubilation to foreboding. The "bad guys" (as our then-Vice-Chairman was fond of calling them) had been driven away, and management retained control of the company. However, we were now very highly leveraged and we faced the prospect of selling a number of our better companies (Ethan Allen, Londontown, Big Yank, and Central Hardware) in order to reduce our debt.

In addition, something else was happening in the fall of 1988 that, had we known of its effect at the time, might have changed the Board's decision to go forward with the dividend payment. The RJR/Nabisco deal was unfolding at that time, and it effectively

drew all demand for junk bonds out of the financial markets. Thus, the free-wheeling purchase and sale of companies by means of junk bond financing – a practice that had driven valuations up during the 80s – was no longer possible. Companies could now fetch only what they were worth. The valuations put on Ethan Allen, Londontown and the rest by our advisors for purposes of reducing our debt were based largely on junk bond-era transactions. Those were now out the window. As I look back, the restructuring was in trouble even before we got started.

Interco, worried that the deal would lead to the barbarians selling off companies for a profit, now had to sell off companies just to stay financially afloat. Among the companies sold were Londontown Corp., Biltwell Co., and the redoubtable Ethan Allen. The Wasserstein Perella defense was brilliant but predicated on the *numbers*, and the *numbers* included assumptions regarding the prices that could be commanded for the assets to be sold. In addition, the *numbers* assumed that the earnings projections for the furniture and shoe companies would be met. Unfortunately, the *numbers* were wrong: The sales and liquidations failed to generate the anticipated revenues, and the operating earnings came in below forecast.

For example, the original projection for Ethan Allen was that it would be sold for $587 million. Experienced furniture people scoffed, and Wasserstein Perella reluctantly sent a team of analysts to division headquarters in Danbury, Connecticut. "The values they put on Ethan Allen were preposterous," said Nat Ancell, chairman of Ethan Allen. "We told them they were crazy. There were loads and loads of nice young kids (from Wasserstein Perella) who didn't know much who were analyzing figures."[5] After doing their diligence, they reduced the projected sales price to $500 million. It eventually sold in May 1989 for $388 million (or $675 million in current dollars) – about two-thirds of the original forecast. Likewise, operating earnings from the furniture companies, following the cyclical pattern of the industry, failed to make forecast.

The real numbers clearly did not support the *projected numbers*, but no matter. Typically, in situations like this, the people generating the projections did not have to generate the earnings. The people in the divisions – those who were expected to make and market the shoes and furniture, the ones who actually did the work that produces the profits that the people in the home office manipulate and convert to *numbers* – were burdened with impossible-to-meet budget requirements and told they would be fired if they failed to do the impossible. For good measure, salaries were frozen, workers were laid off, marketing expenses were chopped, and capital expenditures were postponed. This Procrustean formula made the divisions less competitive, the work force less productive and destroyed morale . . . right when it needed all the help it could get. It was like slashing the tires of a race car during the final pit stop. If Interco had been like so many of the other furniture companies of the '80s and '90s, it might have failed to reach the finish line. But Interco was not typical and minimized the negative impact of the reorganization.

ANOTHER VICTORY FOR GENERAL PYRRHUS

In 1989, Interco earnings from operations were only $70 million, including the sale of assets. In 1990, the company reported massive losses and hit bottom by 1991. Its stock was trading at less than one-eighth, derisively called "drill bit" sizes by Wall Streeters. Its market capitalization was down to $7 million, prompting the Standard & Poor's rating service to remove Interco from the S&P 500 Index after almost 55 years of being included. Interco filed a voluntary petition of Chapter 11 bankruptcy in January 1991, after lengthy negotiations with its creditors broke down.

While this move was not very surprising, it was sobering, especially to the factory workers and their families. The Broyhill workers, accustomed to the paternalistic attitude of the family, were distraught at the thought of bankruptcy. Their fears materialized shortly after the bankruptcy filing, when a North Carolina National Bank branch in Lenoir refused to cash payroll checks until the bank could confirm that funds were available.[6]

So while bankers were collecting their fees, executives were covering their tracks, analysts were "numbering" their forecasts, and lawyers were petitioning the courts, plant workers kept making furniture, supervisors kept the lines running, and people like Furniture Brands' Mickey Holliman held things together.

The Rales assault and the Interco defense have echoes of Greek mythology as it laid waste to a once-proud company. Neither side could claim victory, but they could go to court – and that they did with a vengeful spirit.

Forbes reporter Laura Jereski framed the Interco debacle within the context of the times:

As leveraged takeovers reached a crescendo in the late 1980s, a financial trend that had once made sense no longer did. The leveraged recapitalizations worked only so long as the debt taken on did not exceed the ability of the business to support it. But as the stock market rose from under 1000 on the DJI to nearly 2800, takeover premiums mounted, and so accordingly did the amount of debt needed to finance a deal. Pretty soon deals were being made that could not be financed out of cash flow or by selling properties at a profit; they were predicated on increasing sales or cutting costs.

In the final analysis, the takeover wave subsided, not because federal prosecutors put Drexel, Burnham, Lambert and Michael Milken out of business, but because it was no longer possible to buy public companies for less than their intrinsic value. So the deal machine rolled on, but it was producing products doomed to fail.

In some ways, Interco Inc., in November 1988, was the crest of the wave. It was one of the biggest deals of the Eighties and one of the quickest to fail. This St. Louis-headquartered apparel and furniture conglomerate distributed $2.6 billion to its shareholders, $2 billion of that borrowed, to thwart a hostile takeover. It was an outrageous deal. The price was over 18 times cash flow and over 2 times book value. Just 12 weeks after the deal was done, it was in trouble. . . . Everybody, just about everybody, got so carried away with making deals that they forgot that two and two can never equal six.[7]

It was outrageous to think that any company could support that debt load. It was doubly outrageous to think that a furniture company could.

APOLLO COMES TO ST. LOUIS

After 18 months in Chapter 11, Interco emerged with a plan of reorganization that called for fully repaying all secured debt and trade creditors. The shareholders received nothing, but remember they had been given $38.50 per share when the Rales bid was rejected. Perhaps now that the bankers and lawyers were gone the real work could resume, but there were some impediments. In the process of ridding themselves of the Wassersteins, the Perellas, the Rales and the rest, Interco picked up an ominous shareholder. During the Chapter 11 proceedings, the Wall Street firm Apollo Partners bought much of the company's secured debt and, upon the distribution of equity to secured debt-holders, owned two-thirds of Interco stock. This let Apollo fill a majority of the seats on the board and to control the company. Disparaged by some as "vulture capitalists," Apollo's partners were the country's largest holder of distressed securities and a force to be reckoned with. "A whiff of controversy surrounded Apollo right from the start,"[8] was *Forbes'* gentle way to say that Apollo was ruthless.

Leon Black, the lead partner, had been closely involved with Michael Milken at Drexel Burnham during the height of the junk bond craze in the 1980s. He made a pile of money off the distasteful Executive Life bankruptcy by "buying its portfolio of busted junk bonds that Black had helped push on investors at Drexel years earlier, a move *Forbes* likened in 1991 to a "polluter going into the pollution cleanup business." This aggressive Dartmouth graduate, who also had an MBA from Harvard, was no gentlemanly banker. The *St. Louis Business Journal* said of him, "Talk of Black invariably brings up a wide range of adjectives. 'Obnoxious' and 'arrogant' appeared in the pages of James B. Stewart's book, *The Den of Thieves*, which flayed Drexel's former star Michael Milken. . . . A March 16, 1991, *Wall Street Journal* story referred to him as a "habitual worrier with a shrill, somewhat whiny negotiating style," but a man "with a remarkable knack for focusing on Wall Street opportunities before other people discern them."[9] Like the Rales brothers, Black saw more money in the breakup of the divisions than he did in keeping them together.

Insiders said the relationship with Apollo at the corporate level was good. The New Yorkers realized that the Missourians knew what they were doing, so they did not interfere with operations. And the operating types learned a lot about balance sheet management from the visitors. Again, Interco CEO Dick Loynd acted as a shield between Apollo and the rest of the company. His demeanor and skill served him well as he navigated through the straits.

By 1992, Interco was down to four divisions: Broyhill and Lane in furniture, and Florsheim and Converse in footwear. The strategy of re-formulating the corporation into a furniture company, not a conglomerate, was proceeding swiftly. Florsheim and Converse were spun off to Interco shareholders in 1994, which let the company concentrate on one industry. During the course of its 160-year history, this St. Louis firm had transformed itself from a shoe manufacturing company to a retail-oriented conglomerate to a furniture manufacturing company. But Leon Black and friends still owned 38 percent. Mickey Holliman was still in Tupelo, but he was not exempt from the tension emanating from St. Louis. In spite of the distractions, he remained focused on his customers and operations in Tupelo. During the 1988 to 1994 period, his division grew sales and earnings at an impressive rate.

The Black Prince is Taken Out of St. Louis

While Interco was disposing of divisions it no longer wanted, the furniture companies it kept were gearing up to expand market share. It expanded further on the last day of 1995, spending $331 million to buy Thomasville from Armstrong World. The deal made Interco the world's largest residential furniture producer, at $1.6 billion in annual sales. Recognizing the company's new direction and wishing to help investors forget some of the unpleasant recent history, management decided to rename the venture. After much internal discussion and external advice, managers decided the new name should start with the word "furniture" in hopes that Wall Street would simply refer to the company by its first name. The middle name was intended to draw attention to the famous "brands," and the last name was to be "international" in the hopes the company would export products to markets beyond the continental United States. Ironically, within a few years the company became a huge importer of products as the tide of globalization began flowing into the Briar Patch. The official name, Furniture Brands International, was chosen on March 1, 1996 – precisely 30 years to the day the name had been changed to Interco.

In October 1996, Mickey Holliman was chosen to be the new president and chief executive officer. He wasted no time in dealing with the Apollo group. He knew they wanted to turn their money and reinvest it elsewhere, and they had no particular love for the furniture business. In March 1997, he led Furniture Brands to complete a stock repurchase and secondary offering. In June, Apollo's ownership was liquidated and its representatives resigned from the board. With the departure of Leon, "The Black Prince of Wall Street," the company now known as Furniture Brands International could finally get back to focusing on the business of making and selling furniture.

Sales and earnings took off under Mickey Holliman's direction, despite a soft economy during his first four years at the helm. By 2000, sales passed the $2 billion mark and net profits topped $100 million, an increase of 138 percent. Though growth stopped during the middle of 2001 and sales dropped back to $1.89 billion, the downturn was likely due to the mid-year recession.

As for the state of individual companies, two were doing well and two were not. Lane Wood was still recovering from the shock of moving to Tupelo, and the numbers were not good. Part of the problem was the company's insistence that top executives move to Mississippi. This made recruiting difficult, and several key people resigned rather than move. Lane upholstery (Action) continued to grow and make excellent margins under the capable leadership of division President Tom Foy.

Broyhill was producing good numbers, but competition from upstart import companies was beginning to cause concern. And Thomasville was a bit of a problem child as the newest member of the group. As a semi-upper-end company, Holliman and Foy were unfamiliar with the subtle differences that made it unique.

ALTAVISTA MOVES TO TUPELO

Holliman recognized as early as 1998 that China was becoming a serious threat to American producers, but he also viewed it as an opportunity. Continuing production and sales problems in the Lane Altavista division bothered him. In spite of the brand name, the balance sheet and the reputation they had developed, the original section of the Lane Co. was in a long slow death spiral. Sales fell to $50 million, compared to $400 million at Action. Even the venerable

Hickory Chair Co. was out-producing the parent company. Hickory Chair, a specialist in eighteenth century style casegoods and upholstery, had been acquired by Lane in 1967. Now the acquisition was outperforming the parent. Holliman could no longer tolerate this imbalance and he announced in June 2001 that Lane's Altavista operations would be merged with Action and moved to Tupelo. The manufacturing would be moved offshore and the company would become more of a marketing entity. Jerry Ruff, at one time the president of Jamestown Sterling, was named the CEO.

Three Jewels for the Crown

Toward the end of 2001, Holliman patiently waited for the implosion of his chief rival, Lifestyle Furnishings. All he wanted at first was to acquire Henredon, but the more he saw of Maitland-Smith the more he liked it as well. Drexel Heritage was of little interest because of its overlap with Thomasville, but Lifestyle's Alan Cole insisted that all three had to go together. Months of negotiation paid off on the last day of 2001, as Holliman closed on a deal to acquire Henredon, Drexel Heritage and Maitland-Smith. The Man in Motion was really moving now. The addition of these upper-end brands to the existing Furniture Brands International stable thrust the company to the industry's dominant position. Furniture Brands had the market covered – from $99 dining chairs to $15,000 dining tables, from $199 beds to $10,000 armoires. With the exception of La-Z-Boy and Ethan Allen, Holliman had captured all the top brands in the business.

Investors responded favorably. Henredon added profitable luster, Maitland-Smith added profitable import capabilities, and

Drexel Heritage brought a Thomasville rival into the company. The deal involved a combination of Furniture Brands stock and cash going to Masco with the shares valued at $27. Shares hit $42 a share within weeks, and Masco ironically made more money on paper by getting free of furniture than it ever made making furniture.

As the thrill of the acquisitions died down, Holliman turned his attention to the long list of strategic issues facing him. Drexel Heritage was foundering, trying to pursue a moribund dedicated store program. Henredon's dominant position in the upper end made it difficult to grow unless the entire segment expanded, and trying to reach a less expensive segment would tarnish the image. Maitland-Smith's lack of exciting styling was causing it to lose market share to Theodore and Alexander, its new rival created by the redoubtable Paul Maitland-Smith.

In the meantime, the legacy divisions were not immune from trouble. Lane had begun to slow down. Broyhill was beset with retail bankruptcies. Thomasville was in the midst of transferring sales from several large independent chains to company stores, a process similar to overhauling the engines of a 747 while crossing the Atlantic. Skeptics noted that all these brands under one corporate banner resulted in a high degree of complexity. Running the entity effectively while sustaining focus on so many segments would not be easy. Ironically, Furniture Brands, then named Interco, had passed on acquiring the Masco furniture group in 1995 because some felt it was "too complicated."

Under normal conditions, Mickey Holliman could contend with these problems as long he could recruit and retain strong division CEOs. His "loose tight" style required astute leadership at the division level, and the old problem Masco faced in the 1980s had not gone away. There simply were not enough qualified people to fill the positions. Many said the average furniture Insider was not sophisticated enough to run a division the way Holliman expected, and Outsiders had a habit of self destructing in the Briar Patch. Successful CEOs know how to get the most out of their designated niches. However, they live in fear that when they bump into the boundaries, their ability to expand into another niche is severely limited. Owners and outsiders do not always see this, and the result is a recurring phenomenon of growth directed by a capable CEO as he maximizes his share of his niche, followed by a slowdown as the niche fills up, followed by turnover at the top. All too often the turnover leads to decline and more turnover until the companies become meaningless. Holliman would have to avoid this death spiral in order to save his divisions and to protect his reputation.

From Relationships to Transactions

Dealing with these internal issues was more than most executives could handle, but Holliman stayed on track because of his experience, his direct, common-sense style, and his intense concentration. What concerned him was the new set of problems that had emerged. The Civil War of the Briar Patch seemed tame compared to World Trade War now underway.

The internal issues were pale next to the cataclysmic changes taking place in the furniture supply chain, causing it to break down in both directions. Historically, manufacturers relied on retailers to interpret and meet consumer needs. As time passed, it became

obvious that the conventional methods were not working. There
were exceptions, but consumers generally felt alienated by furniture stores. Shoppers considered upscale "carriage trade" outlets to
be snooty and lacking excitement. Buying from mass market "big
boxes" – with their aggressive salesmen, tasteless displays and boring assortments – was not much fun either.

The traditional alliance between independent retailers and
privately owned manufacturers did not hold up well during these
stressful times. The ownership turnover rate eliminated many of
the buyer-seller relationships that had sustained loyalties. At issue
was the ability to make a decent profit. Manufacturers and retailers alike had always struggled with low margins, as Adam Smith's
"invisible hand" pressured both to keep prices low. By refusing
to grant exclusives or even limited distribution, the producers
coerced stores into driving prices down. In retaliation, the stores
kept factory prices low by adding competitive lines to their assortment. The intensely competitive nature of the business made sure
that no one made too much money.

What this meant was that the number of retail outlets declined
steadily over the years. When Laura Carpi first arrived, she could
shop at an abundance of stores. New York City, by itself, featured
large upscale furniture displays at Bloomingdale's, B. Altman,
Macy's, Gimbel's, Abraham & Strauss, Lord & Taylor, Stern's, and
the inimitable W&J Sloane's. Each of these emporiums had major
furniture displays at multiple branch locations in addition to the
flagship store. Add to this three major design centers, multiple independents stores, chains such as Seeman's and Sacks, scores of loft
operators, along with hundreds more in the suburbs. Across the
country, nearly every major trading area had comparable lineups of

department stores, chain stores, design centers, and independent furniture stores. Even the small towns had one or more "Mom & Pop" stores.

As real estate values rose in the 1970s and 1980s, profits were not sufficient to justify the occupancy costs, and the number of retail "doors" kept declining. Before long, Bloomingdale's and Macy's were the only remaining major accounts. The rest had disappeared. A number of nontraditional stores, such as Crate & Barrel, Ralph Lauren, and ABC Carpet and Home, stepped into the void, but these stores bypassed traditional suppliers. The net result was a severe constriction of the channel of distribution as defined by the typical manufacturer. Manufacturers have not been able to ascertain how to sell to the new retail formats. Instead they bemoan the shrinking dealer base. The old-line stores kept closing their doors, and the new venues simply ignored the historic suppliers. The balance of power had thus tilted in favor of the retailer, but profit margins remain slim.

Retail success rarely lasts long as the forces of Joseph Schumpeter's "creative destruction" attack the leaders and yesterday's winners become tomorrow's Chapter 11 prospects. Ethan Allen, to its credit, has withstood the assaults of time, but other formats have not. The list of failures is endless: major chains such as Sears and Ward's, furniture chains such as Levitz, Heilig Myers, and Rhodes, even carriage trade stores such as Payne's in Boston, Sloane's in New York, Washington, San Francisco, and Los Angeles, Barker Brothers in Los Angeles, Breuner's in San Francisco, Colby's in Chicago, and Van Sciver's in Philadelphia. All gone. Bankruptcies, closings, contraction and consolidation added up to a huge level of uncertainty for retailers and manufacturers.

A big contributor to this decapitation was the North Carolina "800 Number" epidemic that struck the industry in the 1970s and permanently changed the face of the business. Legend says Plato Wilson, a North Carolina sales rep for Henredon, noticed that some of his retailers did a lot of business with out-of-state customers. This was especially true with stores along interstates that carried northerners back and forth to Florida vacations each year. These dealers had some competitive advantages over their counterparts up north. Labor, occupancy, and inbound freight costs were lower, and they could easily undersell retailers in New York, Boston, Detroit and Philadelphia. The allure of buying furniture at a deep discount at a store in "furniture country" proved to be powerful. Before long, hundreds of "800 Number Stores" appeared all over the state. Some were merely phone banks with no display while others built huge stores; all could undercut the full-service stores in the rest of the country. Many brazenly told shoppers to "visit the local store, have their designer plan your purchase, write the numbers down, and call our 800 number."

Consumers loved it, just as they love Internet buying today. The volume to the factories was too good to refuse, even as the hurt it put on out-state retailers was too corrosive to ignore. The Federal Trade Commission's price-fixing laws made it difficult for the manufacturers to discontinue the parasitical "free riders," and the old-line stores went crazy. Their outrage was justifiable. Without their displays of the product, the North Carolina formula would not work. There can be no rational excuse for the manufacturers' willing complicity with this competitive sucker punch. The out-state retailers never saw it coming and could not defend themselves. The in-state retailers struck it rich. The biggest loser was the industry, however, because it hastened the closing of many fine stores.

Inevitably, manufacturers could not resist trying to open their own stores. Ethan Allen had done it on a global scale, and Stickley had done it in select markets. La-Z-Boy had success with its hybrid store program. Masco could have done it, but its manufacturing bias got in the way. Furniture Brands had the names and the pedigree. Mickey Holliman had the nerve. It made sense on paper to combine the brands into two clusters – with Henredon, Hickory Chair, and Drexel Heritage at the upper end; and a mass-market combination of Thomasville, Lane and Broyhill – but the complexity of the transition was staggering. Thomasville already had a decent store program; Drexel Heritage had been trying to have one for 20 years; and Henredon was not inclined to be associated with its fellow divisions.

Many attempts were made to put two or more brands together without success as each division stubbornly resisted giving up its inalienable right to select its own dealers. Instead, Furniture Brands launched five different, competing store programs. The results were mixed. It is rare to find a manufacturer who can "think like a retailer" and vice versa. It's as if there is a genetic difference between the two, and we are predetermined at conception to be one or the other, not both.

Shoppers like to compare brands and are not satisfied by single-brand stores. Manufacturers quickly learned that managing store programs was a lot tougher than it looked, and they learned how inadequate a lot of their programs were. Vertical integration, in which manufacturers develop their own proprietary retail outlets, is not the solution many thought it would be. And so, the bond between suppliers and retailers was broken. What used to be a relationship business built on trust and mutual respect has now become a transaction business based on numbers.

A candid assessment of the front of the distribution channel, where the consumer interacts with the retailer, could only conclude that it was collapsing downstream. The new stores such as IKEA, Pottery Barn, and Rooms-To-Go were meeting consumer needs without buying from the old producers. They bypassed American suppliers and sourced their goods directly with Asian vendors. The channel was collapsing upstream also. Creative destruction combined with Globalization was working overtime to eliminate the middle man.

If the furniture leaders had paid more attention to consumers and what was going on in other parts of the economy, they might have spotted a trend that would soon silence the rip saws and the dust collectors and turn their factories into bare, shuttered monuments to America's industrial past. All they had to do was notice the "Made in China" labels on their TaylorMade drivers or the clothes they wore.

The American economy was rapidly moving from being manufacturing-based to being service-based, and the furniture industry was among the many industries soon to be engulfed in the Made in China Syndrome. Few U.S. companies were prepared for the transformation. Fewer still were prepared for the radically different New World Order that America faced. Mickey Holliman thought he was. Time, and the Chinese, would tell.

THE ASIAN INVASION

China's entry into the war immediately altered the balance of power. . . . With Mao's approval, The Red Army adopted a strategy of inducing the enemy to march forward and then eliminating them with superior forces striking from the rear and on their flanks.

This setback should have sent a strong warning to U.N. forces, but General MacArthur was too arrogant to heed it. He, like many policy makers in Washington, underestimated the size and determination of his Chinese adversaries.

In late November, advancing U.N. forces entered areas where Communist People's Volunteer troops had laid their trap. Starting on November 25, Chinese troops began a vigorous counter offensive. Under tremendous pressure, U.N. troops had to undertake what the political scientist Jonathan Pollack has called "the most infamous retreat in American military history. By mid December, the CPV and the reorganized Korean People's Army had regained control of nearly all North Korean territory.

Chen Jian, *China's Road to the Korean War*

JUST AS THE UNITED STATES NEGLECTED to look beyond Korea's northern border during the Korean War, the furniture leaders defending the Briar Patch failed to keep an eye on the global horizon. In both cases, China was on the march, and American forces were vulnerable to attack. But American forces had just won World War II in the first instance, and Insiders had just routed the Outside invaders in the second. In both instances, Americans were overconfident.

The first off-shore furniture companies – Universal in Taiwan and Hyundai in Korea at the low end, along with Maitland-Smith in the Philippines at the upper end – had been shipping products to America for a long time, yet none of those companies had disrupted the status quo. American furniture manufacturers were not particularly worried about them.

True, there was talk of new furniture plants being built in mainland China, but why would they bother with something as quirky as furniture? Profit margins are low, capital requirements are high, and it is hard to make, especially high quality furniture. How could the Chinese do it, and why would they even bother?

But the signs were obvious by the mid 1980s that the Chinese were coming, even though the American furniture veterans didn't anticipate – and perhaps were even in denial – that China would overtake furniture manufacturing. Most furniture makers just didn't read the signs. The myopic furniture leaders should have noticed that clothing companies such as Land's End were selling men's oxford cotton shirts for less than they did five years earlier. They should have asked how Wal-Mart could offer such good values. They should have asked where IKEA sourced the incredibly good values they had in their stores. They should have paid attention to the new "lifestyle" stores opening in shopping malls. Where did Restoration Hardware and Pottery Barn get their well-designed, well-made, and well-priced goods? They should have and they could have, but they did not. Astute furniture merchants could look at almost any piece of domestic furniture and tell you what plant had produced it, but not these goods. They came from "elsewhere."

GLOBALIZATION COMES TO THE BRIAR PATCH

America and China in November 1999 signed the Sino-U.S. Trade Accord, which allowed for the phasing in of free trade between the two countries, starting with textiles. This paved the way for China to join the World Trade Organization, something China had wanted for years in order to gain recognition as a serious trading partner. The political implications of the country's admittance into the WTO were enormous, because it firmly set China on a free market economic course and made it far less likely to start a war. Economically, it remains to be seen what America gained in return for giving away access to its markets. Almost overnight, the Chinese began making textiles and furniture for the American markets and by 2006, their share of the American market was said to be greater than 60 percent. How did this happen?

Ironically, Westerners were the ones who brought the American furniture industry to Asia, when the likes of Paul Maitland-Smith and Larry Moh built their furniture factories in the Philippines and Taiwan. A select few of these pioneers discovered how to exploit the tremendous advantage of low-cost labor for manufacturing furniture in Asia, which far surpassed the benefits of moving a factory from Virginia to Mississippi. The original plan, developed by Larry Moh of Universal, was to make furniture components in Asian factories using American veneers, ship them to America for assembling, and sell them to the American market at highly competitive prices. The goal was to earn margins that were greatly improved over domestically crafted furniture.

The plan worked. It worked so well, in fact, that other American furniture corporations noticed the success of their competitors and felt compelled to take advantage of similar low-labor costs. More American companies began sourcing parts from factories in Asia and guided the manufacturing of American furniture on Asian soil. As labor costs rose in Korea and Taiwan and the import restrictions on China were eased, new factories were built in southern China, Vietnam, and Indonesia. It was illegal for Americans to trade with Vietnam until the late 1990s, but the World Trade Organization and Congress changed all that.

As successful as Universal became, its assembly system and logistical techniques were cumbersome, and its designers had to make design compromises so components could be packed and shipped efficiently. When the new Chinese industrialists began, they decided to make completely assembled and finished furniture – which made their products better looking than the "assemble-to-order" goods made by Universal. The freight costs were higher, but the trade off was worth it.

Many of these entrepreneurs were from mainland China families who had escaped to Taiwan. With the Westernization of the New China economy, they could now return to the mainland and apply their business acumen with the full support of the government. One of the more prominent of these entrepreneurs is

Samuel Kuo, chairman of Samson Holdings. Kuo, whose original family business made pool cue sticks in Taiwan, now runs LacquerCraft and several other brands. In 2005, his Chinese furniture plants were shipping 2,200 containers a month to America.

The Chinese government not only provided low-cost loans to native entrepreneurs who were creating jobs, it simultaneously made it nearly impossible for foreigners to open their own facilities. Property could only be leased, which made it impractical to build a factory. In order to survive, Americans had to show Asian locals how to run the furniture factories themselves. The Chinese were no strangers to the art of cabinetmaking, having crafted their own fine furniture for thousands of years. Culturally, the Chinese were skilled at replicating artwork and they grasped the visual qualities of designs without much instruction. Very quickly, the Chinese became proficient at churning out Western-style furniture and delivering it to America's shores. The styles and processes it had taken the American furniture industry decades to acquire and perfect were handed over to the Asian furniture warriors within three years.

The American furniture companies that had trained their Asian counterparts in the art and science of Western furniture-manufacturing had started to look like middlemen who were no longer necessary to cut the deal. A new model of an American company was born. It had no factories at home or abroad, just a relationship with one or more Chinese producers. The old-line manufacturers dismissed them as "upstart jobbers," but the new American furniture companies kept growing and – because they had no factory overhead costs – could offer better value than the old-line companies.

NOT A THIRD WORLD COUNTRY

The American furniture industry's response to the arrival of Chinese products in the U.S. domestic market was reminiscent of the American armed forces' reaction to the intervention of the Chinese army in the Korean War. Like MacArthur, the furniture Insiders did not view Chinese furniture manufacturers as a credible threat.

In September 1950, General Douglas MacArthur predicted that American troops would be "home by Christmas" from Korea. By late October, United Nations forces had pushed the North Koreans to the Manchurian border. The supremely confident MacArthur had notions of taking his assault into China, believing there would be no opposition. Suddenly, the Chinese Army attacked to start what MacArthur called "a New War." In large measure, American intelligence failed to detect the Chinese presence, which was cleverly disguised. Carrying only small arms, leaving behind artillery, and advancing strictly at night, the Chinese secretly moved 300,000 troops more than 300 miles in 18 nights from the Manchurian provinces to the Korean mountains.

At first, the Chinese engaged our troops. Then, they pulled back, making American commanders think they had withdrawn. The U.S. Eighth Army was among those that took the bait and advanced northward. This stretched supply lines and made America vulnerable to counter-attack. During the night of Oct. 25, the People's Volunteer Army attacked near the Chosin Reservoir. Their "human waves" of infantrymen simply overwhelmed the U.N. forces. Our troops, outnumbered 5 to 1, never had a chance against this assault. There were no defensible positions and no place to regroup. As a reporter later noted, the Chinese too "were disciplined, aggressive, and tenacious. Envelopment was their favorite tactic, from battalion to army. And, once an advantage was attained, they were quick to exploit it."[1]

The Chinese tactics worked. MacArthur's forces were in full retreat by early December, a mere 17 days after he had dreams of taking all of Korea. By year end, the Chinese had pushed the Americans and their allies all the way out of North Korea. Instead of being home for Christmas, American troops were "home" in South Korea. The American forces could not win the offensive against China during the Korean War.

Likewise, the American furniture manufacturers never had a chance against the threat of Chinese movement into our markets. American manufacturers simply could not compete with Asian labor costs. Just as U.N. commanders should have known the Chinese would intervene during the Korean War, the American furniture manufacturers should have known the Chinese would invade our markets. As soon as the bulk of American manufacturers noticed that the Chinese could replicate American styles at a fraction of the cost, they rushed to move their own production offshore in hopes of becoming more competitive. Americans took the bait, taught the Chinese how to build and finish the pieces, and hastened the demise of their domestic factories.

While 2004 Democratic presidential candidate John Kerry condemned companies that outsourced manufacturing as "Benedict Arnold" traitors and CNN commentator Lou Dobbs castigated their off-shoring sins, the reality is that these companies had no choice. They could either stay with domestic production at domestic costs, and helplessly watch their market share disappear, or they could radically transform their companies from producers to importers.

Mickey Holliman of Furniture Brands International opted to change. Early on, he had the foresight to convert Lane's wood operation to a pure import company, and he pioneered the importing of cut-and-sewn leather. He reminded his division presidents about the law of the jungle: "The fast eat the slow. In a rapidly changing environment, those who drag their feet, or resist change altogether, will not survive." Unfortunately, Briar Patch residents were never known for their speed.

No Foxholes in This War

This global war offered no hiding places. The whole American industry was under siege and there seemed to be no way to save it. Product development and merchandising people flocked to mainland China to work on new designs or, more likely, to copy American-made best sellers. They traded stories and vied with each other for design ideas to copy as they filled the Western-style Hiatt Hotel in Guangdong Province – even the name of the hotel was a knockoff. Back home, companies closely guarded their new furniture designs until Market. Now, with multiple companies sourcing their products in the same Chinese plants, it was impossible to protect your designs. Some Chinese site managers concealed clients' samples in a secure room during the client's visit, only to show them to the next visitor as proof of what they were capable of making.

This transfer of the product development function was only part of the story. Leather and fabrics were also now being made in

Asia. American finishing material suppliers rushed to set up laboratories staffed with American stylists to help the Chinese copy American finishing techniques, and American retailers rushed to connect with Chinese producers so they could eliminate the middle man – the American manufacturer.

American visitors to China could not help but be amused at first. The roads were terrible; the drivers used to drive trucks for the Red Army; the factories were a mess, and some were owed by the government and run by the army. It was chaotic. But you also quickly noticed the energy, the willpower, the almost desperate determination to make it work. Then you would visit a brand new facility, nicer than any in the States, and the owner would proudly tell you about his new plants under construction. Everyone was expanding. You wondered if they might be crazy. If all this furniture is going to end up in America, supply will greatly exceed demand and the disruption will be huge.

On your next trip, you would be astonished at the progress. New hotels, super-highways, public transportation, expanded port facilities, and more furniture factories – all completed since your last visit. The numbers told the story dramatically. In 1994, China exported $241 million of wood furniture to the United States. In 2004, they shipped $4.2 billion! Gradually it dawns on you – yes, lower labor costs are a huge factor in China's expansion into the furniture industry, but it is more than that. Modern factories, technology, machinery, low front-office costs, and relentless energy helped fuel this fabled growth.

It is worth noting that the Chinese did not so much come after us as America pursued them. When American managers were given the task of developing imported furniture to sell in the

American market, the Americans showed the Asians how to do it. Only now the factory was not their own, and there was nothing to stop Asian owners from using what they learned on somebody else's line of furniture. The so-called export of technology was accomplished quickly and innocently. The American manufacturers dug their own graves by teaching the Chinese how to make furniture for the American market, but what else could they do? They were becoming obsolete either way – and so were American factory workers.

A DIRECT HIT ON AMERICAN FACTORIES

The Asian Invasion cut through the defenders' heartland of factories with unchecked fury. The Feb. 4, 2002, issue of *Furniture Today* headline shouted, "U.S. case goods in survival fight, 25,000 U.S. factory jobs disappear in 2001." In the five-year period between 2001 and 2005, the industry closed at least 230 furniture plants and cut 55,800 factory jobs. Among the total, Ethan Allen, Furniture Brands, and Life*Style* Furnishings eliminated 3,500 jobs when closing 6 million square feet of manufacturing space. Thomasville lost 11 plants; Drexel Heritage and Broyhill lost five each; Lane lost four. Pulaski closed its manufacturing facilities completely to become a pure importer.[2]

The odds were overwhelmingly in favor of the invaders. First, recently created trade policy, such as the Sino-U.S. Accord, offered no protection to American manufacturers. One group of American furniture producers petitioned Congress to stop the alleged "dumping" of goods by China, but this merely caused a lot of production to be shifted to Vietnam. Second, the American furniture factories were old – typically 50 or more years in age. Meanwhile, the attackers were opening brand new factories filled with equally new machinery.

As a result, the Americans were forced to shut down their antiquated facilities almost as fast as the Chinese were putting them up. "We have built fewer new case goods plants here in the past 30 years than the Chinese have built in the past few months," lamented Jerry Epperson of Mann, Armistead, and Epperson.[3]

INDUSTRY-WIDE DAMAGE

As the Chinese factories came on line and began making good looking product at amazingly low prices, there was no shortage of American takers. New distribution companies formed quickly as entrepreneurs bought containers of goods and resold them in the United States. Many retailers cut out the middleman and bought directly from the Chinese. Enterprising sales reps created their own companies; manufacturers became importers; and the established producers saw their market share drop sharply. Furniture Brands International, the largest producer of furniture in the world, was hammered. Arch rival La-Z-Boy was hit even harder. No established producer could avoid the attack. The weak and the strong, the big and the small, the good and the bad – all were hurt by the tsunami wave of imports that hit American shores. In 1994, wood furniture imports from China had only amounted to 3 percent of domestic production levels, but by 2002 topped 42 percent of the U.S. wood furniture market. Shipments rose 13 percent even in a down year, which marked the first time in seven years that the increase was less than 30 percent. Within only a handful of years, China had infiltrated and captured a critical mass of furniture territory. By 2005, 60 percent of all the wood furniture sold in America was imported.

WOUNDED WORKERS

The shutdowns were not pretty. Working in a case goods plant was noisy, dirty, and hard. It could be hot or cold or dangerous, but this was offset by the camaraderie that invariably formed. The work was hard, but hardly anyone wanted to leave. Not only were workers' livelihoods tied to the factory, they felt like part of a family. The mere *idea* of having a factory shut down was painful; the *reality* was simply unthinkable.

Nonetheless, the force of globalization had no sympathy for workers as it rolled straight through the Briar Patch. When incoming orders decline, manufacturing rates must be adjusted downward or you will run out of cash. At first you simply shut down for a day or two, then for a week. But this starts to hurt profits and the workers' pocketbooks, so you "downsize" by letting a percentage of your people go – that is to say, you fire them. Eventually, you are forced to shut a plant in order to "consolidate" production and to fire more people. And the spiral continues until little or nothing remains. It's one thing when it happens because your own sales and marketing team failed to generate enough orders, but this time it was all spurred by global forces beyond your control. When the time came for these closures, the workers who made up the factory "family" were let go in sad batches that corresponded in perfect synch with the chronology of the production line.

To an economist, this is a "temporary dislocation." To the worker, it is a disaster. The typical hourly furniture factory worker had dropped out of school to work in the plant, which limited his or her job options. The government safety net could only soften the blow; it could not get a factory worker a new job.

According to a University of Santa Cruz study of the effect of increased furniture competition, 38 percent of the half million furniture workers who lost their jobs in the 1980s and 1990s could not get new jobs. Of those who did get jobs, 1 in 5 took a pay cut of at least 30 percent.[4] It is the opposite in China, where "furniture making is one of the country's fastest-growing categories, exceeding the growth of all other exported commodities except high tech products."[5]

Some in the industry made a point to show government officials that the game was stacked against them. In 2002, Treasury Secretary Paul O'Neill paid a visit to High Point to drum up support for Bush's Social Security proposal, but at lunch he heard an earful from furniture company presidents who complained about Chinese imports. O'Neill shrugged it off and called it a dislocation that could be solved by implementing more up-to-date manufacturing methods. After lunch, when O'Neill toured the Henredon factory, the company's president showed O'Neill how the company had made a "lean conversion" to very "up-to-date" manufacturing seven years ago yet was still losing sales to imports. O'Neill was smart enough to see that the loss of business was caused more by external factors than internal, but he had his own problems. In December, he was forced to resign and has since become a critic of Bush's fiscal policies.

A Confederacy of Niches

The compelling values of the offshore goods disrupted a long-standing pattern of price points that the American industry had come to expect. The furniture industry was long comprised of a series of interlocking segments, or niches, that companies tried to defend or capture. You could grow within your niche up to a point, but once you hit your limit you had to start the difficult task of attacking another niche. Your limit depended on the size of your niche, how many rivals you had for that niche, and how effective you were. Large niches existed in the center of the market and attracted lots of attention. Only the big kids could play in this game – Thomasville, Broyhill, and Action, for example. Smaller niches could be found outside of the main field, but these were usually occupied by fiercely focused specialists – Hancock & Moore, Stickley, and Durham, for example. Then there were scraps to be found in the margins.

This Confederacy of Niches was inherently understood by industry gurus but was a mystery to outsiders. On a grid-type layout, price points would be on the vertical axis and style choices would be on the horizontal axis. Previously there had been a fairly logical progression up and down the price points. If one brand was more expensive than another, it meant it had more labor or more material in it. But the niches were blown apart when the low-cost imports arrived. Now, price differences were more abrupt, and lower-cost imports actually might have more labor and material in them.

In many cases, the imported products were better than the domestic products they replaced. Ethan Allen, for example, developed a Chinese-made collection so good looking and so well priced that it disrupted sales of the rest of its line made in the States.

HIGH-END CONSOLIDATION & CONTRACTION

Drexel Heritage had a similar experience. It historically occupied two distinct but adjacent niches – Drexel's multi-style, moderately priced fine furniture niche, and Heritage's multi-style, expensive fine furniture niche. Yet the company was rocked by the import wave as the boundaries of these niches were changed.

After three decades of good results, the Briar Patch Wars had badly damaged the company. It drifted aimlessly through the 1990s and until Mickey Holliman hired Jeff Young to replace Dan Grow as CEO. Young, who had been part of a successful run at Lexington, surveyed the company and concluded he had little to work with other than a brand name. He also had little to lose. Moving swiftly, he tried to transform the company into a retail-oriented importer with limited manufacturing. He set up offshore sources, reduced overhead costs, closed plants, hired a new team, and rebuilt the store program from the ground up. At its peak, Drexel Heritage had 5,000 workers in 20 separate facilities. By 2005, it was down to 900 workers and two plants.

Henredon was a different story. Most observers conceded Henredon had won the Battle of the High End by defeating challenges from Baker, Century, and Drexel Heritage. By 2002, Henredon continued to dominate the luxury category with its "drop-dead" styling, the largest market share, the highest profit margins, and the most compelling brand image. The company seemed secure, but appearances were deceiving. Historically, the company's carefully designed products were hard to copy. Suddenly, they could be copied faster and better than ever . . . by anyone with access to a plant in the Far East. Previously, it took years to copy the Henredon "looks," and the copies were no match for the originals. Now it only took months for the Chinese to make copies that were frighteningly close to the originals in appearance – but for much less cost. Henredon's preeminent position atop of the American furniture industry was suddenly precarious. Like a well-defended fortress, Henredon was never attacked directly by the Chinese. They simply went around it and made "Henredon-type" products for dozens of other companies. This took away Henredon's exclusive image and dramatically reduced its supply of orders.

Some in the industry believed that the upper-end American furniture producers would be able to resist the invaders who presumably did not have the patience or the skills to make top-quality merchandise. They were wrong. The Chinese started making very good furniture and at prices so low that they stunned American competitors and consumers. Furthermore, the best American firms were not as battle-ready as they needed to be. Always vulnerable to cheaper copies, the high-end firms had watched sales decline starting in the 1980s as consumer lifestyles became more casual and "disposable" furniture became fashionable. The top-of-the-line stores gradually began to disappear. Many carriage trade stores succumbed to rising real estate costs; still more suffered from generational indifference; then the "top-down" recession of the early 1990s nearly wiped out the last of them. The rest of the distribution channel was largely comprised of mass-market merchants who either shunned the upper end or carried it with reluctance.

So, in the face of off-shore competition, the upper end manufacturers struggled to preserve their tenuous positions. The "China Price" made them appear more expensive than ever. If these companies cheapened their products, they would risk their brand images. If they did nothing, they would be hurt by much cheaper imports. As one manufacturer put it, "I feel like a country dog in the city. If I stand still, they'll knock me over; if I run, they'll bite me in the tail."

In 2004, the Henredon CEO announced his retirement after 17 years at the post. Although he was at retirement age, his decision to leave was based partly on the knowledge of how much the industry had changed and how difficult the coming years would be. His carefully groomed successor, former retailer Steve McKee, took over in November. He was left with the tough task of re-defining a company that had a lot to lose. Things did not go as planned, and sales and earnings declined. Henredon's total employment, which had been as high as 2,800 people in the '90s, fell to 1,200 by 2005.

Numbers Give Birth to HDM

Henredon held on to its precarious perch at the top, but costs climbed and margins suffered. Before long, Mickey Holliman decided to combine the management of his three upper-end stalwarts – Henredon, Drexel Heritage, and Maitland-Smith – into one division. The logical choice to lead this group was Jeff Young of Drexel Heritage. This was one of those risky moves that large companies make because of the *numbers*. The *numbers* say, "It makes sense to consolidate, to eliminate redundant costs, and to leverage the various division strengths across the other divisions."

The *numbers* ask, "Why do we have three CFOs and three In-formation Technology chiefs when one CFO and CIO would be substantially more cost effective?" Then Wall Street analysts join the chorus until the CEO has no choice but to take action even if his intuition tells him not to. What the *numbers* and the ana-lysts don't say is, "But morale will be destroyed and the driving competitive spirit will be lost." Nor do the *numbers* ask, "How will the customers respond?" and "Will all those savings really be there when the post-consolidation period is over?" The name chosen for Holliman's new entity, HDM, was as uninspired as the move itself. It's as if the people involved were not excited enough to give it a real name, so they just tossed out a few less-than-memorable let-ters. Competitors began calling it "Drexeldon" and predicted dire consequences.

The move did drive some costs out of the business, but the consolidation did not go smoothly. The Drexel Heritage team got the top positions; the Henredon team viewed the so-called merger as a hostile takeover; morale plummeted; Henredon's driv-ing competitive spirit was shattered. Inevitably, ongoing efforts to put the Henredon and Drexel Heritage cultures together did not work because the cultures are too divergent to be melded. Mean-while, Maitland-Smith languished, and veteran President Seamus Bateson resigned to become head of CF Industries and left Jeff Young as acting CEO of Maitland-Smith. In the summer of 2006, Larry Milan, an accountant by training, was the curious choice to become the company's fourth president since the founder left.

The merged company made plans to combine facilities as well as departments. Henredon upholstery was moved to a Drexel

Heritage plant in High Point. Heritage wood was moved to Henredon's Morganton plant, and rumors flew that the two big trade showrooms in High Point would be combined. Many key customers objected and the plans were shelved . . . for now. Proponents of the put-together argued that the *numbers* demonstrated the logic. Opponents countered that the Henredon consumer would be turned off by the inevitable homogenization of styles that would result from the merger, and the brands would be damaged. Subtle differences in product styling – the amount of "crown" in sofa cushions, for example – gave brands their distinctive points of differentiation. Without them, brand homogenization would develop, and undoubtedly the two product lines would look alike. It reminded one of Disneyworld with multiple restaurants all over the Magic Kingdom, but only one gigantic kitchen underground to serve them all.

When furniture competitor Whitt Sherrill heard of the news that plants were being combined at HDM, he retorted, "I hear Henredon and Drexel Heritage are going to make their upholstery in the same plant. My, my. I don't understand why big companies like that kind of thinking. My dad [Buddy Sherrill] always says each line has to stand on its own with its own management and its own plant. If you run two different lines in the same plant, you're just going to get messed up."[6]

The consolidation that looked so good on paper did not work. Sales continued to drop and profits disappeared. Henredon frantically tried to hit lower price points by importing more, and it lost its exclusive reputation. Drexel Heritage's dedicated store program stalled, and Maitland-Smith failed to recapture any style excitement. New order-entry systems caused customer service nightmares. More key people left the company. Retailers blamed Holliman for failing to understand the high end, and competitors feasted on the opportunity.

Elsewhere in the high end, the results were mixed. The attrition of carriage trade stores accelerated. For example, in the Washington, D.C., trading area, all four of the top-of-the line stores went out of business in 2006. Turnover of key executives accelerated. The Baker president left to become president of Ferguson Copeland, an import company owned by Darrell Ferguson. Century downsized and then smartly shifted its focus from retailers to interior designers. Stickley opened a plant in Vietnam and expanded its retail division. Paula and Bob Fogarty somehow managed to keep Kindel going until their equity partner decided to take over. The results were predictably disastrous.

Collateral Damage at Thomasville, Broyhill & Lane

The middle of the American furniture market was also impacted, but the major players here were able to shift to imports faster than the upper end. This allowed them to adjust to the rules of survival in the flat world. The Chinese liked the big cutting sizes in the mid-market range so they were willing to supply imports to these companies. The Chinese generally did not want to bother with the small production runs that the high end would need to convert to an import model. Nevertheless, the import wave caused heavy damage to the major mid-market players such as Thomasville, Broyhill and Lane.

Thomasville was barely recovering from the trauma of converting its dealer network from independents to dedicated stores when it had to convert from domestic production to imports. Things were moving slowly, and Mickey Holliman surprised many people in September 2005 by appointing Nancy Webster, a high-level merchandising executive from the Target chain, as the new head of Thomasville. This marked the eighth major division CEO change he made in four years. Naturally, a change at the top triggers other organizational changes as the new president creates his or her own team, and the de-stabilizing effect keeps rolling.

Still, it was Holliman's belief that the furniture business needed a new type of leader because so much had changed so fast. The key, in his view, was in the retail side of the equation. After leading the insider forces in the Briar Patch Wars to a victory, Holliman now was turning to an outsider to run his highest profile, highest potential division.

Thomasville had been at the center of the battlefield since its 1965 sale by the founding family. Now it had to contend with the import wave. Armstrong World had made a lot of wrong "outsider moves" over the years. Starting with the false logic of, "We make carpets and rugs; furniture goes on carpets and rugs; therefore we should make furniture," it never figured out how to make money in the industry. It did many things right – including some effective brand building and hiring some capable people – but Wall Street kept harping on the numbers until Armstrong raised a white flag and sold the whole thing to Interco. At Interco, Thomasville thrived at first. It introduced a well-designed and well-priced collection based on the Ernest Hemingway license, and it sold like crazy. It accelerated the opening of dedicated Thomasville stores, generating one-time orders for floor samples beyond normal consumer-sold orders. Sales hit historic levels, and profits flourished.

But good times do not last long in the furniture business. Hemingway was largely made offshore. It got knocked off fast, and the flood of copies hurt Thomasville's sales. Attempts to develop a follow-up fell short, and the store program began to conflict with some large customers who resented competing with the new Thomasville stores. Orders declined; shipments declined; profits declined. The increased competition from imports was hurting the Thomasville stores, and the CEO felt he could not cut costs fast enough to offset the loss of domestic volume and he was replaced. His successor, Tom Tilley, was an experienced product development executive who was able to strengthen the line considerably. However, the Thomasville store program did not progress as swiftly as Mickey Holliman expected, so Tilley was moved to Henredon and Webster moved in from Target. To shore up her obvious lack of manufacturing expertise, the president of the HBF office furniture division, Steve Gane, was brought in as executive vice president of operations.

Broyhill held out a little longer against the import assault, but eventually the competition overwhelmed it and another divisional CEO was replaced. Harvey Dondero, former president of Universal Furniture, was hired in 2005 to steer the company into the new world. It seemed to be a wise choice. He was a globalist with years of experience with imports, and he wasted no time converting Broyhill from a manufacturer to an importer. The conversion, however, proved to be costly, and the new imported goods did not sell well. Massive Broyhill factory layoffs have driven the unemployment rate to 13 percent in Caldwell County, North

Carolina. Harvey Dondero did not see eye to eye with Holliman about the pace of the conversion, and he resigned abruptly in June 2006 – less than a year on the job. Tom Foy took over as interim president.

Holliman's new chieftains were not holding up very well on the battlefield. Soon after Dondero quit, Broyhill's vice president of marketing followed suit, and Steve Gane abruptly left Thomasville along with several other key managers. Tom Foy was assigned to run Broyhill on an interim basis until another replacement could be found. Even more unusual was the choice of the sales and marketing chief at Broyhill, an executive from the distillery company, Brown Forman. One must hope his wood experience with oak casks will serve him well. The only Furniture Brands CEOs with anything close to normal longevity were at three small divisions, Lane Venture, Hickory Chair, and Pearson. Each continued to generate good results. Each was led by an experienced furniture person.

SOLID WOOD SPLITS

Even though Furniture Brands' three "aircraft carriers" – Thomasville, Broyhill, and Lane – were easy targets for importers, Insiders believed the solid wood category would be relatively impervious to import aggression. The Chinese had already stripped their native timberlands to fuel the steel-making furnaces ordered by Mao during one of his Great Leaps Forward. Popular hardwoods like cherry, maple, and oak were indigenous to America and supposedly unavailable in the Far East. And surely the Chinese would not be able to handle the most difficult part of making solid wood casegoods: maintaining the strict humidity controls needed to keep solid panels from splitting. The three key players in the solid wood mid-market niche – Pennsylvania House, Kincaid, and Durham – felt safe.

Much to the chagrin of the American solid wood companies, the Chinese found timber in their northernmost provinces as well as in Russia. The irony of the quintessentially American Pennsylvania House product made by Chinese from Russian wood was too much for some old hands. The Chinese controlled the humidity and entered the U.S. market with incredibly low prices that undercut even the low-end American players, hurting them the same way they had hurt upper-end players. In addition, Durham had trouble keeping their prices steady because of currency fluctuations between the Canadian and U.S. dollars. When the Canadian dollar strengthened against the American dollar, Durham's price advantage weakened and leveled off a phenomenal growth spurt.

With John Scarsella leading merchandising and sales and Orville Mead leading manufacturing, Durham had flourished for a decade. Scarsella and Mead both knew their trade. They trusted and respected each other. Sales in Canadian dollars grew from $9 million to $90 million with pre-tax margins above 15 percent, an unheard of number. But Mead died of cancer, and ownership control changed hands. An investment group from Toronto with no furniture experience wanted to keep sales growing and did not understand that this solid wood bedroom producer was close to reaching the upper limits of its potential. Durham built a new plant and expanded into dining rooms just as the Chinese arrived. Sales and profits dropped. John Scarsella resigned, and the new owner put in charge a 34-year-old banker with no furniture experience. It remains to be seen how successful the company will be as it copes with imported solid wood furniture and a strong Canadian dollar. In 2008 they hired industry veteran Ed Fritz to help restore the luster.

Pennsylvania House just kept staggering, like a boxer who has been knocked unconscious but refuses to fall. Now owned by La-Z-Boy – its eighth owner since 1965 – the company was kept alive by the power of its brand and the loyalty of its customer base. By 2004, Pennsylvania House was being run by its 10th president. The spirit was gone, as were the differentiating factors that once set the company apart from the rabble. Each new owner new president tried to make improvements, but they usually went about it in the wrong fashion.

HYPOTHETICAL CONVERSATIONS

At some point along the way, a new Pennsylvania House president or owner probably noticed that the company's dealer base was composed of low-profile "Mom and Pop" retailers. "We should be selling the big name accounts, not these small stores," the president or owner likely said. The then sales manager probably replied, "But these small stores are loyal and profitable, and they love the line. It would be a strategic mistake to abandon our network of dealers and try to go after the 'big name' guys. The big guys never pay full price and will drop us in a New York minute if they get a better deal." It wasn't long before that sales manager was let go, and his replacement made discounted deals with some big name stores. The Mom and Pops who were affected cut back on their Pennsylvania House display. The line sold poorly at the "big name" retailers, who dropped it after a few seasons.

At a similar point along the way, another new president probably spoke out: "We make everything out of solid wood. Veneer has more look. We should introduce a veneered product." "But," said the merchandise manager, "Our dealers don't look to us for that. It would be a strategic mistake to abandon our solid wood specialty. We will risk losing control of our niche." His replacement debuted a line of veneered furniture. The dealers said they did not look to Pennsylvania House for that type of product. Where the product did get placed, it cannibalized existing product and the plants had trouble producing it. As the long list of new presidents moved the company away from its lucrative niche, upstarts like Jamestown Sterling and Durham moved in to take advantage of the void. They followed the French battle command "*Cherchez le Creneau*" – look for the opening.

Pennsylvania House had been a special company with a great brand, a narrow but effective dealer base, and a fast moving product line that made money. It is now ordinary. Sales are estimated to be in the mid-$50 million range, back to 1968 levels. The erstwhile Lewisburg Chair Co. no longer makes chairs. The big plant in Lewisburg has been shut down. The free-standing showroom in High Point was put up for sale. Bob Zimmerman is not around to fire up the troops. The productive sales reps, like Joe Alfery and Jim Floyd, are gone. And the infamous Steve Sealy is not there to entertain with his latest colorful adventure.

Not surprisingly, La-Z-Boy in July 2006 announced it was merging Pennsylvania House with Clayton Marcus and terminating still another president. For sure this move looks good, *on paper*. The top job has been given to the Clayton Marcus president, meaning the Pennsylvania House organization will be getting its seventh president in 12 years. No mention was made of the respective cultures – perhaps the two divisions have none left – but La-Z-Boy president Kurt Darrow provided the standard corporate rationale for the move by saying "the merger will create synergy among the brands."[7] Don't bank on it, Kurt.

In May 2007, La-Z-Boy said it was "seeking buyers" for both companies. In October, Universal Furniture bought the Pennsylvania House name for $1.65 million.[8] Sales at Pennsylvania House were estimated to be as low as $20 million.

Kincaid was another story, a successful family business that sold out to LADD, which then sold out to La-Z-Boy. Figures are closely guarded, but it is safe to assume the results are not good. The parent company has openly admitted that its wood business has been marginally profitable at best for some time. The old LADD properties, American Drew and Lea, along with Kincaid and American of Martinsville, struggled with low brand recognition and competition from imports. With 75 percent of its sales in relatively import resistant upholstery, La-Z-Boy should be able to avoid the import disease. Still, profits fell from $36 million in 2003 to $4 million in 2007 – including write-offs of $15.6 million on discontinued operations. In the second quarter of 2008 they lost $54 million on sales of $331 million, and the stock price dropped to 75 cents.

ASHLEY RISES FROM THE ASHES

The declining performance of these traditional mainstays of the American furniture industry was in sharp contrast with the rapid growth of the upstart newcomer, Ashley of Arcadia, Wisconsin. It began as a selling organization, but went into manufacturing in the early 1970s. It started with simple oak tables but soon expanded into a full line. By 2005 it had become the largest furniture manufacturer/importer/retailer in the world, with sales of $2.72 billion, a 27 percent increase over the prior year. Furniture Brands fell into second place with sales of $2.4 billion, down 2.4 percent. La-Z-Boy held on to third place at $1.97 billion in sales.

Ashley rose to the top of the industry by stressing fundamentals – delivery and quality, for example. "With patience, planning, and persistence, Ashley has found our industry's Holy Grail," wrote Jerry Epperson, "offering timely delivery at the value end of the price spectrum."[9] Next Ashley became more innovative with extensive market research and sophisticated information technology. No stranger to imports, it set up a division in Taiwan as early as 1984 and was among the first to secure production from factories in mainland China. When Ashley had the product line assortment right, it launched a store program that is considered by many to be the best in the industry. Retailer Keith Koenig said of Ashley: "They have the best supply chain in the home furnishings industry. They have great product at great values. They are extraordinarily responsive. They are the best in the business."[10]

Ashley's retail stores are well on their way to becoming the number one volume producer in the country, and a visit reveals why. The store projects a friendly atmosphere, replete with Otis Spunkmeyer cookies at the checkout counter. The displays are loaded with well-made, commercial looking furniture and accessories at astonishingly low prices. A reasonably well-done knock-off of Henredon's Amalfi Coast bed, made in China, was priced at $2,400. The original design, made in Spruce Pine, North Carolina, achieved legendary status in 2003 when it became a big seller at $12,999. Most importantly, the Ashley stores lack any pretension. They are simply a well-thought-out assortment of low-priced furniture designed to appeal to blue-collar customers. And to add to the experience, they can deliver most of the assortment right away.

How did Ashley do this? They did it by emphasizing basics, avoiding the Seven Deadly Sins, being patient while waiting for results, getting to China before others, and taking care of customers. Being far from the Briar Patch, with all its conventions and distractions, must have been to Ashley's advantage. Avoiding the civil war and remaining privately held likely helped even more.

Focused Specialists

Focused niche players – such as Jack Glasheen at Hancock and Moore, John Bray at Vanguard, the Audi family at Stickley, Jay Reardon of Hickory Chair, and Don McCreary of McCreary Modern – also managed to hold their own in the face of the Asian Tsunami. They did so because they:

✝ Were entrepreneurial in spirit, with strong leaders who were relentless in staying in touch with customers.

✝ Stayed within their niches. If they decided to go after another, they did so carefully and with a separate organization. The model at this was Eliot Wood.[11]

✝ Were not so big that they lost focus.

✝ Avoided alienating their dealers and generated substantial loyalty, especially against the big companies.

✝ Had a passion for their companies and inspired their workers and managers to share in that passion.

Amidst the devastation that the Asian invasion caused with the large mainstream divisions, a few managed to escape, at least for now. Two Virginia-based companies, Stanley Furniture and Pulaski, are included in this small group. The former had the vision to install a lean manufacturing system in their plants that allowed them to avoid turning to imports. The latter saw globalization coming early on and went over to the "other side." They sold their plant to Ethan Allen and became a distributor of imports. Still another who maneuvered out of the way was Jay Reardon at Hickory Chair. He did so by converting his plant to lean manufacturing while following the five practices above. Remarkably, he did this while being a part of a large company and was subject to plenty of friendly fire.

Names Change Along With Everything Else

The Asian Invasion also left its mark on the American Furniture Manufacturer's Association, which had always limited its membership to domestic manufacturers. Originally, AFMA had been two associations, the Southern Furniture Manufacturer's Association and the National Association of Furniture Manufacturers. The two groups merged in 1984 to form the AFMA, ending many years of needless separation of the Northerners who had the money, thanks to a successful machinery show they sponsored, and the Southerners, who had the membership of the bigger companies. In 2003 the association leadership concluded that the old ways no longer applied and began the process of re-invention. Now called the International Home Furnishings Association, it opened its gates and invited foreign manufacturers and retailers to join in – not unlike how the Roman Emperor invited the barbarians at the gates to join the government rather than having to fight. It remains to be seen whether the trade group's move will dilute and diminish it efficacy or strengthen it. It seems unlikely that the domestic members will ever agree on issues with their Chinese adversaries. Its once-influential lobbying efforts have been lost, and membership has declined.

RETAILERS DRAWN INTO THE FRAY

As noted, large non-furniture retailers such as Wal-Mart were the instigators of the Asian Invasion. But after unleashing the dogs of war, many retailers were getting hurt. As the imports flooded the American market at sharply lower prices, retailers found that their dollar sales actually declined. The most pernicious effect was price deflation, which seems benign at first but is anything but. Economists teach that when prices go down, unit volume goes up because people buy more. This is based on the Theory of Price Elasticity and it makes sense – except with furniture. Why? Because consumers don't buy two dining rooms when the price comes down. They only need one. So sellers must handle the same number of goods, leaving their costs at the same level, but taking in less revenue. This puts tremendous pressure on margins.

Also, the manufacturers' experimentation with company stores caused disruptions in longstanding relationships. Vertical integration strategies often cause severe friction between buyers and sellers, and the furniture retailers were no exception. The comfortable relationships of the past became worn, if not torn. For example, Henredon struck a deal to open a series of dedicated stores with Robb & Stucky in Florida, Dallas, and Phoenix. The result was that two of Henredon's biggest dealers, Baers and Gabberts, stopped carrying the line. Gabberts' Dallas stores ended up closing after many years of being the best showcase Henredon account in the country. In the meantime, retail consolidation was taking place. In the time before the Invasion, department stores were great showcases for home furnishings, and each big city had more than one department store that sold furniture. Over time, however, the May Co. and Federated Department Stores ran off the other department stores or bought them. Among the casualties were Jordan Marsh in Boston; B. Altman, Bamberger's, A&S, and Gimbel's in New York; Strawbridge & Clothier and Wanamaker's in Philadelphia, Woodward and Lothrop in D.C., Rich's in Atlanta, and many more across the country. These accounts were difficult for suppliers to deal with, but they sold a lot of goods and were wonderful at showcasing new styles. In the eyes of the furniture companies, one department store stood tall amidst the predatory crowd: Dayton's in Minneapolis. Everyone's favorite department store customer, Dayton's acquired the Hudson stores in Detroit and then the estimable Marshall Field's in Chicago to build a formidable Midwest chain. They displayed the product well. They promoted effectively. They serviced it well. And, unlike Federated and May Co., they treated their vendors in a professional way.

In 2003, May bought out Dayton Hudson Fields and promised not to destroy its unique brand. In 2005, Federated bought out May. With typical big merchant insensitivity, Federated CEO Terry Lundgren announced it would change the Marshall Field's name to Macy's. Cries of anguish could be heard across the Great Lakes as well as in Boston where the venerable Filenes name was to be erased and Atlanta where Rich's was already gone. Even New Yorkers were amazed. Macy's was a store brand that discriminating shoppers avoided if possible. Now, instead of having multiple choices of where to shop in each city, the whole country would be offered the same homogenized middle-brow assortment wherever they shopped. This might be the first indication of a future with large production runs of homogenized middle-brow furniture made in some place like China. It could also make it easy for the Chinese to bypass the middle man as well by cutting a deal with Macy's. Instead of being offered merchandise tailored to local tastes by people who lived and worked in the locality, shoppers would see merchandise selected by people who lived and worked in New York. Lundgren's dream seems to be to create another Wal-Mart. The reality might well be a less-efficient version of Kmart with more overhead and the innocuous Macy's banner overhead.

Place Your Bets

The one constant during the long Briar Patch Wars was the semiannual High Point Furniture Market. It appeared that the geographic center of action for sales, merchandising, and design would remain steadfast. Good old High Point, the drab mill town adjacent to "old money" Winston-Salem and "new South" Greensboro, where buyers and sellers meet every April and October to decide what will be shown in the upcoming season. Oh, sure, the hotels and restaurants are inadequate, the parking and registration logistics are impossible, and the showrooms are scattered all over a 40-mile radius, but this is High Point. What do you expect, luxury hotels, fancy restaurants, night clubs, and casinos? Besides, buyers come here to work, not have fun, or so they thought. But what if you could have all those amenities and more? What if you could have the furniture market in a place like Las Vegas?

In 2002, the Las Vegas Convention Bureau decided to go after the furniture market, and it is beginning to look like they might be successful. Perhaps not overnight and not completely, but attendees at the first "Las Vegas market" in 2005 raved about how much fun it was to experience a well-planned trade show in a big city with all those amenities. Manufacturers and importers continually announce their decisions to lease showroom space in Las Vegas. No longer perhaps will all roads to the furniture market go through High Point.

DESTROYING THE OLD, CREATING THE NEW

Capitalism, then, is by nature a form or method of economic change and not only never is, but never can be stationary. . . . The fundamental impulse that sets the capitalist engine in motion comes from the new consumers, goods, the new methods of production or transportation, the new markets, the new forms of industrial organization that capitalist enterprise creates. . . . This process of Creative Destruction is the essential fact about capitalism. It is what capitalism consists in and what every capitalist concern has got to live in. . . . It must be seen in its role in the perennial gale of Creative Destruction.

Joseph A. Schumpeter,
Capitalism, Socialism, and Democracy

BETWEEN 2002 AND 2008, the furniture business experienced the full frontal force of what Joseph Schumpeter termed "creative destruction."[1] His 1942 theory states that capitalism can never be stable because the economic structure supporting it is under constant attack. For the furniture industry, however, the force was much more destructive than creative. It hit furniture hard and swiftly, destroying even the most respected creations. The companies and brands featured in this book – Pennsylvania House, Henredon, Drexel Heritage, La-Z-Boy, and others – were not immune from what Schumpeter called the "process of industrial mutation that incessantly revolutionizes the economic structure from within, incessantly destroying the old one, incessantly creating a new one."

In 2002, Mickey Holliman and his divisions were seemingly poised to resume growing and to take advantage of the end of the civil war among American companies devouring each other. He knew the Chinese invasion was well underway, but his natural optimism kept this from ruining his good spirits. Furniture Brands' earnings had dropped 45 percent from 2001, but he had been one of the first American furniture manufacturers to establish an effective quality control team on the ground in the Far East. He moved Lane wood production off shore five years earlier. Surely, his divisions could make the gradual transition from manufacturers to importers and remain leaders in their niches. To make this happen, he needed the right people in key management spots, and he needed to do something about the weak retail dealer base. He suspected those right people and strong retailers might be different from the generation of executives who had been running the industry. His suspicions were well founded, but finding capable new managers and retailers would prove to be just as difficult for him as it had been for Masco and others. And furthermore, there was nothing gradual about the Chinese invasion.

THE YEARS OF LIVING DANGEROUSLY

In 2002, the industry looked to a recovery. The previous year had hurt, but it was widely assumed the accompanying adversity would make the survivors leaner and stronger. Instead, the industry was hammered even harder. In spite of a record-setting housing boom, domestic shipments dropped by double digits, and factory payrolls were slashed even more. At mid-year, UBS Warburg's analyst Margaret Whelan reported that imports were 71 percent higher than 1999, comprising more than 40 percent of the U.S. market.[2] Imports grew by 8 percent in 2003, and the rout continued in 2004 with another double-digit increase.

Furniture Brands and other established companies responded by shutting domestic plants and cutting costs wherever possible, only to find themselves overwhelmed by the profound changes. In addition to the flood of imported goods and the resulting price deflation, these companies faced a rash of dealer bankruptcies, higher costs for raw materials, the willingness of large retailers to bypass the middleman and buy directly from offshore, the increase in price-off promotions and deferred billing offers, and market share gains by non-traditional retailers who did not use domestic brands.

By 2005, Mickey Holliman continued to stress the importance of people as he made a number of executive changes. However, people who came from outside the industry interested him more than before. In February, the "furniture man's furniture man" hired Denise Ramos as chief financial officer. Her career had no furniture experience but included stops with Kentucky Fried Chicken, YUM! Brands, BP, and Atlantic Richfield. In April he hired Joseph McClelland as vice president for logistics and supply chain management, calling him "a perfect fit for our industry." Mc-Clelland had no furniture experience. In June he dismissed Randy Spaak, who had been the president of Lane Action for only a year. The versatile Tom Foy was appointed interim head of the division. In August Holliman hired Nancy Webster as the new president and chief executive officer of Thomasville. Her background was with Target stores, where she held the position of vice president of Hardlines Product Design and Development. Like Ramos, she had no furniture experience. Holliman showed his frustration with insiders with an off-the-cuff but not off-the-record remark he made at an investors' conference in June 2005. "This industry has not been accustomed to having had an abundance of brain power on board," he said. That may well be an accurate indictment of furniture Insiders, but the track record of Outsiders has been disastrous. True to form, Ramos, Webster, and McClelland were all gone by the end of 2007, each lasting only two years on average.

Meanwhile, Jeff Young, the head of the fledgling Henredon Drexel-Heritage Maitland-Smith Group (HDM), created a layer of overhead to watch over the players. For the proud Henredon people to report to managers they considered to be inferior was a bitter pill to swallow, and dozens of key people left as a result. The heavy-handed Drexel style could be seen in a letter they sent to all their suppliers demanding a 7 percent permanent price concession. The letter found its way to the trade press, and the move was treated with derision. One supplier called it "outrageous" and "an arrogant approach to vendor relations." Another called it "ridiculous."[3]

Internally, the Drexel management dismantled Henredon's information systems and downgraded its production methods in order to "consolidate and cut costs." Unfortunately, this disrupted Henredon's customer service and cheapened the look of the product. The company's long time adviser on finish quality protested the change and was let go after 18 years. Quality, like water, seeks its own level, and that level is always lower. Sales declined along with profits, and the brand was tarnished. In 2007 the HDM structure was eliminated.

TURNAROUND OR TUMBLEDOWN?

Meanwhile, back in Tupelo, Mickey Holliman struggled to get the Furniture Brands armies on the move again. In July 2005, Margaret Whelan of UBS-Warburg issued a report that ripped Furniture Brands. Citing "share losses, deflation, inefficiencies, plant closings, and excess overhead," she questioned the defensive strategy of pushing dedicated stores that would put the manufacturer in competition with its own customers and further dilute margins. In downgrading the stock, she concluded "compounded by the revolving door of senior execs, results continue to underperform better-managed peers. While the industry environment is challenging, we believe the main problem at FBN is management's inability to execute."[4] At year-end, the FBN stock price was $22 a share. When the yearly results were reported, sales had declined slightly, but net earnings were down 33 percent.

The sheer number of executive changes was disconcerting. In a short time span, seven of the 10 Furniture Brands divisions absorbed a leadership change. Each of these "decapitations" rippled through the ranks as the incoming CEO brought in his or her own team and the departing CEO took a few people with him. These changes led to other changes and so on, until nearly every division was roiling by the end of 2007.

On average, the six large divisions had a new leader every 10 months. It was a total for 21 CEO changes: four each at Lane, Thomasville, and Broyhill, and three each at Henredon, Drexel Heritage, and Maitland-Smith.

Sales in 2005 declined 13.3 percent, and earnings fell 90 percent. At year-end the stock was trading at $25, and by the end of 2005 it hit $20. In 2006, sales and earnings fell further, and the stock price hit $16. The company flirted with red ink in 2007 and saw the stock go below the $10 level.

THE CANDY MAN CAN

The arrival of 2007 marked the fifth consecutive year of declining results for the Furniture Brands armies. The executives kept changing, but the results were not there. In March, Jeff Cook became the fourth president of Broyhill in slightly more than two years. In March, Nike executive Michael McBreen replaced Joseph McClelland as the head of logistics in St. Louis. In May, Denise Ramos resigned to take a position at ITT. In August, Jeff Young quit as the head of the ill-fated HDM group. In October, Nancy Webster was let go at Thomasville and replaced with a furniture person.

Most significantly, Mickey Holloman in June 2007 announced

he himself would retire at the end of the year and be succeeded by Ralph Scozzafava, an executive at the Wrigley Co. Neither the board nor Holliman believed they could find a person within the industry to fill the position. Instead they went outside and recruited someone with extensive experience with chewing gum, Life Savers, and Band-Aids. Immediately dubbed "the Candy Man," Scozzafava would face a credibility hurdle with industry insiders, especially retailers.

In his first interview with *Furniture Today*, he expressed surprise at how big and how fragmented the industry was, but noted that "in many ways this business is similar to the industries I have been in."5 He did not elaborate on the similarities he saw between furniture and Juicy Fruit or Hubba Bubba. He did, however, echo the familiar outsider refrain about how the industry has been out-marketed.

A few months later, he unveiled a new strategy during a meeting with securities analysts. Rather than continuing with the "holding company" model followed by Interco and Furniture Brands, the new strategy will create an "operating company" model – whatever that means. The new strategy calls for a more scientific approach to product development – including new product testing, the separation of the brand identities, the targeting of distinct distribution channels, and the consolidation of "back-room" costs. These are all admirable goals but not exactly innovative. For at least 50 years, product development people have expressed the need for product testing but failed to get it. Brand development has always appealed to marketers. The problem is where to find the money to pay for it. Channel selection is more likely to be determined by the consumer than by the producer. And these companies have been slashing costs and consolidating support functions for decades. What makes Scozzafava think there is much left to cut?

As he sees it, "a centralized, shared services model will not only generate cost savings but, more importantly, promote the collaborative culture that is essential to Furniture Brands' true success."[6]

The whole plan has "outsider logic" stamped all over it, as if Masco or Burlington Industries were brought in to shape it. Most curious of all, the offices will be in St. Louis. This means hundreds of experienced "back room" people in North Carolina will be replaced with hundreds of inexperienced people in Missouri. To house all these new hires, Furniture Brands moved to a 40 percent larger building in the suburb of Clayton. In addition to costing a lot of money, this massive project cannot help but disrupt routine processes, alienate customers, and cause turmoil. It will not reduce costs. If the wheels come off – and it's likely they will – Scozzafava or his replacement, will probably eliminate the St. Louis office and rehire people who know what to do at what is left of the divisions.

According to the new strategy, Henredon's direction will be to target the designer market. This makes sense in view of the shortage of high-end retailers, but it could be lead to the mistake of not understanding Rule No. 3 mentioned in Chapter Three – the alignment among factory, sales reps and retailers. Consider these questions:

✝ How will designers react? Throughout its 60-year history, Henredon has cultivated retail distribution and treated interior designers as secondary distribution channels. Designers know this and resent the Henredon attitude.

✝ How will retailers respond? The two distribution routes do not mix well. Retailers view designers as parasites who siphon away business, and designers view stores as their rivals. The channels simply do not mix; and the stronger you are at one, the weaker you are at the other.

✝ Where will the case goods be made? Interior designers expect customized finishes, sizes, and features in case goods delivered quickly. This can only be done domestically, and Henredon is shutting down its remaining domestic plant.

✝ How profitable will designer showrooms be? To access the design trade, you need showrooms in all major markets. Rental costs are high and profits typically are low. Remember the previous experience with Beacon Hill, when Masco invested heavily in trying to establish a national chain of showrooms.

✝ How will Henredon service these customers? Not all salesmen are skilled at caring for designer whims. Customer service representatives are not accustomed to dealing with designers. Home deliveries are a challenge, as are freight claims, collections, and the resolution of quality disputes.

By July 2008, less than a year into the new direction, the stripped down division management combined with the gargantuan corporate office was not working. The Scozzafava model resembled a super cargo ship with too many decks above the waterline. It would not take much to tip it over. At Henredon, after months of negotiation, the company lost the Polo Ralph Lauren license. Originally signed in 1993, the license was arguably the most successful designer collection in the industry and comprised a third of Henredon's sales volume. As a direct result, division president, Tom Tilley, was dismissed along with the VP of sales. To make matters worse, Drexel Heritage announced the same week that it had lost its license with Lillian August. And, oh yes, Furniture Brands revised their sales and earnings forecast downward. In April, they had forecasted sales for the year to be between $1.9 billion and $2.0 billion with earnings from continuing operations in the range of 40 to 60 cents per share. Now they were predicting sales of $1.75 billion to $1.8 billion and a loss of 49 to 55 cents per share. According to industry analyst Budd Bugatch, "it is clear that CEO Scozzafava is breaking a lot of old eggs at Furniture Brands. It is less clear to us and others, yet, whether he is creating a soufflé or just some scrambled eggs."[7]

"We are aggressively reshaping Furniture Brands into a company that will succeed in our industry regardless of macroeconomic conditions," the Candy Man boldly proclaimed.[8] Soon he would find out how well the reshaping process would hold up.

MASCO ON STEROIDS

Things got worse in the third quarter of 2008 as St. Louis reported an 18 percent drop in sales and a tripling of losses compared to the prior year. The forecast for the year was now lowered to $1.7 to $1.75 billion in sales and a per share loss of $2.25 to $2.45. Then, in the 4th Quarter, the worldwide economy collapsed and propelled Furniture Brands closer to the abyss. Ralph Scozzafava's "Masco

on Steroids" strategy was not working anyway, and now, it was going to be tested by a severe economic environment.

The overhead in St. Louis kept growing as more inexperienced
people were hired to perform the back office functions previously
handled by "locals" in Mississippi and North Carolina. Waves of
layoffs continued to hit the divisions; morale dropped further;
dealer defections climbed as service and quality levels deteriorated.
In December of 2008, a layoff of 1,400 people, about 15 percent
of the total workforce was announced. No one in St. Louis was
let go, but the Board of Directors did approve an astonishing executive incentive compensation plan. Budd Bugatch of Raymond
James found aspects of the plan to be "very disturbing, if not outrageous." Bugatch's "angst with the plan begins with the gargantuan award given to CEO Scozzafava, who stands to receive up to
$10 million in extra cash compensation in two to five years."[9]

SAMSON EYES DELILAH & HERE COMES THE SUN

It remains to be seen how the company will be able to pay for this
lavish package. On February 4, 2009, one month after it was announced, Furniture Brands reported a staggering fourth quarter
loss of $341 million on sales of $403 million, or $7 a share. The
FBN stock price dropped below $2 a share and stockholders could
only wonder why the company had rejected two earlier offers to
sell at higher prices. As Mike Myers's "Dr. Evil" character in the
movie "Austin Powers" opined, "Why make trillions when we
could make billions?"

In July 2007, Samuel Kuo of Samson Holdings, the parent of
Chinese producer, Lacquer Craft, had proposed a merger with

FBN after acquiring 14.9 percent of the stock. His offer was believed to have been $15 a share. It was rejected. Then, in February 2008, investment group Sun Capital offered to buy FBN at a "substantial premium to its latest closing price of $10.18." This offer was also rejected, but in the process, Sun won a contentious proxy fight and gained three seats on the board of directors.

Who knows what these two suitors have in mind. Is Kuo another Colin Carpi with visions of industry consolidation or just another carpetbagger seeking to make money? If he captures the Furniture Brands names, he could link them up with his low-cost production facilities off shore and tighten his grip on the industry. Even if he only gets Thomasville and Drexel Heritage, it would be quite a coup, especially when you consider the stores it would include.

Is Sun Capital another Webb Turner attracted to the thrill of the deal or just another investment group with no particular industry focus? Having already grabbed Lexington, Rowe, and Berkline-Benchcraft, they just might be serious. However, we have seen this kind of outside investor before and they rarely stick around long enough to understand what they bought.

Either way, Furniture Brands is not likely to survive in its current form. If by some quirk of fate, the stock manages to hit $6.26, Ralph Scozzafava will pocket an additional $5 million as part of his new package. Should it reach $9.39, he gets still another $5 million.

LITTLE HELP FROM POLITICIANS

The global invasion of the U.S. furniture industry came with obligatory sound and fury from U.S. politicians, but it signified nothing. Everyone from aldermen to senators insisted, if elected, that they would help the industry and its workers. But their rhetoric was hollow. The Americans were saddled with the twin burdens of excessive regulation and unprecedented competition from Third World producers. Perhaps these weights could be borne by cleaner, more profitable industries, but not by Briar Patch producers. They were forced to comply with so many state and federal regulations that their prices became less competitive in the world marketplace.

For decades, American furniture producers were engaged in competition with a known set of opponents and governed by a known set of regulations. Then – seemingly overnight – the competitors and rules changed. The U.S. government imposed duties and tariffs on foreigners who tried to compete by undercutting prices, and the wonderful American economy kept demand in balance with supply.

It was a sweet arrangement, and the Insiders did their best to repel Outsiders in general and foreigners in particular – especially those who knew nothing of the old ways but insisted on making changes. Potential Insiders were made to join one of two ancient secret societies. Those involved with production were inducted into the Secret Amalgamated Wood Butchers Society, the SAWS, and pledged to do everything within their power to preserve the old ways of making furniture. Those involved with sales were inducted into the Fraternal Order of Peddlers Society, the FOPS, and pledged to concentrate on low price to the exclusion of all other marketing variables. Atop both of them were the owners who had their own fraternity – the Good Old Boy Society, or GOBS – who swore to defend the industry against Outsiders.

The combination of these three groups resulted in profit

margins so low that the industry could not afford to invest in new technology and marketing. The result was that they kept losing ground to other forms of competition. And the U.S. government did not realize how difficult it was to make money, so it kept piling more regulations and taxes on the organizations. Each regulation took on a life of its own, often with unintended consequences. The original intentions may well have been admirable, but the results were not.

No matter what anyone said or did, the combined impacts of the Free Trade movement and the Save the Planet mentality were too much. The American furniture industry's cause was doomed, or so it seemed. Perhaps it could rally and repel the invaders, but this prospect was highly unlikely. The first battle of the global war was for the factories. Next would be the battle for marketing and merchandising jobs; eventually, the retail outlets would be up for grabs.

What happened to the furniture industry parallels Japan's successful attack on the American consumer electronics industry in the 1970s. Japan started with production and moved on to the marketing. At first the offshore producers were content to make original equipment for powerful American brands like Magnavox, Zenith, Raytheon, RCA, Motorola, and Emerson. In time, however, these producers broke away from their American patrons and began marketing their own electronics. Today the top brands are Sony, Mitsubishi, Toshiba, Samsung, and Panasonic – none based in America. How long might the top furniture brands last in the face of the present global attack?

How It Started

It is clear that the furniture industry gave away its markets and received little in return. Assigning blame accomplishes very little, even as it's easy to find guilty parties when looking in any direction. The origins of the free trade concept go back to Plato. Notably, proponents of free trade sometimes justify the theory by citing Thomas More's *Utopia*, written in the sixteenth century. What they miss is that the book is satire, and More was trying to tell us that there is no Utopia. Utopian ideas do not work because they are predicated on benevolent assumptions about human nature. In spite of More's warnings, the idea did not die.

† Eighteenth century economist Adam Smith said, "Protectionism is bad," and most agreed.

† His disciple, David Ricardo, said, "Without protectionism, each country will develop its own comparative advantage," and most agreed.

† Paul Samuelson's economics textbooks indoctrinated nearly all college students from 1950 onward. "Free Trade is the only way to go," he taught, and no one objected.

† Milton Freedman and his University of Chicago gang went further. "Protectionism is evil," he claimed, and no one objected.

✝ Richard Nixon needed help with his sagging approval ratings. "I'll go to China," he boasted, and no one objected.

✝ Alan Greenspan and the Federal Reserve spread the word. "Stop inflation," he warned, and no one objected.

✝ With full congressional approval, the World Trade Organization invited China to join, and the chorus sang the "Globalization Blues":

> Listen, oh listen, if you are able
> To a logic that's unassailable
> From the song of the old Econ bluesman
> Whose voice is quite confused, man.
>
> Banish all your foolish trade barriers,
> From cheap socks to big aircraft carriers
> And costs will be reduced
> On everything we produce.
>
> If Wal-Mart agrees to carry it,
> If somehow we can all pay for it,
> Living standards will climb, they say.
> But we worry about it anyway.
>
> What happens to this happy song
> If the Econman is wrong?
> Will our joy be unalloyed
> If we're all unemployed?

Certainly, free trade has its benefits. It holds back inflation, makes a better standard of living available to more people, and helps developing economies to grow. Imagine America without Wal-Mart. Imagine China with xenophobic Chairman Mao still in charge. The problem is that it is too early to tell what the outcome will be. The dislocations have not all been absorbed. Let us hope they will be.

WHERE DOES IT END?

Nearly everyone in the furniture business has been hurt by the advent of the Great War. A few pockets here and there have managed to avoid injury – the cheap bedroom category because freight is currently too high from Asia, and custom upholstery because delivery from Asia is too slow. But the war is not over. Having captured casegoods manufacturing, the foundation of the furniture industry, what is to stop the Chinese from assuming control of other segments? Can America hold on to the merchandising, design, marketing, and selling functions? Perhaps, but it seems unlikely. Why would producers not want to control the functions that make or break the sale? Are American marketing, merchandising, and sales professionals so impressive that the Chinese won't think they can do better?

What if the Americans were to mount a counteroffensive and confront the Asians head on? It's simply not possible. To match the price levels set by China, American companies can forget incremental reductions in costs and gradual increases in productivity, especially if their products are labor intensive. These companies will need to expect to cut much deeper – try by a third to a half – to meet what *Business Week* calls "The China Price, the three scariest words in U.S. industry."[12]

What about external factors? Might there be some event that will disrupt trade with China? This is possible, but the odds are the disruption would be so catastrophic – a real war, for example, or a nuclear device in an oceangoing container – that trade would not matter much.

Could any internal factors change the picture? The Chinese now know that furniture manufacturing has its faults. A survey by the Ministry of Commerce recorded an average margin of 1.1 percent in the first half of 2008.[13] The housing slump in the States has sharply reduced sales; higher oil prices have increased freight costs; and currency revaluations have driven prices up. The likelihood of another Tiananmen Square event seems remote, but anything could happen. As the Chinese economy grows, the country will need new furniture for its own people and this may cut back further on exports. But America should not count on the return of the furniture industry. Other Asian nations will be glad to pick up anything China abandons.

What about trade policy? Can Congress intervene and restrict trade with China by imposing duties? Yes, they can and yes, they might, but a protectionist trade policy now would bring with it some wicked inflation.

No, there is no magic wand, no silver bullet, no *deus ex machina* that can clean up the mess we are in. We have gone too far down the road of Free Trade to turn back now. We did it to ourselves, and now we have to work our way through it ourselves. We have to figure out how to make it pay. Otherwise, China will have a hard time getting paid for all the well-priced goods they are selling us.

New Rules vs. Old Formulas

The furniture industry needs to discard some of the old familiar formulas, the dogmas that have lost their meaning and to adopt new rules that work in a global economy. The old formulas simply do not work any more.

OLD FORMULA NUMBER ONE worshipped at the Altar of Growth and doomed many companies in the process of getting and staying big. Size kills. The economies of scale never materialize and things become more difficult to manage as you cope with smaller, more agile competitors.

NEW RULE NUMBER ONE warns you to stay small and stay private. Better to let growth come naturally, as a result of great products and service. Don't force it. At any size, think twice about going public, no matter how rich you will become on paper. Public companies become slaves to investors and investment bankers who don't care and the inevitable cyclical earnings drive them crazy.

OLD FORMULA NUMBER TWO urged you to attack on a broad front with a full line. Upholstery makers could not wait to add wood, just as wood producers felt compelled to add upholstery. Bedroom specialists rushed to produce dining rooms, and so on. But neither consumers nor retailers seemed to care. Consumers preferred to mix and match styles and brands and retailers preferred to have multiple resources.

NEW RULE NUMBER TWO tells you to *cherchez le creneau* – to

look for the opening, define a niche and exploit it with passion. It is not easy, but when you have mastered your area of expertise, it will be difficult for others to dislodge you.

OLD FORMULA NUMBER THREE taught that traditional manufacturing methods were fine and there was no need for lean practices much less the Toyota Production System. The lean conversion is expensive and demands a total commitment, but it works and ignoring it is foolish.

NEW RULE NUMBER THREE assumes, if you are still manufacturing anything, you have already made the lean conversion. If not, it may be too late. But either way, you must think globally and develop a group of offshore suppliers who look after your needs. Outsourcing makes sense and today it is better to own a supplier than to own a factory.

OLD FORMULA NUMBER FOUR prayed for brand awareness and told you to develop and extend your brand. Those who had awareness were grateful, but aware of its limitations. Those who did not lusted for it. Again, consumers and retailers were not particularly impressed.

NEW RULE NUMBER FOUR stresses the value of reputation over brand. Many people are aware of brands like Broyhill, Bassett, and Drexel Heritage, but what are they known for? What is their reputation? Brands like Henredon, Stickley, and Baker are less well known, but they have strong reputations for style, quality and design integrity. Regardless of brand awareness, the reputation of the management team is a game changer. The industry values integrity over competency. The combat readiness and the fighting strength of the American furniture industry can be restored, but not with short-term solutions. An excessive short-term emphasis is what drained the Briar Patch of its strength and brought it to the brink of defeat. It will take long-term efforts to restore its competitive velocity.

Not that long ago, America was the acknowledged International King of Furniture. We worked hard at it and we had fun. Then, we became distracted and we lost focus. Somehow we let this uniquely American industry get away. It is unlikely we will ever get it all back. Let us hope we will learn from the experience. Having captured furniture, electronics, textiles, clothing, shoes, sporting goods, and a host of other industries, what will the Asian Tigers go after next? Will they take over all our manufacturing so that we become totally dependent on imported goods? And if so, how will we pay for them?

The answers are not clear and a walk through an abandoned factory provides no clues. The yard is vacant. There are no lumber stacks waiting to be kiln dried. The rough mill no longer whines. There are no boards to cut. The machine room is empty. The tenoners and routers are gone. The finishing room is dark. There are no cases on the conveyor. The rub and pack area is silent. There are no inspectors needed. The warehouse is empty. There are no trucks to be loaded. The smokestacks are clean. There is no pollution. There are no factory workers. There is no need for them. But in the empty silence, perhaps there is some hope.

The pendulum of global competition may have swung as far as

it can go. After all, some domestic manufacturers are increasing their production levels. The top five "lifestyle" retailers had sales of $3 billion last year. The Chinese have their eye on more sophisticated things to make and they have some serious environmental concerns. There are easier ways to make a living than by making furniture, even in China. Several Chinese factories have closed down in recent months and the new Democratic Congress may well introduce legislation containing some import tariffs. Maybe some day Americans will be able to reclaim a bigger share of the furniture business, and this time, maybe we will get it right.

APPENDIX

FURNITURE WARS CHRONOLOGY

1964

General Interiors formed. Acquires Pennsylvania House.

1965

General Interiors acquires Cushman.

General Interiors IPO listed as GIT on April 12.

Stock closes year at 17.

1966

General Interiors acquires Kittinger.

Burlington acquires United and Globe.

GIT stock ranges from 9⅛ to 2⅝, closes year at 11.

1967

GIT stock ranges from 10⅝ to 27⅛, closes year at 25¼.

1968

Armstrong acquires Thomasville.

General Interiors acquires Shaw and Dunbar.

GIT stock hits 35½.

1969

 General Interiors acquires Baker but, deal collapses.

 Magnavox acquires Baker.

 General Interiors acquires Biggs Antique Co. and DUX.

 Iroquois attempts to raid General Interiors.

 S&H acquires Lea.

 GIT stock drops to 9½.

1970

 McClure replaces Carpi as CEO of General Interiors.

 Action Company founded by Mickey Holliman and Bo Bland.

 S&H acquires American Drew and Daystrom.

 GIT stock closes year at 5¾.

1971

 GIT stock closes year at 5⅝.

1972

 Laura Carpi disappears.

 Chan and Fogarty acquire General Interiors for $1.70 per share.

 Robert Fogarty replaces McClure.

 GIT stock ranges from 3 to 9, closes year at 6⅝.

 Lane buys Action.

1973

 General Interiors acquires Brown Saltman.

 GIT stock closes at 4.

1974

GIT stock closes at 6½.

1975

General Mills Acquires General Interiors for $27.00 per share.

1980

Victor Posner attempts to raid Lane.

Interco acquires Ethan Allen.

1981

Baldwin United acquires S&H and spins off LADD.

Turner acquires Union Furniture.

Interco acquires Broyhill.

1982

Turner acquires Sterlingworth.

Jamestown Sterling is formed.

1983

LADD goes public.

LADD puts Kittinger put up for sale.

Turner acquires Williams Furniture.

1984

Turner buys Burlington Furniture, State of Newburgh, Deville,
and Stone Hill.

1985

Burlington Furniture files for bankruptcy.

General Mills spins off fashion, toys, and restaurants.

1986

Masco acquires Henredon.

Kohler acquires Baker.

Masco acquires Drexel Heritage.

General Mills sells furniture group to Chicago Pacific.

Masco stock (MAS) ends the year at 45.

1987

Masco buys Lexington.

Fred Copeland named Group President Home Furnishings Group.

LADD goes public. Stock hits 25.

MAS stock hits 16.

1988

Masco acquires Robert Allen and Ametex.

Interco buys Lane.

Rales Brothers try to buy Interco.

Chicago Pacific merges with Maytag.

Ron Jones named President–Home Furnishings Products.

Fred Copeland made Chairman–Home Furnishings Products.

MAS hits 13.

1989

LADD buys General Interiors furniture group from Maytag.

Masco buys Universal.

Masco launches Lineage.

Interco sells Ethan Allen.

MAS hits 12.

1990

Interco stock bottoms out at 9 cents.

LADD stock hits 4½.

MAS hits 9.

1991

Michael Carlow buys Kittinger.

Discover the World of Masco launched.

Interco files for bankruptcy.

Leon Black's Apollo group buys into Interco.

MAS moves up to 12.

1992

Allen and Carol Wyatt resign from Robert Allen.

Copeland and Ferguson take over Marge Carson.

MAS moves to 15.

1993

Copeland resigns from Marge Carson. Ferguson takes over.

MAS at 18½.

1994

Interco spins off shoe companies to focus on furniture.

Interco stock hits 6¾.

Masco buys Berkline from Ron Cordover.

Universal launches Alexander Julian line.

MAS at 16.

1995

Masco announces it will divest furniture holdings.

Interco buys Thomasville.

Lexington launches Arnold Palmer Collection.

Jamestown Sterling files for bankruptcy.

Lineage folded into Drexel Heritage and disappears.

Morgan Stanley group agrees to buy furniture holdings.

MAS at 16.

1996

Morgan Stanley deal called off.

Ron Jones leaves Masco to become president of Sealy.

Citicorp group led by Wayne Lyon buys furniture holdings.

LifeStyle Furnishings International (LFI) formed.

Interco renamed Furniture Brands International (FBN).

Henredon signs Polo Ralph Lauren license.

Mickey Holliman named CEO of FBN.

MAS at 18.

FBN stock hits 14.

1997

Project Delphi with Oracle software launched.

Lean manufacturing crusade led by Don Barefoot.

MAS up to 25.

1998

LFI's IPO fails.

MAS hits 29.

1999

Sino–U.S. Trade Accord signed by China and U.S.

2000

Lyon moved "upstairs" as Alan Cole is made CEO of LFI.

La-Z-Boy buys LADD.

2001

Life*Style* Home Furnishings raises white flag.

FBN buys Henredon, Drexel Heritage, and Maitland Smith.

Samson Holdings (Lacquercraft) buys Universal.

Management led group buys Sunbury Textile.

Lane's Altavista operations moved to Tupelo.

2002

Sun Capital group buys Lexington.

Management led group buys Benchcraft and Berkline.

FBN stock hits all time high at $42.74.

2003

FBN stock at 29.

2004

Randy Spaak made president of Lane Action.

Tom Foy made COO of Furniture Brands.

Michael Dugan retires as president of Henredon.

Steve McKee named as replacement.

FBN stock ends year at 25.

2005

Harvey Dondero replaces Dennis Burgette as president of Broyhill.

Randy Spaak let go at Lane Action.

Nancy Webster replaces Tom Tilley as president of Thomasville.

Tom Tilley replaces Steve McKee as president of Henredon.

FBN at 22.

2006

Seamus Bateson resigns as president of Maitland Smith.

Harvey Dondero resigns as president of Broyhill.

Larry Milan named as president of Maitland Smith.

Broyhill closes its last remaining domestic casegoods plant.

FBN stock dips below 16.

2007

Jeff Cook named president of Broyhill.

Mickey Holliman announces retirement.

Ralph Scozzafava named as successor.

Jeff Young steps down as president of HDM.

FBN stock drops below 8.

2008

Tom Tilley departs Henredon.

FBN stock dips below 2.

NOTES

INTRODUCTION

1. This figure accounts for the value of wood and upholstered furniture sold at retail. It does not include bedding.

2. The author is grateful to Jerry Epperson of Mann, Armistead, and Epperson, Richmond, Virginia., for providing these and other furniture industry statistics. See *Furnishings Digest*, Volume 9, Number 8, Aug. 2001.

3. According to a 1967 *Fortune* article, America had 5,350 companies in the furniture industry at that time and factory shipments of $4 billion. In the 1997 census, after some 30 years of "consolidation," there were 5,843 companies in the industry.

4. *The Hardwood Review*, Charlotte, North Carolina

5. "Imports Hammer Furniture Makers," by Jon Hilsenruth and Peter Wonacott, *Wall Street Journal*, Sept. 20, 2002, page 2.

CHAPTER ONE

1. On Sept. 29, 1993, President Bill Clinton and his wife Hillary hosted a White House dinner for a small group of home furnishings executives who had contributed to redecorating the private quarters of the executive residence. After dinner, the president spoke about the powerful influence of furnishings in our lives, even referring

to the fact that he had signed an important treaty that day while using a desk that had belonged to Thomas Jefferson. The speech was short, but insightful and perceptive. The Clinton Library has denied repeated requests to provide a copy of the talk.

2.   Kenneth R. Davis, *Furniture Marketing*, University of North Carolina Press, 1957.

3.   Ibid., page 214.

4.   Ibid., page 214.

5.   E. A. G. Robinson, *The Structure of Competitive Industry*, (New York: Harcourt Brace, 1959), page 174.

6.   Michael E. Porter's writing demonstrates a marvelously clear understanding of how industry structure determines strategy. In particular, see *Competitive Strategy* (New York: Macmillan, 1980), and *Competitive Advantage* (New York: Macmillan, 1985).

7.   Porter, *Competitive Strategy*, page 200.

8.   "5,350 Companies = A Mixed-Up Furniture Industry," by Tomas O'Hanlon, *Fortune*, February 1967.

CHAPTER TWO

1.   Jerry Epperson of Mann, Armistead and Epperson, *Furnishings Digest*, Vol. 9, Number 8, August 2001.

2.   Joe Carroll, Furniture Today.

3.   *Cherchez le creneau* is French for "Look for the opening."

4.   *Furnishings Digest*, Volume 9, No. 8, August 2001.

CHAPTER THREE

1. John Brooks, *The Go-Go Years* (New York: Weybright and Talley, 1973), dust jacket.
2. Colin Evans, *Blood on the Table*, (Berkley Books, New York, 2008), page 163.
3. "5,350 Companies = A Mixed-Up Furniture Industry," by Tomas O'Hanlon, *Fortune*, February 1967.

CHAPTER FOUR

1. General Interiors Corp. Annual Report, 1967.
2. General Interiors Corp. Annual Report, 1968.

CHAPTER SEVEN

1. Michael E. Porter, "From Competitive Advantage to Corporate Strategy," *Harvard Business Review*, May–June, 1987.
2. Lee Smith, "The Wrecking Crew," *Fortune*, July 10, 1995, page 50.

CHAPTER EIGHT

1. *Buffalo News*, March 1, 1991.
2. *Fortune*, July 10, 1995.
3. *Fortune*, July 10, 1995.

CHAPTER NINE

1. In addition to owning office buildings, factories and warehouses, Hillenbrand's owned several houses, a hotel, the country club, a restaurant, the airport, and even a bank for a while.

2. "The Rise and Fall of United Globe," *The Lexington Dispatch*, Aug. 16, 1985.

3. Bill Bamberger and Cathy N. Davidson, *Closing: The Life and Death of an American Factory* (New York: W. W. Norton & Co., 1998).

CHAPTER TEN

1. "Merger Mania Strikes Again in Furniture Field," by James Flanigan, *The Los Angeles Times*, Feb. 27, 1987, page 1.

2. The Household Furniture Industry in 1986, Harvard Business School, Dec. 3, 1998.

3. *Furniture Today*, Sept. 29, 1986, page 26.

4. *Masco Corp.* (A), No. 9-389-186, Harvard Business School. Revised Dec. 12, 1998, by C. W. Moorman and Cynthia A. Montgomery in collaboration with Michael E. Porter; *Masco Corp.* (B), No. 9-389-187, revised Nov. 23, 1998.

5. *Furniture Today*, March 9, 1987, page 8.

6. Ibid.

7. "Faucet Maker Masco Makes a Daring Move," *Detroit Free Press*, Sept. 28, 1986.

8. "Masco Targets Hefty Profits With Missionary Zeal, Tight Discipline," *Furniture Today*, March 9, 1987.

9. First Call Research, May 1988, page 27.

10. "Masco Targets Hefty Profits With Missionary Zeal, Tight Discipline," *Furniture Today*, March 9, 1987.

11. *Furniture Today*, Aug. 3, 1987, page 25.

12. "Masco Has Rare Profit Decline," *Detroit Free Press,* Jan. 6, 1990, page 9A.

13. Masco 1989 Annual Report, page 2.

14. "From Competitive to Corporate Strategy," *Harvard Business Review,* Reprint No. 87307.

15. "How Competitive Forces Shape Strategy," *Harvard Business Review,* Reprint No. 79208.

16. "The Lessons of Masco," *Furniture Today*, July 17, 1995, page 1.

17. The 1989 Masco Annual Report gave this attribute top billing. "Entrepreneurial Innovation. It is the spirit on which Masco was founded, and it remains the spark igniting our growth some 60 years later. . . . To facilitate the independent thinking that is fundamental to our management style, our organization is structured into decentralized, autonomous profit centers that are entrepreneurially managed, functional business units."

CHAPTER ELEVEN

1. "Masco picks name for newest firm," *Greensboro News and Record,* April 16, 1990.

2. "Tilley to head Masco's new furniture unit," Furniture Today, Nov. 13, 1989, page 1.

3. "Lineage plans about 50 new Pavilion galleries in 1992," *Furniture Today*, Dec. 31, 1991, page 59.

4. A reference to the fake villages placed along the railroad line

followed by the Tsar of Russia before the revolution. Potemkin, a consultant to the royal family, knew he could not fix all the social problems as the Tsar had ordered him to do, but he could fake it so that, from the train at least, it would look as though conditions had improved.

5. Masco press release, Jan. 24, 1992.

6. For some reason, it seems that the only way to leave Masco is through the attic. People always were kicked upstairs even when they quit as Pastrone had done.

7. Howard Haworth retired in 1985 and was succeeded by Fred Copeland, Paul Monroe in 1988, John Pastrone in 1990, and Dan Grow in 1991.

8. "Masco studies exit options," *Furniture Today*, June 12, 1995, page 1.

9. Ibid.

10. *Detroit Free Press*, June 9, 1995, "Disappointed by Profits, Masco Ready to Give up Furniture Group."

CHAPTER TWELVE

1. *Forbes*, May 5, 1997.

2. Jones seemed to thrive in the marketing oriented bedding environment and greatly expanded Sealy's market share during his tenure. Profits, however, never reached expected levels, and attempts to go public fell short. In April 2002, Jones gave up his CEO responsibilities but remained as Sealy's chairman until 2004.

3. Jack Welch and John A. Byrne, *Jack: Straight From the Gut* (New York: Warner Books, 2001), page 391.

4. "Interco to pay $339M for Thomasville," *Furniture Today*, November 27, 1995, page 1.

5. *St. Louis Post Dispatch*, May 19, 1997.

6. "Lifestyle: New Name, Same Plan," *Greensboro News and Record*, Oct. 10, 1997.

7. Tyler Best, a talented information technology specialist, came from a large ad agency in Detroit and had no furniture experience.

8. "Life*Style* Furnishings International Ltd. Announces First Quarter Results," *Business Wire*, May 6, 1998.

9. *Greensboro News and Record*, Aug. 15, 1998, page B8.

10. "Lifestyle Shuffles Top Management," by Amy Joiner, *Greensboro News & Record*, Feb. 22, 2000, page B8.

11. "Life*Style* breaking up," *Furniture Today*, Dec. 10, 2001, page 1.

12. *InFurniture*, March 2002, page 61.

13. *Furniture Today*, May 28, 2002.

CHAPTER THIRTEEN

1. "A Bundle of Sticks," by Janet L. Fix, *Forbes*, Nov. 18, 1985.

2. Ibid.

3. "Some of Interco's Holders Oppose Bid for Lane Co.," *The Wall Street Journal*, (Eastern edition) April 1, 1987, page 1.

4. Lynn Chipperfield, Furniture Brands' chief counsel, November 2005, in conversation.

5. *The Wall Street Journal*, July 11, 1990, page A1.

6. *The Wall Street Journal*, January 28, 1991, page B5.

7. "Fiction In, Fiction Out," by Laura Jereski, *Forbes*, Dec. 9, 1991, page 292(2)

8. "Black is Back," by Bernard Condon, *Forbes*, Nov. 15, 2003.

9. "Leon Black, Ready to Snare Interco," by Julie Quick, *St. Louis Business Journal*, June 22, 1992, vol. 12 no. 40, page 1.

CHAPTER FOURTEEN

1. John Toland, *In Mortal Combat: Korea, 1950–1953* (New York: William Morrow, 1991), page 340.

2. Courtesy of George Barrett of the American Hardwoods Association, Charlotte, North Carolina.

3. *Furniture Today*, Feb. 3, 2002, page 14.

4. "Imports Hammer Furniture Makers," *Wall Street Journal*, Oct. 1, 2002.

5. Ibid.

6. Personal communication with Whitt Sherrill, Nov. 2005.

7. "La-Z-Boy Consolidates," *Furniture Today*, Aug. 7, 2006.

8. "La-Z-Boy Completes Pennsylvania House Deal," La-Z-Boy press release, Oct. 16, 2007. N.B.: Carpi paid $4.5 million in 1964.

9. "Our industry's Wal-Mart just keeps growing," by Jerry Epperson, *Furniture Today*, June 12, 2006.

10. "At 2.72 Billion, Ashley Takes Top Spot," *Furniture Today*, Feb. 20, 2006, page 16.

11. After co-founding and then selling Heritage Furniture, Wood started a focused chair specialty company called Woodmark, a focused sofa company called Stanton Cooper, a contemporary specialist called Dansen, a motion company called Bradington Young, and a decorative fabric company. Each had its own president, factory, and sales force. Each was a niche player with outstanding products. Each was successful.

CHAPTER FIFTEEN

1. Joseph A. Schumpeter, *Capitalism, Socialism, and Democracy* (New York, Harper, 1975), pages 82–85.

2. "Imports Hammer Furniture Makers," *The Wall Street Journal*, Oct. 10, 2002.

3. "HDM Seeks 7% Price Cut From Suppliers," *Furniture Today*, June 17, 2005.

4. "Turnaround or Tumbledown," UBS Investment Research, July 8, 2005.

5. *Furniture Today*, July 23, 2007.

6. *Furniture Today*, July 7, 2008.

7. Budd Bugatch, Raymond James & Associates, July 16, 2008.

8. Company Press Release, August 6, 2008.

9. Budd Bugatch, "Furniture and Furnishings Suppliers Company Comment," Raymond James & Associates, December 24, 2008.

10. In 2001, Henredon received word that it would cost $2 million to comply with the new Clean Air Act's requirement called Maximum Allowable Control Technology. The plant boilers which efficiently used scrap lumber and sawdust as fuel would all have to be modified to reduce the emissions from burning oak, cherry and other hardwoods. The cost was the equivalent of six months of normal capital investment. The law was aimed at the huge power plants burning soft coal, but it hit the furniture industry because of the way it was hastily written. During the same week, Henredon made the decision to "downsize" the company in the face of soft orders.

11. In late 2001, Greenpeace decided to go after the American

furniture companies who had the nerve to use Brazilian mahogany to make furniture. It mattered not that the few trees used for this time-honored practice were insignificant compared to the countless acres of rainforest trees cut down and burned by peasant farmers to clear for planting crops. The Chinese continue to import wood from all over the world without fear of protest. They had already defoliated much of their country by cutting down their native hardwoods to fuel their steelmaking industry during the Cultural Revolution.

12. "The China Price," *Business Week*, Dec. 6, 2004.

13. "China Furniture Makers Feel Global Slowdown Pain," July 26, 2008, Reuters.

ABOUT THE AUTHOR

MICHAEL K. DUGAN is currently the Chair of the Business School at Lenoir-Rhyne University. Previously he was the President and CEO of Henredon Furniture Industries, a position he held for 17 years. Widely recognized by Insiders as an industry pioneer and marketing guru, he played the lead role in building the Pennsylvania House brand and co-founded his own furniture company, Jamestown Sterling.

He is a contributing editor to *Home Furnishings Business* magazine and writes book reviews for the *Hickory Daily Record*.

A frequent guest lecturer at other colleges and universities, Dugan teaches a graduate course in Leadership and an undergraduate course in Marketing at Lenoir-Rhyne.

His business career involved working with many influential people, including Polo chief Ralph Lauren, longtime Bloomimgdale's CEO Marvin Traub, and designer Barbara Barry. A graduate of the University of Toronto, where he majored in English Literature and Medieval Philosophy, he holds an MBA degree from Syracuse University.

2786950

Made in the USA